Summerhill School

A.S. Neill was born in 1883 in Forfar, Scotland, and worked during his youth as a pupil teacher in his father's school. At twenty-five, after holding various assistant-teacher roles, he gained his M.A. in English from Edinburgh University. In 1915, while working as acting head of a Scottish school, Neill published his first book, *A Dominie's Log*. It was not until he was thirty-eight years old that Neill began the real work of his life when he founded, with others, an international school in Hellerau, Dresden, which afterwards moved to Sonntagsberg in Austria. Returning to England, he continued the school in a house on a hill at Lyme Regis called Summerhill, a name he kept when the school moved to Leiston, in Suffolk.

Neill lectured widely and published twenty-one books in his lifetime as well as working as headmaster of his beloved Summerhill. His school became famous around the world for its pioneering of freedom and self-government for children and Neill became well known for his radical philosophy of life. He was influenced not by educationalists but by psychologists such as Freud, Stekel, Reich and Homer Lane. A compilation of Neill's books called *Summerhill, A Radical Approach to Child Rearing* (1960), edited by his American publisher, Harold Hart, sold millions of copies around the world. A.S. Neill died in 1973.

Zoë Readhead, the daughter of A.S. Neill, is the headmistress of Summerhill School. She lives with her husband, Tony, and her four children on a large farm near the school. Her mother Ena, who ran the school for twelve years after Neill's death, still lives next door to the school. Zoë is a qualified riding instructor and, as well as being principal, currently teaches riding to children at the school.

Albert Lamb, the editor, was part of the American invasion of students to Summerhill in 1961. After being away from the school for twenty-two years he came back to England to help out on the staff. Albert has worked as a cartoonist and musician and has four children. He now travels back and forth between Summerhill and his home in the Cotswolds where he lives with his second wife, Popsy, and his stepdaughter.

Summerhill School
A New View of Childhood

A. S. Neill

edited by Albert Lamb

St. Martin's Griffin
New York

Library of Congress Cataloging-in-Publication Data

Neil, Alexander Sutherland
     Summerhill School : a new view of childhood / by A.S. Neil ;
edited by Albert Lamb.
     p.   cm.
     ISBN 0-312-14137-8
     1. Summerhill School.   I. Lamb, Albert.   II. Title.
LF795.L467N42   1995
372.9426'4—dc20   95-33481
                                                             CIP

First published in Great Britain by Penguin Books.

10

Contents

A Foreword by a Former Summerhill Student

A. S. Neill was adventurous in his vision of a school for children. A large part of that vision was that at root there weren't any bad children. There were only problem parents, problem teachers, and problem schools that together contributed to problem children.

He decided on a school that would give children an environment of freedom for themselves plus the responsibility of governing themselves. Adults would only have the final say about fire and safety hazards. Each and every child had to work out his problems and difficulties within the social situation of the peer groups. Of course, if difficulties had to be dealt with, there were always Neill's "Private Lessons." Intrinsic to the success of such an undertaking was Neill's great sense of humor—he could be on a six- or seven-year-old level in a flash and could send the child off laughing.

I remember walking with my father and Neill one day during a January visit of my parents. They were deep in conversation when I decided I wanted a sweet. There was a sweet shop adjacent to the school grounds. I asked Neill for a shilling. He didn't want me to have it. Each child received an allowance of double his age in pence. This was done in order to have all the children on an equal footing. Neill always carried a small notebook in which he recorded notes and transactions of the day. He turned to me and said, "I can't give you the shilling, Bobby, because I don't have my notebook with me, and if I forget, you'll have done me out of it." That sent me skipping off across the field—denied, yes, but with a smile on my face for having understood. He had a way of presenting a negative to a child without it being either offensive or authoritarian—and always with a warm twinkle in his eyes.

Once my mother had left her purse on the main building landing while visiting another school area. When she returned, the purse was missing. She told Neill about it. He asked a few kids in the building about it, but they had seen nothing. "Well," said Neill, "there's nothing to do but to organize a search, call Tubby." Tubby was known by one and all as the school thief. Neill in his wisdom asked Tubby to lead the search. The purse was not found by the search team. One of the kids had found it earlier on the landing and had safely tucked it away in Neill's office. What a wonderful way Neill picked to show support for Tubby without any moralizing about him being known as the school thief.

One of the major problems at Summerhill was bullying. Kids were always bringing other kids up on charges at the school meetings. The following incident demonstrates the wondrous insight and intelligence of children when left to their own devices.

Johnny was a handsome, redheaded boy who was brought up on charges of bullying his girlfriend. After the children heard both of them out, they voted to fine Johnny one week's allowance. The fine didn't seem to work. She brought him up on charges again at the next meeting. This time the children fined the girl! The circumstances were the same—why fine the girl? The answer seemed to lie in the fact that the children knew of Johnny's background. He was punished often by his parents; therefore, he expected punishment when he behaved badly, but could not deal with someone else being punished for his behavior.

Recently, when I enrolled my five-year-old son at his first school, it proved to be an interesting experience for me. Both the school principal and interviewing teacher concentrated on the psychological profile and emotional make-up of my son so that they would have a full view of the child with which to work. This total approach to the child-person indicated to me that Neill's books and the Summerhill experience had made inroads over the years both with teachers individually and teacher college curriculum in general. This was further born out when I later revealed to the principal and teachers that I had attended Summerhill in the early sixties. They were quite surprised and happy to meet someone who actually went to school there. Summerhill is a way of life, living with others in society and expressing oneself through the passion of interest in love, knowledge, and work.

Robert Gottlieb

(Note: Robert Gottlieb attended Summerhill School in 1960–61–62. During that time he evinced no interest in learning to read or write. That desire didn't arrive until the age of eleven, largely as a result of the influence of Summerhill. Today he is an Executive Vice-President of a large talent agency and, in fact, is head of their Literary Department.)

Editor's Preface

Summerhill School: A New View of Childhood presents A. S. Neill looking back on fifty years of running his pioneer self-governing Free School, Summerhill. Extracts from many of his twenty published books and other material are here woven into a narrative to give the impression of being his final word on his favourite subject. We hear Neill at eighty-eight, in 1971, telling us the story of his famous school. In the second part of this book Neill goes on to tell his own story and describe the many changes that he lived to see.

I first got the idea for this book last spring after talking on the phone from Summerhill to a woman from the USA who was concerned because the book *Summerhill* was now out of print in the States. Colleges across America were dropping discussion of Summerhill from their education courses because the book was no longer available.

I talked to Neill's daughter Zoë about it the next day and we agreed that if Neill was to be put back in print he should be re-edited. We decided that I should devote most of my efforts for the school during the summer term to editing Neill's writings into a new book. Neill had never liked the original book *Summerhill* because his American publisher (and editor), Harold Hart, had included Neill's dated Freudian explanations of child psychology from the 1920s and early 1930s and had twisted Neill's prose to fit the American market; Hart had also taken out all but passing references to Neill's friend and mentor Wilhelm Reich because he thought Reich was too much of a hot potato for 1960s America.

We had our own reasons for believing Neill could be better served by a completely new edition of his work. The book *Summerhill* did not adequately represent the school that we have known and loved. I first came to Summerhill in 1961 as part of the American invasion of pupils when the book *Summerhill* was first published. At the time the school was already forty years old. I had a rude awakening as I realized the place was very different from the book. Most of the description of the school in *Summerhill* was lifted out of *That Dreadful School*, published in the mid-1930s. Neill was now an old man and no longer a benign presence at the centre of every good story. More to the point, co-existing in 'freedom' was harder work than I had imagined and 'self-government' was a much more living presence within the school than I had anticipated. By the time I had awakened fully I realized that I preferred the reality to the book.

In editing Neill I have tried to limit his description of the workings of the school to what I have personally witnessed or what he describes as particular to one time and moment. Part of the 'freedom' of the school has been that many things have been organized in different ways at different times. Readers should bear in mind that many aspects of the self-government at Summerhill are open to change as the community changes.

Coming back to work at the school after eighteen years without a visit I was struck by many elements of school life that were run in exactly the same way as when I was a boy. Only later did I find out that in the intervening years some aspects of the school's self-government had been managed very differently, and that only recently had they come full circle. The most important thing about the school is its attempt to provide a structure which will allow the school to fit the child.

A week after the end of the summer term the school plays host to the annual conference of the Friends of Summerhill Trust. The Trust was set up by a group of Summerhill's friends, parents and old pupils soon after Zoë took over running the school. It is a charitable organization to help raise money for the school and also promote the ideas of Summerhill around the world. I would like to thank members of the Trust and the Trust's secretary, Freer Spreckley, for advice and encouragement during the preparation of this book. By the way, if you wish to join the Friends of Summerhill Trust you can write to them, care of Summerhill.

This summer's Friends' weekend conference was entitled 'Self-government at Home and at School'. Half of the hundred and twenty people who attended came from Germany. It looks as if Eastern Europe may be the next part of the world to become interested in democratic education.

While in the States I showed this book to some people who are

connected to an educational foundation and are particularly concerned with free schools, and they had many thoughtful suggestions
for changing this book. Some of their criticisms were local to the
USA; for instance it was suggested that I should take out the
paragraph on fluoridization and the whole chapter on Reich (since
Reich is such a controversial issue there). These people had been
connected with a day school and they wanted to leave out the
arguments in favour of boarding-schools in the chapter 'Other
Schools' because Americans have no tradition or belief in
boarding-schools for younger children. Their sternest criticism was
that they felt Neill spoke in a way that in the 1990s could be
interpreted as sexist.

After giving it a lot of thought I have decided not to make these
changes. Neill always supported freedom of expression for others
and I think we ought to give him the same courtesy. In the last
twenty years the world has quite rightly come to expect careful
avoidance of even the appearance of prejudice in writers. Neill was
a man of his times but, however casual his language might seem by
today's standards, he had no intention of displaying prejudice and
would be shocked at the charge. He strongly believed in self-
determination for everyone.

Neill spent a lifetime trying to bring his message to the world
and now, thirty years after the publication of the original *Summerhill*, my hope is that the world will be big enough to set him in
his time and love him in spite of his flaws and limitations. His
message about the nature and meaning of childhood is still unique
and his democratic working model still backs it up with living
proof.

Albert Lamb
November 1990

Editor's Introduction: Neill and Summerhill

Alexander Sutherland Neill was thirty-seven years old when he started his school Summerhill back in 1921 and he was already well established in England as a radical educational theorist through his early books on education.

Neill had grown up in a Scottish village as the son of the local schoolteacher. Unlike his seven brothers and sisters he was not deemed worthy of being sent on to the local secondary school so he was put out to work at fourteen. Several years later he drifted into schoolteaching and at the age of twenty-five he took up his formal education again as a student at Edinburgh University. He began writing about education and as a young graduate, working as the acting head of a Scottish village school, he wrote his first book, *A Dominie's Log*.

By the time I got to know him he was an old man. Gone were the days when he would join a young hooligan in throwing stones through the greenhouse windows. Neill's burly old figure was enormously comforting but he remained something of a quietly canny Scot right to the end. He combined diffidence with mild impatience in a way that does not come across in his writing. Still, we kids always found him very easy to approach. He had none of the adult pride that is so common in strong grown-ups. He managed to carry great personal authority while being a non-authoritarian presence.

He seemed very good at old age but I don't think he really enjoyed it. He greatly enjoyed his late blossoming fame, however, even though it brought him a host of troubles in the form of huge stacks of letters and busloads of visitors.

Summerhill first become well known during the 1930s in Britain and for a while Neill was much in demand as a speaker. During the period he had a profound effect on many British teachers as well as on parents. Since that time Summerhill has been best known abroad and has had its greatest effect on schools and parents in other parts of the world. In the 1960s Neill's book *Summerhill* sold two million copies in the United States; it also did well in Britain. In the 1970s in Germany a translation of the book sold well over a million copies. Recently, in the 1980s, there has been a great vogue for books about Summerhill in Japan. The effect of the school on modern education has always been way out of proportion to the numbers attending the school; in the whole history of Summerhill there have been only about six hundred students. Perhaps the most profound effect of Neill's work has been on parents and their attitude to their children.

Neill was unusual among educational pioneers in caring more about 'psychology' than about 'education'. His creation is the oldest self-governing school offering non-compulsory lessons in the world. During the early years Neill took many maladjusted children but in the 1930s he shifted the emphasis of the school and tried to take mostly children without psychological problems.

Neill at this time came to see Summerhill as a therapeutic school for normal children. The goal was to use childhood and adolescence to create emotional wholeness and personal strength. Neill thought that once this wholeness had been achieved children would be self-motivated to learn what they needed academically. The key to this growth was to give children freedom to play for as long as they felt the need in an atmosphere of approval and love. The children were given freedom but not licence; they could do as they pleased as long as it didn't bother anyone else.

After Neill's death in 1973 his wife Ena, who had been sharing the burdens with him for many years, took over and ran the school for twelve years on her own. In 1985 Neill's daughter Zoë Readhead (pronounced 'Redhead'), who had grown up as a pupil in the school, became the current headmistress.

Summerhill's living reality seems so powerful and right that it is surprising how little interest the world has shown in what actually goes on there. The year 1991 is the seventieth anniversary of the world's most famous progressive school and yet there has never been a systematic study of Summerhill's actual mode of operation, its effect on pupils and its potential consequences for educational theory and practice in the larger context of the wide world.

An example of the latter . . . young kids at Summerhill almost always go to lessons eagerly. Older kids also seem very interested in their studies, often working much more cheerfully than adolescents in other schools. However, kids between ten and twelve at

Summerhill spend very little time in lessons. At this particular age they seem to have a great need to get out from under the weight of adult expectations. Understanding why these children make this choice might help educators design schools that would work with a child's nature instead of fighting against it.

The social control at Summerhill has always been invested in the whole community through the Meeting and that control has always been greater than the word 'freedom' would seem to imply. Children like rules and they provide themselves with a great many of them. At any time during the history of the school there have been hundreds of 'laws' on the books.

Every week during term time for the last sixty-nine years Summerhill kids have settled down after supper on Saturday night to make and change the laws that administer every facet of their life together. This General Meeting is concerned with announcements to the community, questions about areas of general concern, and the proposal of new laws. Although they are not compulsory, anyone, child or staff, can come to any Meeting and use their vote.

Each week the community picks a new chair (at Summerhill always called chairman or madam chairman) to run the Meetings for the next week. The secretary, who keeps the record of business, proposals, and new laws, often holds the position for weeks at a time. The General Meeting starts with a Tribunal report (explained in the next paragraph). The chairman then calls on those who have put themselves on the agenda. Each item is handled separately and the chairman himself cannot speak on a subject without having someone take his place. A chairman has no vote but he has a great deal of power over the Meeting. If people disrupt the Meeting he can fine them or make them leave. The chairman's job is to choose who can speak from the raised hands being offered, to take proposals and bring each matter to a conclusion with a vote.

On Friday afternoon at two o'clock we have Tribunal. Tribunal is a form of lawcourt where people can bring up a personal case if they feel they have been wronged in any way. After individual complaints have been heard the community can decide on the appropriate fines. As well as the regular Tribunal and General Meetings, it is also possible to call Special Meetings. You have to go to the secretary and the current chairman and convince them of the need for immediate community action. Special Meetings are run in the same way as a Tribunal case except that the school is free to speak more generally and make new laws.

The Meetings at Summerhill combine formality and flexibility in a way children instinctively understand and believe in. Each new generation of Summerhill kids quickly learns all the subtleties of their self-government. The General Meeting and Tribunal take up a tiny part of each week's time but their presence is constantly felt throughout the school. The number of cases that actually come to the Meeting is small compared to the times in the week that someone talks about changing a law or 'bringing someone up'.

The part that Zoë takes in the meetings is very different from that taken by her father. Most of Neill's proposals in the Meeting were intentionally silly and were voted down. He felt it was important as headmaster and therapist not to take sides on issues that involved personalities; Neill had a profound ability to be non-judgemental. His whole aim was to stay in the background and make the kids run their own school.

Zoë behaves more like one of the big kids, speaking her piece with the rest of the community and voting for her convictions. Sometimes, watching the swift wave of her raised hand when she wants to be heard, I am swept back almost thirty years to when we were teenagers together. Zoë's lifelong involvement with Summerhill has made her something of a natural democrat in this community of children. She has a sure sense of how she can empower the kids of Summerhill to take charge of their own school.

As well as the Meeting, the school administers itself through the use of committees elected by a general vote and by ombudsmen. At the beginning of each term there are often several committees to be formed or in need of new members. As well as the members of the regular ongoing committees like the bedtimes committee, the library committee or the social committee, the ombudsmen are also voted for at this time.

Each week three ombudsmen are on duty to help people who need to bring in someone from the outside when they are in some kind of row. Sometimes ombudsmen can settle a disagreement there and then but more often they act as a witness or a representative when the case is bought to the Meeting. Even the staff make frequent use of the ombudsmen, as they don't want to be seen as authority figures handing down the law.

The place of ombudsmen within the school shows how the school has evolved structurally over the years. Older kids always made an effort to arbitrate in the disputes of the younger ones but an official title was only found for this role in the mid-1960s. At the time I was seventeen and the rest of the school was very young. As I remember it, it was Ena's son Peter Wood who first read about how Sweden was employing ombudsmen to settle disputes between individuals and local government. It was discussed in the Meeting and a proposal was made that we should have our own ombudsman. I took on the job for the rest of that term. The idea seemed a natural for Summerhill and there was a constant parade of little kids coming to my door with complaints against each other.

Summerhill is such a unique community that there are probably many ways to describe what is going on there. Neill's is only one description. Danë Goodsman, who was one of the little kids when I was there, has written about the school in anthropological terms, seeing the big kids as the true elders of the social structure. According to Danë . . .

As a big kid the child can be seen as a custodian of the school's culture, and we can see that being a big kid becomes a role which is understood as having high status. The effect of this on the social structure of the school is most interesting. It means that effectively children are sent not to the care of adults, but to the care of other children.

An important aspect of the school is certainly the range of ages and interests represented in a community of under a hundred people, similar in size to a traditional extended family. Zoë's mother, Ena, had her eightieth birthday recently and is the oldest member of the community. The student population goes from seventeen right down to five years old. The structure provided by Summerhill includes both the democratic forms of self-government and a hierarchical structure of social expectation by age. This pluralistic variety of age, sex, and interests helps keep the school from being what Margaret Mead once asserted that it was, a 'tyranny of the community' over the individual.

I like to look at Summerhill as a democracy on the Athenian

model. Above the free citizens stands the central figure of the headmistress. Matters that are not of real concern to children or that would weigh them down with responsibility are reserved for the staff and Zoë. For instance the children do not have a final say in hiring new staff or expelling children. Standing to the side of the free citizens there is a kind of hidden support similar to the 'slave class' in Ancient Athens. Many issues that would be divisive to the community do not come up because the food is cooked, the floors are cleaned and the clothes are washed without the children having to say a word about it. These are important differences between Summerhill and some other free schools and part of why our community of children is such a strong one. Our children are given great responsibility over their lives but are still provided for in such a way that they can enjoy their childhood unhampered by social concerns that are beyond them.

Many things that at other schools are now being taught as part of the curriculum are at Summerhill dealt with within the course of daily life. Children do not need to be taught about racial tolerance when they are in a sort of extended family that is an inter-racial group; the same could be said for respect for women's rights. The school is effectively run by the oldest children. When there is a body of older girls at the school, because they are so quick to mature, they usually have a leading role in the management of the school – and another lesson is learned without a teacher.

No sooner did we decide that I should edit a new version of the book *Summerhill* than the word came down from Her Majesty's Inspectorate that they wanted to come and settle in with a team of inspectors for their longest-ever visit to the school. In the past these occasions have cost the school a lot of sleepless nights and ultimately a lot of money too, repairing and rebuilding old facilities. The inspectors arrived at the end of the first week of the summer term.

Soon after they left Zoë wrote, 'Having Her Majesty's Inspectors visiting for five days is something akin to having a distant, nosy, and somewhat prudish relative poking around your house, looking in the oven, smelling the fridge, and rummaging through your knicker drawer. It can only be described as an imposition.' In their verbal report they were friendly and respectful – perhaps Summerhill is at last becoming a kind of grand old British institution –

but they gave the impression that they will be keeping their eye on the place. In the future, red tape may be the tie that binds.

After the inspectors left us the summer term settled down. The big kids took their General Certificate exams during the first half of the term and then the school relaxed into its comfortable summer routine that resembles a very loose American summer camp more than anything else. Lots of kids running around outside (or rolling around on skateboards) and lots of swimming in the pool. As always the end-of-term committee closed the lounge for the final week of term to prepare for the big end-of-term party. The walls of the lounge were covered with drawing paper and huge murals were painted and streamers and balloons were hung. The actors stuck themselves into the theatre to prepare for the end-of-term play (appropriately entitled 'The Inspectors are Coming').

On the last Saturday of term, after the play, everyone trooped over for the opening of the lounge and the traditional end-of-term party began. During the evening the school's rock and roll blues band played a long set. At midnight the kids who were leaving went into the middle of a human circle and 'Auld Lang Syne' was sung by all those who were staying on.

While Summerhill provides a traditional academic education and is proud of the academic achievements of its pupils the real benefits of its educational programme are more profound. Many children come to Summerhill with emotional problems and go away whole and strong. At the moment over a third of the children in the school are Japanese, quite a few are from other countries, but all of them are Summerhillians. Warmth, optimism, independence, and self-reliance are contagious qualities at the school. The structure of the school lets kids be independent and at the same time accept their responsibilities towards each other just as the best families do.

Many of the benefits of a Summerhill education are not apparent until later in life. This 'invisible' aspect of the school is one of the hardest things to describe to visitors or new staff. Neill himself was a late bloomer and in some ways Summerhill is the ultimate environment for late bloomers. With a happy childhood tucked under your belt your future development is almost assured. We at the school believe that in this time of rapid technological change Summerhill has a formula that could help produce the men and women we will be needing in the future.

Introduction to the American Edition

by Albert Lamb

In 1970 A. S. Neill's American publisher, Harold Hart, after a calendar year (1969) where the sale of the book *Summerhill* exceeded 200,000 copies, looked back with pardonable pride on his role in launching *Summerhill*. He wrote: "When *Summerhill: A Radical Approach to Child Rearing* was announced in 1960, not a single bookseller in the country was willing to place an advance order for even one copy of the book, for A. S. Neill was practically unknown in the United States."

Even if they had heard of Neill and his radical ideas, they would have been unlikely to place many orders for this new book. The 1950s had seen a conservative backlash against the ideas of Progressive education, and with fears after the launch of the first artificial satellite, Sputnik, that the Soviets were overtaking America in the production of scientists and engineers, the United States seemed in the mood to tighten its corporate grip on the youth of the nation.

Harold Hart was very clever in his promotion of *Summerhill*. For instance he took the unusual step of taking out full page ads in Parade magazine, distributed around the United States with local Sunday newspapers, where he made his pitch directly to parents. As Erich Fromm had said in his introduction to the 1960 edition: "Even though no school like Summerhill exists in the United States today, any parent can profit by reading this book. These chapters will challenge him to rethink his own approach to his child."

Summerhill, published during the week that John Kennedy was elected president, caught the public's fancy at a turning point in America's history. Neill's book rode the tide of the 1960s by giving a psychological and philosophical underpinning to the special consciousness of that era. Neill applied some home truths to children that Americans had long considered part of their shared assumptions for adults. Neill said that children should have the right to choose freely what they want to do with their lives. He also claimed they had the ability to govern themselves effectively in a working democratic community. The simplicity of these ideas cut through the existing dialogue between conservatives and progressives and touched a raw nerve.

The progressives had worked hard to get their ideas implemented in the public school system between the World Wars and then had seen their ideas watered down and ultimately discredited. The McCarthy era put private Progressive schools on the defensive, and by the end of the 1950s the leaders of the movement were either dead or had run out of steam. At the same time as the publication of *Summerhill*, a new generation of educators and social critics, such as Paul Goodman, John Holt, Herbert Kohl, and Jonathan Kozol, began writing about American schools from a new angle. The American public school had got to be too big and too inefficient on every level not to be seen as an appropriate target.

During the decade of the 1960s, while traditional private schools were in decline, more than 200 Free Schools opened their doors. Most of them didn't open them for very long and by 1980 the number must have been down to a mere handful. The tide had turned and the only growth stock in the alternative school movement was homeschooling. More recently there has been some new growth. Jerry Mintz, who had run his own Free School in Vermont, travelled the country looking for alternative schools and found a great deal of quiet activity. These schools now are in touch with each other and have formed the National Coalition of Alternative Community Schools (N.C.A.C.S.), in Summertown, Tennessee.

Neill never gave much direct help to the founders of Free Schools in America. He never set up a franchise. His descriptions of how Summerhill worked were resolutely anecdotal. Very few people intending to start Free Schools came to Summerhill to see how the place was put together. And Neill distanced himself from other Free Schools when he began to hear disturbing reports: "My school Summerhill has no affiliation with any school in the USA or elsewhere....the words founded on Summerhill principles' do not mean that the school is automatically approved of by my staff or myself. I am proud to have any school acknowledge the inspiration my work has aroused, but each school must stand on its own feet. I don't want any praise for its success, just as I don't want to be blamed by parents who fancy that I had something to do with its failures."

Just as Doctor Spock got the blame for a whole generation of children, so Neill got the blame for many children who were raised in licence rather than in true freedom. This wasn't entirely fair as a great many American adults took Neill's message to heart and were able to change and improve their relationships with children. Many children also were helped to bear up with difficult situations in their homes and schools. George Dennison summed it up well when he said: "I think that Neill has been extremely influential even in schools that don't remotely resemble Summerhill. I don't mean that you find many teachers adapting his attitude *in toto*, but that you find important modifications all down the line, in schools and out, that can be traced to Neill and other libertarians."

All the same it is a pity that America didn't listen more carefully to Neill's message about youth as the time for emotional and social development. That great push for scientists and engineers promised in the 1950s never actually took place. Instead of discovering things or building things, the cream of the expanding college market has been sending itself off to law school or business school with the ultimate aim of making money.

The rat race now begins with first grade and the public school system that was in trouble in the 1950s is in more trouble in the 1990s. The kids who used to run around with their friends out in the neighborhood are now safely at home after school watching videos. One-parent families are becoming the norm, and big families, where the children outnumber the parents, are almost a thing of the past. Kids are still second class citizens whose youth culture has become an annexe of big business. Maybe the mood of the educational community is not as conservative as it looks. Maybe the parents, children, and teachers of America are ready for a change.

Part One

Introduction

Summerhill today (1971) is in essentials what it was when founded in 1921. Self-government for the pupils and staff, freedom to go to lessons or stay away, freedom to play for days or weeks or years if necessary, freedom from any indoctrination whether religious or moral or political, freedom from character moulding.

At other schools the number of enterprising and good teachers is legion, and they should be honoured for their original work in their cramping environment – their often barrack-style schools. But I say they have nothing to give to me because we are not going quite the same way; on parallel lines perhaps, but we do not meet, because they are in school and I am in a self-governing community.

I do see signs of progress in other schools. The modern primary schools can be excellent. One I saw in Leicester was a great contrast to the primary school of forty years ago; happy faces, a buzz of natural conversation, each child busy on his or her own job. The next step is the application of such free methods to the secondary modern and comprehensive school, an almost impossible task within the examination system.

Summerhill has shown the world that a school can abolish fear of teachers and, deeper down, fear of life. Staff at Summerhill do not stand on their dignity, nor do they expect any deference because they are adults. Socially, the only privilege the teachers have is their freedom from bedtime laws. Their food is that of the school community. They are addressed by their first names and are seldom given nicknames; and if they are, these are tokens of friendliness and equality. For thirty years, George Corkhill, our science master, was George or Corks or Corkie. Every pupil loved him.

There is no necessity for a gulf separating pupils from teachers, a gulf made by adults, not children. Teachers want to be little gods protected by dignity. They fear that if they act human, their authority will vanish and their classrooms will become bedlams. They fear to abolish fear. Innumerable children are afraid of their teachers. It is discipline that creates the fear. Ask any soldier if he fears his sergeant-major; I never met one who didn't.

More and more, I have come to believe that the greatest reform required in our schools is the abolition of that chasm between young and old which perpetuates paternalism. Such dictatorial authority gives a child an inferiority that persists throughout life; as an adult, he merely exchanges the authority of the teacher for that of the boss.

An army may be a necessity, but no one, barring a dull conservative, would argue that military life is a model for living. Yet our schools are army regiments or worse. Soldiers at least move around a lot, but a child sits on his bottom most of the time at an age when the whole human instinct is to move.

In this book, I explain why the powers that be try to devitalize children as they do, but the mass of teachers do not understand what lies behind their discipline and 'character moulding', and most do not want to know. The disciplinary way is the easy one. ATTENTION! STAND AT EASE! These are the orders of the barrack square and the classroom.

In the USA, it is the student's fear of bad grades – idiotic grades that mean nothing of importance – or fear of not passing exams; in some countries it is still fear of the cane or the belt, or the fear of being scorned or mocked by stupid teachers.

The tragedy is that fear also exists on the teacher's side – fear of being thought human, fear of being found out by the uncanny intuition of children. I *know* this. Ten years of teaching in state schools left me with no illusions about teachers. In my time, I, too, was dignified, aloof, and a disciplinarian. I taught in a system that depended on the 'tawse', as we called the belt in Scotland. My father used it and I followed suit, without ever thinking about the rights and wrongs of it – until the day when I myself, as a headmaster, belted a boy for insolence. A new, sudden thought came to me. What am I doing? This boy is small, and I am big. Why am I hitting someone not my own size? I put my tawse in the fire and never hit a child again.

The boy's insolence had brought me down to his level; it offended my dignity, my status as the ultimate authority. He had addressed me as if I were his equal, an unpardonable affront. But today, sixty years later, thousands of teachers are still where I was then. That sounds arrogant, but it is simply the raw truth that teachers largely refuse to be people of flesh and blood.

Only yesterday, a young teacher told me that his headmaster had threatened him with dismissal because a boy had addressed him as Bob. 'What will happen to discipline if you allow such familiarity?' he asked. 'What would happen to a private who addressed his colonel as Jim?'

Why do I get hundreds of letters from children? Not because of my beautiful eyes – nay, but because the idea of Summerhill touches their depths, their longing for freedom, their hatred of authority in home and school, their wish to be in contact with their elders. Summerhill has no generation gap. If it had, half of my proposals in our general meetings would not be outvoted. If it had, a girl of twelve could not tell a teacher that his lessons are dull. I hasten to add that a teacher can tell a kid that he is being a damned nuisance. Freedom must look both ways.

Education should produce children who are at once individuals and community persons, and self-government without doubt does this. In an ordinary school obedience is a virtue, so much so that few in later life can challenge anything. Thousands of students in teacher training are full of enthusiasm about their coming vocation. A year after leaving college they sit in staffrooms and think that education means subjects and discipline. True they dare not challenge the system or they will get the sack, but a few do, if only in their minds. A lifetime of moulding is hard to break.

That society is sick no one can deny; that society does not want to lose its sickness is also undeniable. It fights every humane effort to better itself. It fought votes for women, abolition of capital punishment; it fought against the reform of our cruel divorce laws, our cruel laws against homosexuals. In a way, our task as teachers is to fight against a mass psychology, a sheep psychology where every animal has the same coating and the same baa baa ... barring the black sheep, and challengers. Our schools have their shepherds ... not always gentle ones. Our sheep pupils are clad in their nice uniforms.

In psychology, no man knows very much. The inner forces of human life are still largely hidden from us.

Since Freud's genius made it alive, psychology has gone far; but it is still a new science, mapping out the coast of an unknown continent. Fifty years hence, psychologists will very likely smile at our ignorance today.

Since I left education and took up child psychology, I have had all sorts of children to deal with – young arsonists, thieves, liars, bedwetters, and bad-tempered children. Years of intensive work in child training has convinced me that I know comparatively little of the forces that motivate life. I am convinced, however, that parents who have had to deal with only their own children know much less than I do.

It is because I believe that a difficult child is nearly always made difficult by wrong treatment at home as well as at school that I dare to address parents as well as teachers.

What is the province of psychology? I suggest the word *curing*. But what kind of curing? I do not want to be cured of my habit of choosing the colours orange and black; nor do I want to be cured of smoking; nor of my liking for a bottle of beer. No teacher has the right to cure a child of making noises on a drum. The only curing that should be practised is the curing of unhappiness.

One place I have changed over the years is in my attitude to psychology. When my school was in Germany and then Austria (from 1921 to 1924) I was in the midst of the then new psychoanalytical movement. Like so many other young fools I thought that Utopia was in sight. Make the unconscious conscious and the world will be rid of its hates and crimes and wars, so the answer was psychoanalysis.

When I came back to England to a house called Summerhill in Lyme Regis I had only five pupils. In three years the number grew to twenty-seven. Most were problem children sent in despair by parents and schools. Thieves, destroyers, bullies of both sexes. I 'cured' them by analysis, I thought, but discovered that the ones who refused to come to my analysis sessions were cured also, and had to conclude that freedom, not analysis, was the active agent. Luckily, for analysis is not the answer to the sickness of humanity.

I don't say that therapy is wrong, but I know it is wrong for a teacher to be the therapist. The therapist must be neutral, on the outside; at a General Meeting I would ask, 'Who the hell borrowed my spanner and didn't bring it back?' Willie did it, and to him it was father's voice complaining, so he identified me with a cop and at the next session of analysis he shut up like a clam.

The difficult child is the child who is unhappy. He is at war with himself; and in consequence, he is at war with the world.

The difficult adult is in the same boat. No happy man ever disturbed a meeting, or preached a war, or lynched a Negro. No happy woman ever nagged her husband or her children. No happy man ever committed a murder or a theft. No happy employer ever frightened his employees.

All crimes, all hatreds, all wars can be reduced to unhappiness. This book is an attempt to show how unhappiness arises, how it ruins human lives, and how children can be reared so that much of this unhappiness will never arise.

More than that, this book is the story of a place – Summerhill School – where children's unhappiness is cured and, more important, where children are reared in happiness.

Idea of Summerhill

This is a story of a modern school – Summerhill.

Summerhill was founded in the year 1921. The school is situated within the town of Leiston, in Suffolk, and is about one hundred miles from London.

Just a word about Summerhill pupils. Some children come to Summerhill at the age of five years, and others as late as twelve. The children generally remain at the school until they are sixteen years old. In good times we generally have about thirty-five boys and thirty girls, with a good number of the children from foreign countries.

The children are housed by age groups with a houseparent for each group. The intermediates sleep in a stone building, the seniors sleep in huts. The pupils do not have to stand room inspection and no one picks up after them. They are left free. No one tells them what to wear: they put on any kind of costume they want to at any time.

Newspapers have called it a 'go-as-you-please school' and have implied that it is a gathering of wild primitives who know no law and have no manners.

It seems necessary, therefore, for me to write the story of Summerhill as honestly as I can. That I write with a bias is natural; yet I shall try to show the demerits of Summerhill as well as its merits. Its merits will be the merits of healthy, free children whose lives are unspoiled by fear and hate.

Obviously, a school that makes active children sit at desks studying mostly useless subjects is a bad school. It is a good school only for those who believe in such a school, for those uncreative citizens who want docile, uncreative children who will fit into a civilization whose standard of success is money.

Summerhill began as an experimental school. It is no longer such; it is now a demonstration school, for it demonstrates that freedom works.

When my first wife and I began the school, we had one main idea; *to make the school fit the child* – instead of making the child fit the school. I had taught in ordinary schools for many years. I knew the other way well. I knew it was wrong. It was wrong because it was based on an adult conception of what a child should be and of how a child should learn. The other way dated from the days when psychology was still an unknown science.

Well, we set out to make a school in which we should allow children freedom to be themselves. In order to do this, we had to renounce all discipline, all direction, all suggestion, all moral training, all religious instruction. We have been called brave, but it did not require courage. All it required was what we had – a complete belief in the child as a good, not an evil, being. For fifty years this belief in the goodness of the child has never wavered; it rather has become a final faith.

My view is that a child is innately wise and realistic. If left to himself without adult suggestion of any kind, he will develop as far as he is capable of developing. Logically, Summerhill is a place in which people who have the innate ability and wish to be scholars will be scholars; while those who are only fit to sweep the streets will sweep the streets. But we have not produced a street cleaner so far. Nor do I write this snobbishly, for I would rather see a school produce a happy street cleaner than a neurotic scholar.

What is Summerhill like? Well, for one thing, lessons are optional. Children can go to them or stay away from them – for years if they want to. There *is* a timetable – but only for the teachers.

The children have classes usually according to their age, but sometimes according to their interests. We have no new methods of teaching, because we do not consider that teaching in itself matters very much. Whether a school has or has not a special method for teaching long division is of no significance, for long division is of no importance except to those who *want* to learn it. And the child who *wants* to learn long division *will* learn it no matter how it is taught.

Children who come to Summerhill as kindergarteners attend lessons from the beginning of their stay; but pupils from other schools vow that they will never attend any beastly lessons again at any time. They play and cycle and get in people's way, but they fight shy of lessons. This sometimes goes on for months or years.

The recovery time is proportionate to the hatred their last school gave them. One case was a girl from a convent. She loafed for three years. The average period of recovery from lessons aversion is rather less than that.

Strangers to this idea of freedom will be wondering what sort of madhouse it is where children play all day if they want to. Many an adult says, 'If I had been sent to a school like that, I'd never have done a thing.' Others says, 'Such children will feel themselves heavily handicapped when they have to compete against children who have been made to learn.'

I think of Jack who left us at the age of seventeen to go into an engineering factory. One day, the managing director sent for him.

'You are the lad from Summerhill,' he said. 'I'm curious to know how such an education appears to you now that you are mixing with lads from the old schools. Suppose you had to choose again, would you go to Eton or Summerhill?'

'Oh, Summerhill, of course,' replied Jack.

'But what does it offer that the other schools don't offer?'

Jack scratched his head. 'I dunno,' he said slowly; 'I think it gives you a feeling of complete self-confidence.'

'Yes,' said the manager dryly, 'I noticed it when you came into the room.'

'Lord,' laughed Jack. 'I'm sorry if I gave you that impression.'

'I liked it,' said the director. 'Most men when I call them into the office fidget about and look uncomfortable. You came in as my equal.'

This story shows that learning in itself is not as important as personality and character. Jack failed in his university exams because he hated book learning. But his lack of knowledge about Lamb's *Essays* or the French language did not handicap him in life. He is now a successful engineer.

All the same, there is a lot of learning in Summerhill. Perhaps a group of our twelve-year-olds could not compete with a class of equal age in handwriting or spelling or fractions. But in an examination requiring originality, our lot would beat the others hollow.

We have no class examinations in the school, but sometimes I have set an exam for fun. The following questions appeared in one such paper:

Where are the following: Madrid, Thursday Island, yesterday, love, democracy, hate, my pocket screwdriver [alas, there was no helpful answer to that one]?

Give meanings for the following (the number shows how many are expected for each): hand (3) [. . . only two got the third right – the standard measure of a horse]; brass (4) [. . . metal, cheek, top army officers, department of an orchestra].

Translate Hamlet's To-be-or-not-to-be speech into Summerhillese.

These questions are obviously not intended to be serious, and the children enjoy them thoroughly. Newcomers, on the whole, do not rise to the answering standard of pupils who have become acclimatized to the school. Not that they have less brainpower, but rather because they have become so accustomed to work in a serious groove that any light touch puzzles them.

This is the play side of our teaching. In all classes much work is done. If, for some reason, a teacher cannot take his class on the appointed day, there is usually much disappointment for the pupils.

David, aged nine, had to be isolated for whooping cough. He cried bitterly. 'I'll miss Roger's lesson in geography,' he protested. David had been in the school practically from birth, and he had definite and final ideas about the necessity of having his lessons given to him. David is now a professor of mathematics at London University.

A few years ago someone at a General Meeting (at which all school rules are voted by the entire school, each pupil and each staff member having one vote) proposed that a certain culprit should be punished by being banished from lessons for a week. The other children protested on the ground that the punishment was too severe.

My staff and I have a hearty hatred of all examinations. To us, the university exams are anathema. But we cannot refuse to teach children the required subjects. Obviously, as long as the exams are in existence, they are our master. Hence, the Summerhill staff is always qualified to teach to the set standard.

Not that all the children want to take these exams; only those going to the university do so. And such children do not seem to find it especially hard to tackle these exams. They generally begin to work for them seriously at the age of thirteen, and they do the work in about three years. Of course they don't always pass at the first try. The more important fact is that they try again.

Let me describe a typical day in Summerhill. Breakfast is from 8.15 to 8.45. The staff and pupils carry their breakfast from the hatch beside the kitchen door across to the dining-room. Beds are supposed to be made by 9.30, when lessons begin.

At the beginning of each term, a timetable is posted. Thus Derek in the laboratory may have Class I on Monday, Class II on Tuesday, and so on. I have a similar timetable for English and mathematics; Maurice for geography and history. The younger children (aged six to ten) usually stay with their own teacher most of the morning, but they also go to woodwork or the art room.

No pupil is compelled to attend lessons. But if Jimmy comes to English on Monday and does not make an appearance again until Friday of the following week, the others quite rightly object that he is holding back the work, and they may throw him out for impeding progress.

Lessons go on until one o'clock, but the kindergarteners and juniors lunch at 12.30. The school has to be fed in two relays, the staff and seniors sit down to lunch at 1.15.

Afternoons are completely free for everyone. What they all do in the afternoon I do not know. I garden or work in my office, and seldom see youngsters about. I see the juniors playing gangsters. Some of the seniors busy themselves with motors and music and drawing and painting. In good weather seniors play games. Some tinker about in the workshop, mending their bicycles or making boats or revolvers.

Tea is served at four and then classes resume after tea. The juniors school day ends at 5.30 when their supper is served. The staff and seniors have their supper at 6.15.

At seven, various activities begin. The juniors like to be read to. The middle group likes work in the art room – painting, linoleum cuts, leather work, basket making. There is usually a busy group in the pottery; in fact, the pottery seems to be a favourite haunt morning and evening. The wood and metal workshop is full every night.

There is no timetable for handiwork. Children make what they want to. And what they want to make is nearly always a toy revolver or gun or boat or kite. They are not much interested in elaborate joints of the dovetail variety; even the older boys do not usually care for difficult carpentry. Not many of them take an interest in my own hobby – hammered brasswork – because you can't attach much of a fantasy to a brass bowl.

On a good day you may not see the boy gangsters of Summerhill. They are in far corners intent on their deeds of derring-do. But you will see the girls; they are in or near the house.

You will often find the art room full of girls painting. They keep busy with sewing work, making bright things with fabrics, and other creative activities.

Summerhill is possibly the happiest school in the world. We have no taunts and seldom a case of homesickness. We very rarely have fights – quarrels, of course, but seldom have I seen a stand-up fight like the ones we used to have as boys. I seldom hear a child cry, because children when free have much less hate to express than children who are downtrodden. Hate breeds hate, and love breeds love. Love means approving of children and that is essential in any school. You can't be on the side of children if you punish them and storm at them. Summerhill is a school in which the child knows that he is approved of.

Mind you, we are not above and beyond human foibles. I spent weeks planting potatoes one spring, and when I found eight plants pulled up in June, I made a big fuss. Yet there was a difference between my fuss and that of an authoritarian. My fuss was about potatoes, but the fuss an authoritarian would have made would have dragged in the question of morality – right and wrong. I did not say that it was wrong to steal my spuds; I did not make it a matter of good and evil – I made it a matter of *my spuds*. They were my spuds and they should have been left alone. I hope I am making the distinction clear.

Let me put it another way. To the children, I am no authority to be feared. I am their equal, and the row I kick up about my spuds has no more significance to them than the row a boy may kick up about his punctured bicycle tyre. It is quite safe to have a row with a child when you are equals.

Now some will say? 'That's all bunk. There can't be equality. Neill is the boss; he is bigger and wiser.' That is indeed true. I am the boss, and if the house caught fire the children would run to me. They know I am bigger and more knowledgeable, but that does not matter when I meet them on their own ground, the potato patch, so to speak.

When Billy, aged five, told me to get out of his birthday party because I hadn't been invited, I went at once without hesitation – just as Billy gets out of my room when I don't want his company. It is not easy to describe this relationship between teacher and child, but every visitor to Summerhill knows what I mean when I say that the relationship is ideal. One sees it in the attitude to the staff in general. Members of the staff are known as Harry, and Ulla, and Daphne. I am Neill and the cook is Esther.

In Summerhill, everyone has equal rights. No one is allowed to walk on my piano, and I am not allowed to borrow a boy's cycle without his permission. At a General School Meeting, the vote of a child of six counts for as much as my vote does.

But, says the knowing one, in practice of course the voices of the grown-ups count. Doesn't the child of six wait to see how you vote before he raises his hand? I wish he sometimes would, for too many of my proposals are beaten. Free children are not easily influenced; the absence of fear is the finest thing that can happen to a child.

Our children do not fear our staff. One of the school rules is that after ten o'clock at night there shall be quietness on the upper corridor. One night, about eleven, a pillow fight was going on, and I left my desk, where I was writing, to protest against the row. As I got upstairs, there was a scurrying of feet and the corridor was empty and quiet. Suddenly I heard a disappointed voice say, 'Humph, it's only Neill,' and the fun began again at once. When I explained that I was trying to write a book downstairs, they showed concern and at once agreed to chuck the noise. Their scurrying came from the suspicion that their bedtime officer (one of their own age) was on their track.

I emphasize the importance of this absence of fear of adults. A child of nine will come and tell me he has broken a window with a ball. He tells me, because he isn't afraid of arousing wrath or moral indignation. He may have to pay for the window, but he doesn't have to fear being lectured or being punished.

Children make contact with strangers more easily when fear is unknown to them. English reserve is, at bottom, really fear; and that is why the most reserved are those who have the most wealth. The fact that Summerhill children are so exceptionally friendly to visitors and strangers is a source of pride to me and my staff.

The most frequent question asked by Summerhill visitors is, 'Won't the child turn round and blame the school for not making him learn arithmetic or music?' The answer is that young Freddy Beethoven and young Tommy Einstein will refuse to be kept away from their respective spheres.

The function of the child is to live his own life – not the life that his anxious parents think he should live, nor a life according to the purpose of the educator who thinks he knows what is best. All this interference and guidance on the part of adults only produces a generation of robots.

You cannot *make* children learn music or anything else without to some degree converting them into will-less adults. You fashion them into accepters of the *status quo* – a good thing for a society that needs obedient sitters at dreary desks, standers in shops, mechanical catchers of the 8.30 suburban train – a society, in short, that is carried on the shabby shoulders of the scared little man – the scared-to-death conformist.

School Meetings

Summerhill is a self-governing school, democratic in form. Every-thing connected with social, or group, life, including punishment for social offences, is settled by vote at the Saturday night General Meeting.

Each member of the teaching staff (including houseparents) and each child, regardless of his age, has one vote. My vote carries the same weight as that of a seven-year-old.

One may smile and say, 'But your voice has more value, hasn't it?' Well, let's see. Once, at a time when smoking was permitted in the school, I got up at a meeting and proposed that no child under sixteen should be allowed to smoke. The question of children's smoking is of course a controversial one, and I am not going to argue about it here. In the end it generally solves itself.

At the time, during the Second World War, sweet rationing made the spending of pocket money a bit of a problem. Since about the only things that could be bought were cigarettes, there had been an increase of smoking, especially among the younger boys and girls. I was concerned about this, perhaps too concerned when I recall that at least 50 per cent of old pupils who had smoked at the age of ten were non-smokers. I argued my case: a drug, poisonous, not a real appetite in children, but mostly an at-tempt to appear grown up. Counter-arguments were thrown across the floor. The vote was taken. I was beaten by a large majority.

The sequel is worth recording. After my defeat, a boy of sixteen proposed that no one under twelve should be allowed to smoke. He carried his motion. However, at the following weekly meeting, a boy of twelve proposed the repeal of the new smoking rule, saying, 'We are all sitting in the bogs [toilets] smoking on the sly just like kids do in a strict school, and I say it is against the whole idea of Summerhill.' His speech was cheered, and that meeting repealed the law. I hope I have made it clear that my voice is not always more powerful than that of a child.

Once, I spoke strongly about breaking the bedtime rules, with the consequent noise and the sleepy heads that lumbered around the next morning. I proposed that culprits should be fined all their pocket money for each offence. A boy of fourteen proposed that there should be a penny reward per hour for everyone staying up after his or her bedtime. I got a few votes, but he got a big majority. The reward was not to come from me but from the community cash box and its collection of petty fines. Whether it worked or not is a subsidiary matter; the valuable part is that children keep trying different ways and means to keep the community together, to keep it social.

Summerhill's self-government has no bureaucracy. There is a different chairman at each General Meeting, and the secretary's job is voluntary.

Our democracy makes laws – good ones, too. For example, it is forbidden to bathe in the sea without the supervision of life-guards, who are always staff members. It is forbidden to climb on the roofs. Bedtimes must be kept or there is an automatic fine. Whether classes should be called off on the Thursday or on the Friday preceding a holiday is a matter for a show of hands at a General School Meeting.

The success of the meeting depends largely on whether the chairman is weak or strong, for to keep order among sixty-five vigorous children is no easy task. The chairman has power to fine noisy citizens. Under a weak chairman, the fines are much too frequent.

The staff takes a hand, of course, in the discussions. So do I; although there are a number of situations in which I must remain neutral. In fact, I have seen a lad charged with an offence get away with it on a complete alibi, although he had privately confided to me that he had committed the offence. In a case like this, I must always be on the side of the individual.

I, of course, participate like anyone else when it comes to casting my vote on any issue or bringing up a proposal of my own. Here is a typical example. I once raised the question of whether football should be played in the lounge. The lounge is under my office, and I explained that I disliked the noise of football while I was working. I proposed that indoor football be forbidden. I was supported by some of the girls, by some older boys, and by most of the staff. But my proposal was not carried, and that meant my continuing to put up with the noisy scuffle of feet below my office. Finally, after much public disputation at several meetings, I did carry by majority approval the abolition of football in the lounge. And this is the way the minority generally gets its rights in our school democracy; it keeps demanding them. This applies to little children as much as it does to adults.

On the other hand, there are aspects of school life that do not come under the self-government regime. Our aim was to impose nothing on the child, but in actual practice freedom is limited. No general vote is taken to decide who should cook and what should be cooked. New staff are appointed without any official consultation with children. My wife Ena plans the arrangements for bedrooms, provides the menu, sends out and pays bills. I appoint teachers and ask them to leave if I think they are not suitable. I decide about fire escapes, Ena about health rules. We buy and repair the furniture; we decide what textbooks should be bought.

None of these factors comes into self-government. Nor do the pupils want them to. Self-government to them means dealing with situations that arise in their communal life; they can say what they like, vote how they like in a meeting, and they never wait to see how the staff votes. True, a member of the staff can often get his or her motion carried, but the motion is judged on its merits. We never ask children to decide on things that are beyond their ability to grasp.

A Communist teacher in London described our democracy as anarchism, but I do not know what he meant, and wonder if he did himself. If anarchy means literally without law, Summerhill with its self-government is miles from that. On the other hand, if anarchy means being anti laws made by authorities, I am an anarchist.

I expect he meant that we were playing at democracy, that I, the capitalist (a capitalist who too often makes a loss), run the school, giving the children and staff only a shadow which I call democracy. Other schools have tried complete community living, where the staff decide policy – employment of new members, the buying of furniture, etc. But I have not heard of one that allows the pupils to help choose staff in a meeting, or to decide whether the kitchen requires new mops.

What part should adults play in self-government? They should not lead; they should have the gift of standing more or less outside. When a child is charged with some breach of the rules I make it a point never to vote for or against a fine.

The function of Summerhill self-government is not only to make laws but to discuss social features of the community as well. At the beginning of each term, rules about bedtime are made by vote. You go to bed according to your age. Sports committees have to be elected, as well as an end-of-term dance committee, a theatre committee, bedtime officers, and officers who report any disgraceful behaviour out of the school boundaries.

The most exciting subject ever brought up is that of food. I have more than once waked up a dull meeting by proposing that second helpings be abolished. Any sign of kitchen favouritism in the matter of food is severely handled. But when the kitchen brings up the question of wasting food, the meeting is not much interested. The attitude of children towards food is essentially a personal and self-centred one.

In a General Meeting, all academic discussions are avoided. Children are eminently practical and theory bores them. They like concreteness, not abstraction. I once brought forward a motion that swearing be abolished by law, and I gave my reason. I had been showing a woman around with her little boy, a prospective pupil. Suddenly from upstairs came a very strong adjective. The mother hastily gathered up her son and went off in a hurry. 'Why,' I asked at a meeting, 'should my income suffer because some fathead swears in front of a prospective parent? It isn't a moral question at all; it is purely financial. You swear and I lose a pupil.'

My question was answered by a lad of fourteen. 'Neill is talking rot,' he said. 'Obviously, if this woman was shocked, she didn't believe in Summerhill. Even if she had enrolled her boy, the first time he came home saying damn or hell, she would have taken him out of here.' The meeting agreed with him, and my proposal was voted down.

A General Meeting often has to tackle the problem of bullying. Our community is pretty hard on bullies; and I notice that the school government's bullying rule has been underlined on the bulletin board: *'All cases of bullying will be severely dealt with.'* Bullying is not so rife at Summerhill, however, as in strict schools, and the reason is not far to seek. Under adult discipline, the child can become a hater. Since the child cannot express his hatred of adults with impunity, he takes it out on smaller or weaker boys. But this seldom happens in Summerhill. Very often, a charge of bullying, when investigated, amounts to the fact that Jenny called Peggy a lunatic.

How are the General Meetings run? At the beginning of each term, a chairman is elected for one meeting only. At the end of the week, during Tribunal, the community will vote for his successor. This procedure is followed throughout the term. Anyone who has a grievance, a charge, or a suggestion, or a new law to propose brings it up.

Here is a typical example: Jim took the pedals from Jack's bicycle because his own cycle was in disrepair, and he wanted to go away with some other boys for a weekend trip. After due consideration of the evidence, the meeting decides that Jim must replace the pedals, and he is forbidden to go on the trip.

The chairman asks, 'Any objections?'

Jim gets up and shouts that there jolly well are! Only his adjective isn't exactly 'jolly'. 'This isn't fair!' he cries. 'I didn't know that Jack ever used his old crock of a bike. It has been kicking about among the bushes for days. I don't mind shoving his pedals back, but I think the punishment unfair. I don't think I should be cut out of the trip.'

Follows a breezy discussion. In the debate, it transpires that Jim usually gets a weekly allowance from home, but the allowance hasn't come for six weeks, and he hasn't a bean. The meeting votes that the sentence be quashed, and it is duly quashed.

But what to do about Jim? Finally it is decided to open a subscription fund to put Jim's bike in order. His schoolmates chip in to buy pedals for his bike, and he sets off happily on his trip.

Usually, the Meeting's verdict is accepted by the culprit. However, if the verdict is unacceptable, the defendant may appeal, in which case the chairman will bring up the matter once again at the very end of the meeting. At such an appeal, the matter is considered more carefully, and generally the original verdict is tempered in view of the dissatisfaction of the defendant. The children realize that if the defendant feels he has been unfairly judged, there is a good chance that he actually has been.

As an aside . . . recently an irate woman wrote to me asking why I always used the pronoun 'he' and not 'she', accusing me of being a rabid patriarch who feels that woman is inferior. My answer is that if I have to write 'he or she' all the time, grammar becomes too complicated and awkward ... 'He or she must eat his or her supper' type of thing. When I say 'he' I mean any child of either sex.

No culprit at Summerhill ever shows any signs of defiance or hatred of the authority of his community. I am always surprised at the docility our pupils show when punished.

One term, four of the biggest boys were charged at the General Meeting with doing an illegal thing – selling various articles from their wardrobes. The law forbidding this had been passed on the ground that such practices are unfair to the parents who buy the clothes and unfair as well to the school, because, when children go home minus certain wearing apparel, the parents blame the school for carelessness. The four boys were punished by being kept on the grounds for two days and being sent to bed at eight each night. They accepted the sentence without a murmur. On Monday night, when everyone had gone to the town cinema, I found Dick, one of the culprits, in bed reading.

'You are a chump,' I said. 'Everyone has gone to the cinema. Why don't you get up?'

'Don't try to be funny,' he said.

I grant that democracy is far from a perfect system. Majority rule is not too satisfactory, but I can see no alternative barring dictatorship. What has surprised me for years has been that our school minority accepts the majority verdict; if there is a refusal to accept it it comes from some lad of fifteen who has just come and cannot see why he has to obey 'what a crowd of bloody kids vote on'.

There is an argument that democracy is wrong because it penalizes the minority. Say the twelve-year-olds vote that their bedtime is ten o'clock, and two children of that age like to go to bed at nine. They naturally complain that the others waken them when they come to bed at ten. The ideal solution would be separate rooms, which our school does not have. In our school we cannot use the Communist method of persuading the minority that it is wrong and must come round to the majority view; we have no party line to toe. In general the minority does not feel strongly about a majority vote, and when it does it has simply to lump it.

We have a law against dangerous weapons, a law under which airguns are forbidden. The few boys who want to have their airguns in the school hate the law but in the main they conform to it. As a minority children do not seem to feel so strongly as adults do.

I think the test of the value of self-government lies in the determination of the pupils to retain it. Any suggestion of abolishing it, even of limiting its powers, is met by a very strong reaction. I have suggested abolition twice but would not dare ever to do so again.

Some laws are often broken, especially the bedtime law, yet I am sure that if I made the laws more of them would be broken, for then the natural rebellion against father would come in. It is well known that 'the law makes the crime'.

On the whole the laws in Summerhill are pretty well kept, partly, maybe mainly, because children are so charitable with each other. I have marvelled for fifty years about the sense of justice they show. A boy is charged for bullying and reprimanded by the meeting. At the next meeting he brings up a trumpery charge against the victim. The meeting spots that it is a revenge charge and tells him so.

Someone wrote that our self-government is a fake because the staff really makes the rules and pretends that the pupils make them by a show of hands. That is just a libel, as any pupil, past or present would know. As I have said many a time, they will vote for a law on its own merits whoever proposes it. I have more than once proposed that the loud music be played only in the evenings. I am always outvoted. One of the staff will bring up the wastage of good food . . . for many years we had a little shop just outside the school grounds, and often a child would stoke up on ice lollies and then leave his lunch. The staff proposal may be that anyone leaving his or her lunch should be deprived of lunch next day. That motion is never carried. Again and again I have proposed that money sent to pupils during term should be pooled and divided equally. This is always voted down; all the ones with the least pocket money from home vote against it. But I have said enough to show that our democracy is not a fake.

Self-government

One advantage our boarding-school has over a day school: we can have community self-government where the children make their own laws. In a day school there is nothing to govern about, for the school means lessons. In Summerhill one hardly ever hears lessons mentioned in our General Meeting; most subjects dealt with are outside the classroom ... breaking bedtime rules, bullying, riding someone else's bike, throwing food, making a noise during silence periods. To me this community living is infinitely more important in a child's education than all the textbooks in the world.

Democracy should not wait until the age of voting, twenty-one – and then it is not democracy at all; to be one of thousands registering a vote for a candidate is not democracy. In Summerhill we can all meet in one hall, all speak, all vote in a sort of town meeting.

Ours may be a fairer democracy than the political one, for children are pretty charitable to each other, and have no vested interests to speak of. Moreover, it is a more genuine democracy because laws are made at an open meeting, and the question of uncontrollable elected delegates does not arise.

The loyalty of Summerhill pupils to their own democracy is amazing. It has no fear in it, and no resentment. I have seen a boy go through a long Special Meeting for some antisocial act, and I have seen him sentenced. Often, the boy who has just been sentenced is elected chairman for the next General Meeting.

The sense of justice that children have never ceases to make me marvel. And their administrative ability is great. As education, self-government is of infinite value.

Certain classes of offences come under the automatic fine rule. If you ride another's bike without permission, there is an automatic fine of sixpence. Swearing in town (but you can swear as much as you like on the school grounds), bad behaviour in the cinema, climbing on roofs, throwing food in the dining-room – these and other infractions of rules carry automatic fines.

Punishments are nearly always fines: hand over pocket money for a week or miss a cinema.

An oft-heard objection to children acting as judges is that they punish too harshly. I find it not so. On the contrary, they are very lenient. On no occasion has there been a harsh sentence at Summerhill. And invariably the punishment has some relation to the crime.

Three small girls were disturbing the sleep of others. Punishment: they must go to bed an hour earlier every night for three days. Two boys were accused of throwing clods at other boys. Punishment: they must cart clods to help level the hockey field.

Often the chairman will say, 'The case is too silly for words,' and decide that nothing should be done. Often someone will propose that a matter is dropped.

When our secretary was tried for riding Ginger's bike without permission, he and two other members of the staff who had also ridden it were ordered to push each other on Ginger's bike ten times around the front lawn.

Four small boys who climbed the ladder that belonged to the builders who were erecting the new workshop were ordered to climb up and down the ladder for ten minutes straight.

The meeting never seeks advice from an adult. Well, I can remember only one occasion when it was done. Three girls had raided the kitchen larder. The meeting fined them their pocket money. They raided the kitchen again that night and the meeting fined them a cinema. They raided it once more, and the meeting was confounded what to do. The chairman consulted me. 'Give them tuppence reward each,' I suggested.

'What? Why, man, you'll have the whole school raiding the kitchen if you do that.'

'You won't,' I said. 'Try it.'

He tried it. Two of the girls refused to take the money; and all three were heard to declare that they would never raid the larder again. They didn't – for about two months.

Priggish behaviour at meetings is rare. Any sign of priggishness is frowned upon by the community. A boy of eleven, a strong exhibitionist, used to get up and draw attention to himself by making long involved remarks of obvious irrelevance. At least he tried to, but the meeting shouted him down. The young have a sensitive nose for insincerity.

At Summerhill we have proved, I believe, that self-government works. In fact, the school that has no self-government should not be called a progressive school – it is a compromise school. You cannot have freedom unless children feel completely free to govern their own social life. When there is a boss, there is no real freedom. This applies even more to the benevolent boss than to the disciplinarian. The child of spirit can rebel against the hard boss, but the soft boss merely makes the child impotently soft and unsure of his real feelings.

Good self-government in a school is possible only when there is a sprinkling of older pupils who like a quiet life and fight the indifference or opposition of the gangster age. These older youngsters are often outvoted, but it is they who really believe in and want self-government. Children up to, say, twelve, on the other hand, will not run good self-government on their own because they have not reached the social age. Yet at Summerhill a seven-year-old rarely misses a General Meeting and the kindergarten ones register their votes and often make good speeches.

One spring we had a spate of bad luck. Some community-minded seniors had left us after passing their O level exams, so that there were very few seniors left in the school. The vast majority of the pupils were at the gangster stage and age. Although they were social in their speeches, they were not old enough to run the community well. They passed any amount of laws and then forgot them and broke them. The few older pupils left were, by some chance, rather individualist, and tended to live their own lives in their own groups, so that the staff was figuring too prominently in attacking the breaking of the school rules. Thus it came about that at a General Meeting I felt compelled to launch a vigorous attack on the seniors for being not antisocial but asocial, breaking the bedtime rules by sitting up far too late and taking no interest in what the juniors were doing in an antisocial way.

Frankly, younger children are only mildly interested in government. Left to themselves, I question whether younger children would ever form a government. Their values are not our values, and their manners are not our manners.

Communists talk about the class war in society. I have not studied that question and cannot give an opinion on it, but I do know there is a class war in a free school, although it should not properly be called a war; there is no hate in it, no organized aggression – say – against staff or seniors. It is rather a difference of interest that is always there. Later this week it will be Guy Fawkes's day and the noise of fireworks, which has already started, makes me very tired and annoyed, but to the juniors there is bliss in every bang.

One of the biggest problems in all education is the gulf that separates youth from age. For fifty years now I have lived with children's noise. As a rule I do not hear it consciously; an analogy would be living in a hammered-brass factory – one becomes accustomed to the perpetual clang of hammers. Those who live on busy streets come to be unaware of the roar of traffic. One difference is that hammering and traffic are more or less constant sounds, whereas the noise of children is ever varied and strident. It can get on one's nerves.

And I must confess that when I moved out of the main building to live in the Cottage many years ago, the peace of the evening was most pleasant. I have to hear the noise of over sixty children, while the average parent has to deal with the noise of two or three only, but then it is my job. And even when a man's job is in an office or a shop, his children's noise may irritate him in the evening. There has to be a certain amount of sacrifice on the part of the adult if children are to live according to their inner nature.

Good self-government requires some pupils who have grown up in the system. When we enrol boys and girls of fifteen and over they do not help the self-government; they have too many repressions to let off, they do not grasp freedom unconsciously as adolescents do who have had seven or eight years in the school. This means that sometimes our government has too much of the staff element in it. If someone throws food all over the dining-room walls an older pupil will raise the matter in a meeting, that is if he or she is an old-timer, but when at one time we had an influx of teenagers who had no social feeling about food throwing, one of the staff would bring the matter up. We all feel that this is bad, but under the circumstances inevitable.

Stern discipline is the easiest way for the adult to have peace and quiet. Anyone can be a drill sergeant. What the ideal alternative method of securing a quiet life is I do not know. Our Summerhill trials and errors certainly fail to give the adults a quiet life. On the other hand they do not give the children an over-noisy life. Perhaps the ultimate test is happiness. By this criterion, Summerhill has found an excellent compromise in its self-government.

In Summerhill, there is one perennial problem that can never be solved; it might be called the problem of *the individual v. the community*. Both staff and pupils get exasperated when a gang of little girls led by a problem girl annoy some people, throw water downstairs on others, break the bedtime laws, and make themselves a perpetual nuisance. Jean, the leader of the gang, is attacked in a General Meeting. Strong words are used to condemn her misuse of freedom as licence.

A visitor, a psychologist, said to me, 'It is all wrong. The girl's face is an unhappy one; she has never been loved, and all this open criticism makes her feel more unloved than ever. She needs love, not opposition.'

'My dear woman,' I replied, 'we *have* tried to change her with love. For months we have shown her affection and tolerance, and she has not reacted. Rather, she has looked on us as simpletons, easy marks for her aggression. We cannot sacrifice the entire community to one individual.'

I do not know the complete answer. I know that when Jean is fifteen, she will be a social girl and not a gang leader. I pin my faith on public opinion. No child will go on for years being disliked and criticized. As for the condemnation by the School Meeting, one simply cannot sacrifice other children for one problem child.

Once, we had a young boy who had had a miserable life before he came to Summerhill. He was a violent bully, destructive, and full of hate. The other juniors suffered and wept. The community had to do something to protect them; and in doing so, it had to be against the bully. The mistakes of two parents could not be allowed to react on other children whose parents had given them love and care.

On a very few occasions, I have had to send a child away because the others were finding the school a hell because of him. I say this with regret, with a vague feeling of failure, but I could see no other way.

There are other ways the community has to protect itself. In the very early days of the school, the workshop was always open to the children and, as a result, every tool got lost or damaged. A child of nine would use a fine chisel as a screwdriver. Or he would take a pair of pliers to mend his bike, and leave them lying on the path.

I then decided to have my own private workshop separated from the main workshop by a partition and locked door. But my conscience kept pricking me; I felt that I was being selfish and antisocial. At last, I knocked down the partition. In six months, there wasn't a good tool left in what had been my private section. One boy used up all the wire staples in making cotter pins for his motorcycle. Another tried to put my lathe in screw-cutting gear when it was running. Polished planishing hammers for brass and silver work were used for breaking bricks. Tools disappeared and were never found. Worst of all, the interest in crafts died out completely, for the older pupils said, 'What's the good of going into the workshop? All the tools are rotten now.' And rotten they were. Planes had teeth in their blades, while saws had none.

I proposed at a General Meeting that my workshop be locked again. The motion was carried. But in showing visitors around, I had a feeling of shame when I had to unlock my workshop door each time. *What? Freedom and locked doors?* It looked bad indeed, and I decided to give the school an extra workshop which would remain open all the time. I had one fitted out with everything necessary – bench, vice, saws, chisels, planes, hammers, pliers, set squares, and so on.

One day, about four months later, I was showing a group of visitors around the school. When I unlocked my workshop, one of them said, 'This doesn't look like freedom, does it?'

'Well, you see,' I said hurriedly, 'the children have *another* workshop which is open all day long. Come along, I'll show it to you.' There was nothing left in it except the bench. Even the vice had gone. In what sundry corners of our twelve acres the chisels and hammers lay, I never knew.

The workshop situation continued to worry the staff. I was the most worried of all, because tools mean a great deal to me. I concluded that what was wrong was that the tools were used communally. 'Now,' I said to myself, 'if we introduce the possessive element – if each child who really wants tools has his own kit of tools – things will be different.'

I brought it up at a meeting, and the idea was well received. Next term, some of the older pupils brought their own kits of tools from home. They kept them in excellent condition and used them far more carefully than before.

Possibly it is the wide range of ages in Summerhill that causes most of the trouble. For certainly tools mean almost nothing to the very young boys and girls. Nowadays, our woodwork teacher keeps the workshop locked. I graciously allow a few senior pupils to use my shop when they want to. They do not abuse it, for they have arrived at the stage where giving tools the proper care is a conscious necessity for good work. They now also understand the difference between freedom and licence.

Still, the locking of doors has increased recently at Summerhill. I brought the matter up one Saturday night at the General Meeting. 'I don't like it,' I said. 'I took visitors round this morning and had to unlock the workshop, the laboratory, the pottery, and the theatre. I propose that all public rooms be left open all day.'

There was a storm of dissent. 'The laboratory must be kept locked because of the poisons in there,' said some of the children. 'And since the pottery adjoins the laboratory, that has to be kept locked, too.'

'We won't have the workshop left open. Look what happened to the tools last time!' said others.

'Well, then,' I pleaded, 'we can at least leave the theatre open. Nobody will run away with the stage.'

The playwrights, actors, actresses, stage manager, lighting man all rose at once. Said the lighting man, 'You left it open this morning, and in the afternoon some idiot switched on all the lights and left them on – 3 kilowatts at sixpence a kilowatt!'

Another said, 'The small kids take out the costumes and dress up in them.'

The upshot was that my proposal to leave doors unlocked was supported by two hands – my own and that of a girl of seven. And I discovered later that she thought we were still voting on the previous motion, that children of seven be allowed to go to the cinema. The children were learning out of their own experience that private property should be respected.

Have I had to alter my views on self-government in these long years? On the whole, no. I could not visualize Summerhill without it. It has always been popular. It is our show piece for visitors. But that, too, has its drawbacks, as when a girl of fourteen whispered to me at a meeting, 'I meant to bring up about girls blocking the toilets by putting sanitary towels in them, but look at all these visitors.' I advised her to damn the visitors and bring the matter up – which she did.

The educational benefit of practical civics cannot be over-emphasized. At Summerhill, the pupils would fight to the death for their right to govern themselves. In my opinion, one weekly General Meeting is of more value than a week's curriculum of school subjects. It is an excellent theatre for practising public speaking, and most of the children speak well and without self-consciousness. I have often heard sensible speeches from children who could neither read nor write.

After all, it is the broad outlook that free children acquire that makes self-government so important. Their laws deal with essentials, not appearances. The laws governing conduct in the town are the compromise with a less free civilization. The outside world wastes its precious energy in worrying over trifles. As if it matters in the scheme of life whether you wear dressy clothes or say hell.

In their self-government our pupils show a healthy attitude to the outside world. You can swear in the school grounds but not in the local cinema or café. You must look clean and tidy when you go down town. You must follow the law and have two efficient brakes on your bicycle. You must stop at halt signs. We compromise mainly in minor matters partly because of our good manners. One very left-wing teacher used to refuse to stand up in the cinema when the National Anthem was played. He was censured by the children at a General Meeting . . . and went on keeping his seat. Children are troubled if they do anything to give outside critics of the school any ground for antagonism.

Summerhill, by getting away from the outward nothings of life, can have and does have a community spirit that is in advance of its time. True, it is apt to call a spade a damn shovel, but any ditch digger will tell you with truth that a spade *is* a damn shovel.

There was once a time in the early days of the school when no one would stand for election to our various committees. I seized the opportunity of putting up a notice: 'In the absence of a government, I herewith declare myself Dictator. Heil Neill!' Soon there were mutterings. In the afternoon Vivien, aged six, came to me and said, 'Neill, I've broken a window in the gym.'

I waved him away. 'Don't bother me with little things like that,' I said, and he went.

A little later he came back and said he had broken two windows. By this time I was curious, and asked him what the great idea was.

'I don't like dictators,' he said, 'And I don't like going without my grub.' (I discovered later that the opposition to dictatorship had tried to take itself out on the cook, who promptly shut up the kitchen and went home.)

'Well,' I asked, 'What are you going to do about it?'

'Break more windows,' he said doggedly.

'Carry on,' I said, and he carried on.

When he returned, he announced that he had broken seventeen windows. 'But mind,' he said earnestly, 'I'm going to pay for them.'

'How?'

'Out of my pocket money. How long will it take me?'

I did a rapid calculation. 'About ten years,' I said.

He looked glum for a minute; then I saw his face light up. 'Gee,' he cried, 'I don't have to pay for them at all.'

'But what about the private property rule?' I asked. 'The windows are my private property.'

'I know that but there isn't any private property rule now. There isn't any government, and the government makes the rules.'

It may have been my expression that made him add, 'But all the same I'll pay for them.'

But he didn't have to pay for them. Lecturing in London shortly afterwards, I told the story; and at the end of my talk, a young man came up and handed me a pound 'to pay for the young devil's windows'. Two years later, Vivien was still telling people of his windows and of the man who paid for them. 'He must have been a terrible fool, because he never even saw me.'

Play and Self-regulation

Summerhill might be defined as a school in which play is of the greatest importance. Why children and kittens play I do not know. I believe it is a matter of energy.

There have been many theories about play, the one generally accepted being that the young play in order to practise activity for later life, so that when a kitten chases a string it is getting ready for the subsequent mouse. This postulates a purpose in the kitten's make-up, or alternatively a divine power that fashions the animal's behaviour so that later a divine purpose will be fulfilled. If one rejects both assumptions one has simply to believe that a kitten or a puppy plays because it is built that way. In the case of children the energy seems to be chiefly some kind of built-in bodily energy.

Childhood is not adulthood; childhood is playhood and no child ever gets enough play. The Summerhill theory is that when a child has played enough he will start to work and face difficulties, and I claim that this theory has been vindicated in our old pupils' ability to do a good job even when it involves a lot of unpleasant work.

I am not thinking of play in terms of athletic fields and organized games; I am thinking of play in terms of fantasy. Organized games involve skill, competition, teamwork; but children's play usually requires no skill, little competition, and hardly any teamwork. Small children will play gangster games with shooting or sword play. Long before the motion picture era, children played gang games. Stories and films give a direction to some kind of play, but the fundamentals are in the hearts of children of all races.

At Summerhill the six-year-olds play the whole day long – play with fantasy. To a small child, reality and fantasy are very close to each other. When a boy of ten dressed himself up as a ghost, the little ones screamed with delight; they knew it was only Tommy; they had seen him put on that sheet. But as he advanced on them, they one and all screamed in terror.

Small children live a life of fantasy and they carry this fantasy over into action. Boys of eight to fourteen play gangsters or Red Indians and are always bumping people off or flying the skies in their wooden aeroplanes. Small girls also go through a gang stage, but it does not take the form of guns and swords. It is more personal. Mary's gang objects to Nellie's gang, and there are rows and hard words. Boys' rival gangs only play enemies. Small boys are thus more easy to live with than small girls.

I have not been able to discover where the borderline of fantasy begins and ends. To a small child reality and fantasy are very close to each other. When a child brings a doll a meal on a tiny toy plate, does she really believe for the moment that the doll is alive? Is a rocking-horse a real horse? When a boy cries 'Stick 'em up' and then fires, does he think or feel that his is a real gun? I am inclined to think that children do imagine that their toys are real, and only when some insensitive adult butts in and reminds them of their fantasy do they come back to earth with a plop.

It seems to be clear that boys and girls have different ideas about play. Boys play much more than girls do. Sometimes a girl appears to substitute a fantasy life for play, but few boys ever do that.

Boys do not generally play with girls. Boys play gangsters, and play tag games; they build tree huts; they dig holes and trenches and do all the things that small children usually do.

Girls seldom organize any play. The time-honoured game of playing teacher or doctor is unknown among free children, for they feel no need to mimic authority. Smaller girls play with dolls; but older girls seem to get the most fun out of contact with people, not things.

We have often had mixed football teams. Card games, chess, and table tennis are usually mixed. Indoor games, arranged by one of the staff or an older pupil, are always mixed. So are many outside games like 'kick the can'. In the summer swimming in our swimming-pool is very popular with all ages.

The younger children have a paddling pool, a sand pit, a seesaw and swings. The sand pit is always filled with grubby children on a warm day; and the younger ones are always complaining that the bigger children come and use their sand pit. It appears that we shall have to have a sand pit for the seniors. The sand and mud-pie era lives on longer than we thought it did.

We have no artificial gymnastics in the school, nor do I think them necessary. The children get all the exercise they need in their games, swimming, dancing, and cycling. I wonder if free children would go to a gym class.

People have asked if we encourage games in Summerhill. We don't encourage anything, really. We like to see the children play adventure and fantasy games. They can organize team games when they want to, but perhaps they have not the desire to get into teams and win as organized children have, for there is no competition in the school lessons or games. Naturally when they play tennis they play to win, but they do not care much if they lose. Fellow golfers may agree with me that there is more joy in placing a no. 3 iron shot a foot from the pin than in winning a round.

I distinguish between games and play. To me football, hockey, rugby, and baseball are not real play; they lack the imagination of play. When children are free they tend to bypass team games in favour of, for want of a better name, fantasy play.

Our team games depend a lot on the ages of the pupils. With children from five to seventeen it is not easy to get a football team to play the local grammar school, for out of sixty-five boys and girls to get an eleven we should have to put a seven-year-old in goal. About thirty years ago we had quite a few big lads and lasses, who with the young staff played hockey, not usually against schools, but against town teams all over Suffolk.

I take it that the underlying motive for encouraging team games is the wish to cultivate the team spirit ... or in some cases to sublimate sex (but I am glad to say it never does the latter). In Summerhill the team spirit arises out of self-government in community living.

Games are said to be good for the health of children. They should be, yet often I have had pupils who never played a game in ten years, and they look as healthy at forty-five as their neighbours. Most of them, however, cycled and swam a lot.

Perhaps I should not bring in children's books in a chapter headed 'Play' but they ought to be brought in somewhere. Like many parents I had to read bedtime stories for a few years, and, much as I love my daughter, I must confess that those evening readings were a misery to me. There was one dreadful story that made me feel murderous, my daughter Zoë's favourite: I had to read it fifty times.

Luckily only a few of these books point a moral directly. Indirectly many of them do. In many of these books the children are so good and pure. The illustrations show how angelic their faces are, what good manners they have, how obedient they are. They make me sick.

How much should we censor a child's reading? I think we are inclined to exaggerate the effect of bloodthirsty stories on children. Most children can enjoy the most sadistic tales. On Sunday nights, when I tell my pupils adventure stories in which they are rescued at the last moment from the cannibal's cauldron they jump for joy.

Going to the cinema and reading books are in different categories. What is written is not so terrifying as what is seen or heard. Some films fill children with terror, and one is never sure where and when something frightening in the cinema may arise. I have even seen young children afraid of the crocodile or the pirates in *Peter Pan*.

I went to see the play of *Peter Pan* several years ago and was interested to note how much it had dated. To save Tinker Bell's life, the juvenile audience had to cry 'Yes' when asked if they believed in fairies. The 'Yes' was rather feeble, and I could see fond parents nudge their offspring vigorously to make them cry at all. *Peter Pan* is an adult's play; children want to grow up, and it is too often their unfulfilled parents who sigh for the Never Never Land of childhood.

Recently, we saw a film about a man who sold his soul to the devil. The children unanimously agreed that the devil looked very much like me. I always become the devil to boys who have been taught that the sex sin is the sin against the Holy Ghost. When I tell them that there is nothing sinful about the body, they look upon me as a tempting devil. To neurotic children I represent both God and the devil. Years ago one little chap even took up a hammer to kill the devil. Helping neurotics can be a dangerous life.

As a child, I recall being terrified by the biblical story of the children who were eaten by bears, yet no one advocates the censorship of the Bible. Many children when I was young read the Bible searching for obscene passages. As a small boy I knew them all, chapter and verse.

Children's minds seem to be cleaner than those of adults. A boy can read *Tom Jones* and fail to see the obscene passages. If we free the child from ignorance about sex, we destroy the danger in any book. I am strongly against censorship of books at any age.

One time a new pupil, a girl of fourteen, took *A Young Girl's Diary* from my bookshelf. I saw her sit and snigger over it. Six months later, she read it a second time and told me that it was rather dull. What had been spicy reading to ignorance had become commonplace reading to knowledge.

Since Freud discovered the positive sexuality of small children, not enough has been done to study its manifestations. True, books have been written about sexuality, but so far as I know, no one has written a book about self-regulated children.

I had never heard the term self-regulation until my friend Wilhelm Reich used it, and if he did not invent it, he, more than any other man, has understood and used the method. Homer Lane spoke of self-determination and others described self-government; these were not the same as self-regulation, for they referred more to children governing themselves communally than to self-determination of the individual child.

Self-regulation implies a belief in human nature, a belief that there is not, and never was, original sin. Self-regulation means the right of a baby to live freely without outside authority. It means the baby feeds when it is hungry; that it becomes clean in habits only when it wants to; that it is never stormed at nor spanked; that it shall always be loved and protected. Of course, self-regulation, like any theoretical idea, is dangerous if not combined with common sense.

Only a fool in charge of young children would allow unbarred bedroom windows or an unprotected fire in the nursery. Yet, too often, young enthusiasts for self-regulation come to my school as visitors, and exclaim at our lack of freedom in locking poison in a lab closet, or our prohibition about playing on the fire escape. The whole freedom movement is marred and despised because so many advocates of freedom have not got their feet on the ground.

Self-regulation means behaviour coming from the self, not from some outside compulsion. One does not need to be educated or cultured to self-regulate a child. I think of Mary, now a very old woman in a Scottish village. Mary had a wonderful placidity; she never fussed, never stormed; she was instinctively on the side of her boys and girls; they knew that she approved of them whatever they did. Mary was a mother, a comfy warm hen with her chicks around her; she had a natural gift of giving out love without making it possessive love. I am afraid that when we were little boys we exploited Mary's propensity to pile on the second helpings.

Here was a simple woman who never heard of psychology or self-regulation, practising the latter nearly seventy years ago. I have often seen farmers' wives who were like Mary, following their emotions in their dealing with their families and not acting according to any set rules of child rearing. Mind you, those women had better conditions than a mother in London. The children were out of doors much of the time, and indoors there were no expensive gadgets to protect from infant hands. Children should not really be in a kitchen or a drawing-room at all. They should have their own quarters, built by the village blacksmith, I fancy. The ideal home for self-regulation would be one in the country.

Yet we have to face facts, and one fact is that we do not have these quarters. But if a mother has real contact with her offspring, if they do not fear her, she can say 'no' positively without doing any harm. The first thing parents have to do is regulate themselves. Drop all conventional ideas about cleanliness, untidiness, child noise, swearing, sex play, unconscious destruction of toys ... in fact many toys should be destroyed consciously by a healthy child.

Of all her toys, the only one that my daughter Zoë retained a liking for was Betsy Wetsy, a self-wetting doll I bought for her when she was eighteen months old. The wetting arrangement did not interest her one bit; perhaps because it was a puritanical fake, its 'wee-wee hole' having been placed in the small of the back. Only when she reached four and a half did Zoë say one morning, 'I'm tired of Betsy Wetsy and want to give her away.'

Once Zoë received a gift from an old pupil of a wonderful walking and talking doll. It was obviously an expensive toy. About the same time, a new pupil gave Zoë a small cheap rabbit. She played with the big expensive doll for half an hour, but she played with the cheap little rabbit for weeks. In fact, she took the rabbit to bed with her each night.

Some years ago, I tried out a questionnaire on older children. 'When do you get most annoyed with your little brother or sister?' In practically every case, the answer was the same, 'When he breaks my toys.'

One should never show a child how a toy works. Indeed, one should never help a child in any way until or unless he is not capable of solving a problem for himself.

Do not give your children everything they ask for. I may not be entirely objective here, for a father who owes me a lot of money has just sent his son back with an expensive new 'super' racing bicycle and I do not like it. Generally speaking children today get far too much, so much that they cease to have any appreciation of their gifts . . . I stumbled over the 'super' bike last night in the rain.

When Zoë was little I made it a rule that when I went to London I did not bring her a present each time, and in consequence she did not expect one. On the other hand you should not be mean with your children; you are the only one they can rely on.

Parents who overdo the giving of presents are too often those who do not love their children enough, and have to compensate by making a show of parental love by showering expensive presents on them. One of the characters in Barrie's *Dear Brutus* tells his sweetheart that every time she is nice to him he gives his wife a fur coat.

As usual I have wandered from the point. It is one of my major charms, they tell me. A dull writer is one who sticks to the point, too often a blunt one.

Back to the subject of play. Granting that childhood is playhood, how do we adults generally react to this fact? We *ignore* it. We forget all about it – because play, to us, is a waste of time. Hence we erect a large city school with many rooms and expensive apparatus for teaching; but more often than not, all we offer to the play instinct is a small concrete space.

Children love music and mud; they clatter on stairs; they shout like louts; they are unconscious of furniture. If they are playing a game of touch, they would walk over the Portland Vase if it happened to be in their way – walk over it without seeing it.

One could, with some truth, claim that the evils of civilization are due to the fact that no child has ever had enough play. To put it differently, every child has been hothoused into being an adult long before he has reached adulthood.

The adult attitude towards play is quite arbitrary. We, the old, map out a child's timetable: Learn from nine till twelve and then an hour for lunch; and again lessons until three. If a free child were asked to make a timetable, he would almost certainly give to play many periods and to lessons only a few.

Fear is at the root of adult antagonism to children's play. Hundreds of times I have heard the anxious query, 'But if my boy plays all day, how will he ever learn anything, how will he ever pass exams?' Very few will accept my answer, 'If your child plays all he wants to play, he will be able to pass university entrance exams after two years' intensive study, instead of the usual five, six, or seven years of learning in a school that discounts play as a factor in life.'

But I always have to add, 'That is – if he ever wants to pass the exams!' He may want to become a ballet dancer or an engineer. She may want to be a dress designer or a carpenter.

Yes, fear of the child's future leads adults to deprive children of their right to play. There is more in it than that, however. There is a vague moral idea behind the disapproval of play, a suggestion that being a child is not so good, a suggestion voiced in the admonition to young adults, 'Don't act like a baby.'

Parents who have forgotten the yearnings of their childhood – forgotten how to play and how to fantasize – make poor parents. When a child has lost the ability to play, he is physically dead and a danger to any child who comes in contact with him. It is an intriguing thing, yet most difficult, to assess the damage done to children who have not been allowed to play as much as they wanted to.

At Summerhill, some children play all day, especially when the sun is shining and their play is generally noisy. In most schools noise, like play, is suppressed. One of our former pupils who went to a Scottish university said, 'The students make a hell of a row in classes, and it gets rather tiresome; for we at Summerhill lived out that stage when we were ten.'

I recall an incident in that great novel, *The House with the Green Shutters*, where the students of Edinburgh University played 'John Brown's Body' with their feet in order to heckle and tease a weak lecturer. Noise and play go together, but it is best when they go together between the ages of seven and fourteen.

Work and Sincerity

In Summerhill, we used to have a community law that provided that every child over twelve and every member of the staff must do two hours of work each week on the grounds. The pay was a token pay of sixpence an hour. If you did not work, you were fined a shilling. A few, teachers included, were content to pay the fines. Of those who worked, most had their eyes on the clock. There was no play component in the work, and therefore the work bored everyone. The law was re-examined, and the children abolished it by an almost unanimous vote.

In the early days in Leiston, we needed an infirmary in Summerhill. We decided to build one ourselves – a proper building of brick and cement. None of us had ever laid a brick, but we started in. A few pupils helped to dig the foundations and knocked down some old brick walls to get the bricks. But the children demanded payment. We refused to pay wages. In the end, the infirmary was built by the teachers and visitors. The job was just too dull for children, and to their young minds the need for the sanatorium too remote. They had no self-interest in it. But some time later when they wanted a bicycle shed, they built one all by themselves without any help from the staff.

I am writing of children, not as we adults think they should be, but as they really are. Their community sense – their sense of social responsibility – does not develop fully until the age of eighteen or more. Their interests are immediate and the future does not exist for them.

I have never yet seen a lazy child. What is called laziness is either lack of interest or lack of health. A healthy child cannot be idle: he has to be doing something all day long. Once I knew a very healthy lad who was considered a lazy fellow. Mathematics did not interest him, but the school curriculum demanded that he learn mathematics. Of course, he didn't want to study mathematics, and so his teacher thought he was lazy.

I read recently that if a couple who were out for an evening were to dance every dance they would feel little or no fatigue because they would be experiencing pleasure all evening long – assuming that their steps agreed. So it is with a child. The boy who is considered lazy will often run miles during a football game.

I have never seen a child who came to Summerhill before the age of twelve who was lazy. In my opinion the lazy boy is either physically ill or he has no interest in the things that adults think he ought to do. Many a 'lazy' lad has been sent to Summerhill from a strict school. Such a boy remains 'lazy' for quite a long time; that is, until he recovers from his education. I do not set him to do work that is distasteful for him, because he isn't ready for it. Like you and me, he will have many things to do later that he will hate doing; but if he is left free to live though his play period now, he will be able, later on, to face any difficulty.

Anyway, if your philosophy of life is a good one the job you end up doing is not of the highest importance. One of our old boys was a bus conductor and was very miserable when bad health forced him to give it up. He said he enjoyed meeting so many people. Another old boy, a bricklayer, is happy in his work. We have a few old pupils who are farmers; true they are their own bosses, but they do many a menial job on their farms.

The reason we here in Summerhill keep getting such good reports about the industrious performance of our old pupils in responsible jobs is that these boys and girls have lived out their self-centred fantasy stage in Summerhill. As young adults they are able to face the realities of life without any unconscious longing for the play of childhood.

I find it impossible to get youths of seventeen to help me plant potatoes or weed onions, although the same boys will spend hours souping up motor engines, or washing cars, or making radio sets. It took me a long time to accept this phenomenon. The truth began to dawn on me one day when I was digging my brother's garden in Scotland. I didn't enjoy the job, and it came to me suddenly that what was wrong was that I was digging a garden that meant nothing to me. And my garden means nothing to the boys, whereas their bikes or radios mean a lot to them. True altruism is a long time in coming, and it never loses its factor of selfishness.

Small children and teenagers have quite different attitudes

towards work. Summerhill juniors, ranging from ages three to eight, will work like Trojans mixing cement or carting sand or cleaning bricks; and they will work with no thought of reward. They identify themselves with grown-ups and their work is like a fantasy worked out in reality.

However, from the age of eight or nine until the age of nineteen or twenty, the desire to do manual labour of a dull kind is just not there. This is true of most children; there are individual children, of course, who remain workers from early childhood right on through life.

The fact is that we adults exploit children far too often. 'Marion, run down to the' post box with this letter.' Any child hates to be made use of. The average child dimly realizes that he is fed and clothed by his parents without any effort on his own part. He feels that such care is his natural right, but he realizes that on the other hand he is expected and obliged to do a hundred menial tasks and many disagreeable chores which the parents themselves evade.

In a village school I would take the pupils out to the garden on a fine afternoon and we all dug and planted, and I got the idea that children liked gardening. I did not see that the gardening was a pleasant relief from sitting looking at a blackboard.

At Summerhill I have a large garden. A group of little boys and girls would be of great assistance during weeding time. To order them to help me with my work is quite possible. But these children of eight, nine, and ten years of age have formed no opinion of their own on the necessity of weeding. They are not interested in weeding.

I once approached a group of small boys. 'Anyone want to help me do some weeding?' I asked. They all refused.

I asked why. The answers came: 'Too dull!' 'Let them grow.' 'Too busy with this crossword puzzle.' 'Hate gardening.'

I, too, find weeding dull. I, too, like to tackle a crossword puzzle. To be quite fair to those youngsters, of what concern is the weeding to them? It is *my* garden. I get the pride of seeing the peas come through the soil. I save money on vegetable bills. In short, the garden touches my self-interest. I cannot compel an interest in the children, when the interest does not originate in them. The only possible way would be for me to hire the children at so much an hour. Then, they and I would be on the same basis: I would be interested in my garden, and they would be interested in making some extra money.

Maud, aged fourteen, often helps me in the garden, although she declares that she hates gardening. But she does not hate *me*. She weeds because she wants to be with me. This serves her self-interest for the moment.

When Derrick, who also dislikes weeding, volunteers to help me, I know he is going to renew his request for a pocket knife of mine that he covets. That is his only interest in the matter.

A reward should, for the most part, be subjective: self-satisfaction in the work accomplished. One thinks of the ungratifying jobs of the world: digging coal, fitting nut no. 50 to bolt no. 51, digging drains, adding figures. The world is full of jobs that hold no intrinsic interest or pleasure. We seem to be adapting our schools to this dullness in life. By compelling our students' attention to subjects which hold no interest for them, we, in effect, condition them for jobs they will not enjoy.

People are always saying to me, 'But how will your free children ever adapt themselves to the drudgery of life?' I wish that these free children could be pioneers in abolishing the drudgery of life.

I have equally strong feelings about getting children to do our jobs. If we want a child to work for us, we ought to pay him according to his ability. No child wants to collect bricks for me just because I've decided to rebuild a broken wall. But if I offer three-pence a barrowload, a boy may help willingly, for then I've enlisted his self-interest. But I do not like the idea of making a child's weekly pocket money depend on his doing certain chores. Parents should give without seeking anything in return.

I once read about a school in America that was built by the pupils themselves. I used to think that this was the ideal way. It isn't. If children built their own school, you can be sure that some gentleman with a breezy, benevolent authority was standing by, lustily shouting encouragement. When such authority is not present, *children simply do not build schools.*

My own opinion is that a sane civilization would not ask children to work until at least the age of eighteen. Most boys and girls would do a lot of work before they reached eighteen, but such work would be play for them, and probably uneconomical work from the viewpoint of the parents. I feel depressed when I think of the gigantic amount of work students have to do to prepare for exams. I understand that in pre-war Budapest nearly 50 per cent of the students broke down physically or psychologically after their matriculation exams.

Teachers from Israel have told me of the wonderful community centres there. The school, I'm told, is part of a community whose primary need is hard work. Children of ten, one teacher told me, weep if – as a punishment – they are not allowed to dig the garden. If I had a child of ten who wept because he was forbidden to dig potatoes, I should wonder if he were mentally defective. Childhood is playhood; and any community system that ignores that truth is educating in the wrong way. To me the Israeli method is sacrificing young life to economic needs. It may be necessary; but I would not dare to call that system ideal community living.

We must allow the child to be selfish – ungiving – free to follow his own childish interests through his childhood. When the child's individual interests and his social interests clash, the individual interests should be allowed precedence. The whole idea of Summerhill is release: allowing a child to live out his natural interests.

A school should make a child's life a game. I do not mean that the child should have a path of roses. Making it all easy for the child is fatal to the child's character. But life itself presents so many difficulties that the artificially made difficulties which we present to children are unnecessary.

I believe that to impose anything by authority is wrong. The child should not do anything until he comes to the opinion – his own opinion – that it should be done. The curse of humanity is the external compulsion, whether it comes from the Pope or the state or the teacher or the parent. It is all fascism.

Most people demand a god; how can it be otherwise when the home is ruled by tin gods of both sexes, gods who demand perfect truth and moral behaviour? Freedom means doing what you like, so long as you don't interfere with the freedom of others. The result is self-discipline.

The surprising thing is that, with millions reared in sex hate and fear, the world is not more neurotic than it is. To me this means that natural humanity has the innate power of finally overcoming the evils that are imposed on it. There is a slow trend of freedom, sexual and otherwise. In my boyhood, a woman went bathing wearing stockings and a long dress. Today, women show legs and bodies. Children are getting more freedom with every generation. Today, only a few lunatics put cayenne pepper on a baby's thumb to stop sucking. Today, only a few countries still beat their children in school.

There is a great amount of good fellowship and love in humanity, and it is my firm belief that new generations that have not been warped in babyhood will live at peace with each other – that is, if the haters of today do not destroy the world before these new generations have time to take control.

The fight is an unequal one, for the haters control education, religion, the law, the armies, and the vile prisons. Only a handful of educators strive to allow the good in all children to grow in freedom. The vast majority of children are being moulded by anti-life supporters with their hateful system of punishments.

Girls in some convents still have to cover themselves when they take a bath, lest they see their own bodies. Boys are still sometimes told by parent or teacher that masturbation is a sin leading to madness. Nearly every time I go to a town or city, I see a child of three stumble and fall, and then I shrink to see the mother spank the child for falling. On a railway trip I hear a mother say, 'If you go out to that corridor again, Willie, the conductor will arrest you.' Most children are reared on a tissue of lies and ignorant prohibitions. It is a race between the believers in deadness and the believers in life.

Once I saw a boy of three put out in the garden by his mother. His suit was spotless. He began to play with earth and slightly soiled his clothes. Mamma rushed out, smacked him, took him indoors and later sent him out weeping in new clothes. In ten minutes, he had soiled his suit, and the process was repeated. I thought of telling the woman that her son would hate her for life; and worse, hate life itself. But I realized that nothing I could say would sink in.

The tragedy of man is that, like the dog, his character can be moulded. You cannot mould the character of a cat. You can give a dog a bad conscience, but you cannot give a conscience to a cat. Yet most people prefer dogs because their obedience and their flattering tail-wagging afford visible proof of the master's superiority and worth.

The common assumption that good habits that have not been forced into us during early childhood can never develop in us later on in life is an assumption we have been brought up on and which we unquestioningly accept merely because the idea has never been challenged. I deny this premise.

Freedom is necessary for the child because only under freedom can he grow in his natural way – the good way. I see the results of constraint in new pupils coming from other schools. They are bundles of insincerity, with an unreal politeness and phoney manners.

Their reaction to freedom is rapid and tiresome. For the first week or two, they open doors for the teachers, call me 'sir', and wash carefully. They glance at me with 'respect', which is easily recognized as fear. After a few weeks of freedom, they show what they really are. They become impudent, unmannerly, unwashed. They do all the things they have been forbidden to do in the past: they swear, they smoke, they break things. And all the time, they have a polite and insincere expression in their eyes and in their voices.

It takes at least six months for them to lose their insincerity. After that, they also lose their deference to what they regarded as authority. Within a year they begin to flower as natural, healthy kids who say what they think without fluster or hate. When a child comes to freedom young enough, he does not have to go through this stage of insincerity and acting. The most striking thing about Summerhill is this absolute sincerity among the pupils.

This business of being sincere in life and to life is a vital one. It is really the most vital one in the world. If you have sincerity, all other things will be added to you. Everyone realizes the value of sincerity in, say, acting. We expect sincerity from our politicians (such is the optimism of mankind), from our judges and magistrates, teachers and doctors. Yet we educate our children in such a way that they dare not be sincere.

We set out to let children alone so that we might discover what they were like. It is the only possible way of dealing with children. The pioneer school of the future must pursue this way if it is to contribute to child knowledge and, more important, to child happiness. Possibly the greatest discovery we have made in Summerhill is that a child is born a sincere creature.

Problem Children

Many psychologists believe that a child is born neither good nor bad, but with tendencies towards both beneficence and criminality. I believe there is no instinct of criminality nor any natural tendency towards evil in the child. Criminality appears in a child as a perverted form of love.

One day, one of my pupils, a boy of nine, was playing a game and was pleasantly crooning to himself, 'I want to kill my mother.' It was unconscious behaviour, for he was making a boat, and all his conscious interest was directed towards that activity. The fact is that his mother lives her own life, and seldom sees him. She does not love him, and unconsciously he knows it.

But this boy – one of the most lovable of children – did not start out in life with criminal thoughts. It is simply the old story: *if I can't get love, I can get hate*. Every case of criminality in a child can be traced to lack of love.

Crime is obviously an expression of hate. The study of criminality in children resolves itself into the study of why a child is led to hate. It is a question of injured ego.

We cannot get away from the fact that a child is primarily an egoist. No one else matters. When the ego is satisfied, we have what we call goodness; when the ego is starved, we have what we call criminality. The criminal revenges himself on society because society has failed to appreciate his ego by showing love for him.

The young gangsters of the world are seeking happiness, and I make the guess that their unhappiness in home and school is the root cause of their being antisocial. The happiness they should have had in childhood gave place to the spurious happiness of damaging and stealing and beating people up. What should have been joy has become hate because of frustration. I am convinced that the cure for juvenile delinquency is the giving of happiness in infancy, and it is time that all the good people who are trying to diminish youthful crime should concentrate on beginnings, the wrong beginnings of punishment and fear and, supremely, lack of love in childhood. And this is not theory, for, in the early days when Summerhill had many problem children, nearly all went out into the world straight people, simply because they were loved, simply because freedom made them happy.

Hate and punishment never cured anything, only love can cure. Homer Lane proved this fifty years ago. Summerhill was never a school for 'problems' but when it began it got pupils who had been expelled from conventional schools. Thirty-five years ago it had a fair number of thieves and liars and destroyers. I know of only one pupil, among those who were here for at least three years, who went to prison. During the war he was convicted of selling black-market petrol. Unfortunately his garage was two hundred miles from me: I was pretty short of petrol.

I had quite a few problems in those days. I have written this before but it is worth repeating: I thought I was curing them by analysis but those who refused to come for analysis were also cured, so I concluded that it was not psychology that cured them; it was freedom to be themselves.

If humans were born with an instinct for criminality, there would be as many criminals from fine middle-class homes as from slum homes. But well-to-do people have more opportunities for expression of the ego. The pleasures money buys, the refined surroundings, culture, and pride of birth all minister to the ego. Among the poor, the ego is starved.

A boy is born in a mean street. His home has no culture, no books, no serious conversation. His parents are ignorant and slap him and yell at him; he attends a school where strict discipline and dull subjects cramp his style. His playground is the street corner. His ideas about sex are pornographic and dirty. On television he sees people with money and cars and all sorts of luxuries. At adolescence he gets into a gang whose aim is to get rich quick at all costs. How can we cure a boy with that background?

Homer Lane showed for all time that freedom could cure a problem child, but there are few Homer Lanes around. Lane died over forty years ago yet I know of no official body dealing with delinquents which has benefited from his experience. The demand is still curing by authority and too often fear. One terrible result is that juvenile crime increases every year.

Not having seen them I cannot fairly judge borstals and approved schools. A few may be very good, but from what I read, I take it that the methods used are those that made the inmates crooks: discipline from above, strenuous work, obedience without question, shortage of free time. Punishment cannot cure what is individual and social sickness.

Lane took tough boys and girls from the London courts – anti-social, hard-boiled youngsters glorying in their reputation as thugs, thieves, and gangsters. These 'incorrigibles' came to his reform camp called the Little Commonwealth, and there they found a community with self-government and loving approval. These juvenile delinquents were cured by love – cured by authority being on the side of the child. Gradually these youngsters became decent, honest citizens, many of whom I used to count among my friends.

Lane was a genius in the understanding and handling of delinquent children. He cured them because he constantly gave out love and understanding. He always looked for the hidden motive in any delinquent act, convinced that behind every crime was a wish that originally had been a good one. He found that talking to children was useless, and that only action counted. He held that in order to rid a child of a bad social trait one should let the child live out his desires.

Once, when one of his young charges, Jabez, expressed an angry wish to smash up the cups and saucers on the tea table, Lane handed him an iron poker and told him to carry on. Jabez carried on – the very next day he came to Lane and asked for a more responsible and better-paying job than he had been working at. Lane asked why he wanted a better paying job. 'Because I want to pay for them cups and saucers,' said Jabez. Lane's explanation was that the action of smashing the cups brought a load of Jabez's inhibitions and conflicts tumbling to the ground. The fact that for the first time in his life he was encouraged by authority to smash something and get rid of his anger must have had a beneficial emotional effect on him.

The delinquents of Homer Lane's Little Commonwealth were all from bad city slums, yet I never heard of any of them returning to gangsterdom. I call Lane's way the love way. I call giving-the-delinquent-hell the hate way. And since hate never cured anyone of anything, I conclude that the hell way will never help any youngster to be social.

Yet I know very well that if I were a magistrate today and I had a tough, sullen delinquent to deal with, I might be baffled to know what to do with him. For I know of no reform school in England today like the Little Commonwealth to send him to, and I say so with shame. Lane died in 1925, and our authorities here in England have not learned anything from that remarkable man.

However, in recent years, our fine body of probation officers has shown a sincere desire to try to understand the delinquent. The psychiatrists, too, in spite of much hostility from the legal profession, have gone a long way to teach the public that delinquency is not wickedness but rather a form of sickness that requires sympathy and understanding. The tide is flowing towards love instead of towards hate, towards understanding instead of towards bigoted moral indignation. It is a slow tide. But even a slow tide carries a little of the contamination away; and in time the tide must grow in volume.

I know of no proof that a person has ever been made good by violence, or by cruelty, or by hate. In my long career, I have dealt with many problem children, many of them delinquents. I have seen how unhappy and hateful they are, how inferior, how emotionally confused. They are arrogant and disrespectful to me because I am a teacher, a father substitute, an enemy. I have lived with their tense hate and suspicion. But here in Summerhill, these potential delinquents have governed themselves in a self-governing community; they have been free to learn and free to play.

Before psychology discovered the importance of the unconscious, a child was considered a reasonable being with the power to will to do good or evil. His mind was assumed to be a blank slate on which any conscientious teacher had only to write the script. Now we understand that there is nothing static about a child; he is all dynamic urge. He seeks to express his wishes in action. By nature he is self-interested, and he seeks always to try his power.

If there is sex in everything, there is also the drive for power in everything. When a child's wish is thwarted, he hates. If I take a toy from a bright boy of three, he would kill me if he could.

One day, I was sitting with Billy. I was in a deck-chair striped black and orange. I, of course, am father substitute to Billy.

'Tell me a story,' he said.

'You tell me one,' said I.

No, he insisted, he could not tell me a story; I must tell him one.

'We'll tell one together,' said I. 'When I stop, you say something – eh? Well then, there was once a –'

Billy looked at my chair with its stripes. 'Tiger,' he said, and I knew I was the animal with stripes.

'And it lay at the roadside outside this school. One day, a boy went down the road and his name was . . .'

'Donald,' said Billy. Donald is his chum.

'Then the tiger sprang out and . . .'

'Ate him up,' said Billy promptly.

'Then Derrick said, "I won't have this tiger eating up my brother." So he buckled on his revolver and went down the road. And the tiger jumped out and . . .'

'Ate him up,' said Billy cheerfully.

'Then Neill got wild. "I simply won't have this tiger eating up all my school," he said; and he buckled on his two revolvers and went out. The tiger jumped out and . . .'

'Ate him up, of course.'

'But then Billy said that this wouldn't do. So he buckled on his two revolvers, his sword, his dagger, and his machine-gun and went down the road. And the tiger jumped out and . . .'

'He killed the tiger,' said Billy modestly.

'Excellent!' I cried. 'He killed the tiger. He dragged it up to the door and came in and called a Special Meeting. Then one of the staff said, "Now that Neill is inside the tiger we shall need a new headmaster, and I propose . . ."'

Billy looked down and was silent.

'"And I propose . . ."'

'You know well enough it was me,' he said with annoyance.

'And so Billy became headmaster of Summerhill School,' I said. 'And what do you think was the first thing he did?'

'Went up to your room and took your turning lathe and type-writer,' he said, without hesitation or embarrassment.

Billy was a power case. Billy's fantasies were power fantasies. I heard him telling the other boys tall stories of the number of planes he can drive at one time. There is ego in everything.

The thwarted wish is the beginning of fantasy. Every child wants to be big; every factor in his environment tells him that he is small. The child conquers his environment by fleeing from it; he rises on wings and lives his dream in fantasy. The ambition to be an engine driver is a power motive; to control a train rushing along at great speed is one of the best illustrations of power.

Peter Pan has been popular with children – not because he does not grow up – but because he can fly and fight pirates. He is popular with grown-ups because they want to be children, without responsibilities, without struggles. But no one really wants to remain a child. The desire for power urges children on.

The youths who are called delinquents are trying to express power that has been suppressed. I have generally found that the antisocial child, the leader of a gang of window breakers, becomes under freedom a strong supporter of law and order.

In the early days a girl named Ansi came to Summerhill. Ansi had been a leader of lawbreakers in her school, and the school could not keep her. Two nights after her arrival at Summerhill she began to fight with me playfully, but soon she was no longer playing. For a long time she kicked and bit me, saying over and over again that she would make me lose my temper. I refused to lose my temper and kept smiling. It was an effort. Finally, one of my teachers sat down and played soft music. Ansi quieted down. Her attack was partly sexual; but on the power side, I stood for law and order. I was headmaster.

Ansi found life rather confusing. At Summerhill she found there were no adult-made laws to break, and she felt like a fish out of water. She tried to stir up mischief among the other pupils, but succeeded only with the very young ones. She was trying once more to find her accustomed power in leading a gang against authority. She was really a lover of law and order. But in the domain of law and order that the adults ruled there was no scope to express her power. As second best, she chose the side of rebellion against law and order.

A week after her arrival, we had a General Meeting. Ansi stood and jeered at everything. 'I'll vote for laws,' she said, 'but only for the fun of having some laws to break.'

Her housemother got up. 'Ansi shows that she doesn't want laws that everyone will keep,' she said. 'I propose that we have no laws at all. Let us have chaos.'

Ansi shouted 'Hurrah!' and led the pupils out of the room. This she easily did because they were younger children, and they had not reached the age of having developed a social conscience. She took them to the workshop, and they all armed themselves with saws. They announced their intention of cutting down all the fruit trees. I, as usual, went to dig in the garden.

Ten minutes later, Ansi came to me. 'What do we have to do to stop the chaos and have laws again?' she asked in a mild tone.

'I can't give you any advice,' I replied.

'Can we call another General Meeting?' she asked.

'Of course you can, only I won't come to it. We decided to have chaos.' She went away and I continued digging.

In a short time, she returned. 'We had a meeting of the kids,' she said, 'and we voted to have a full General Meeting. Will you come?'

'A full General Meeting?' said I. 'Yes, I'll come.'

In the meeting, Ansi was serious, and we passed our laws in peace. Total damage done during chaotic period – one clothes-pole sawed in two.

For years Ansi had found pleasure in leading her school gang against authority. In stirring up rebellion, she was doing something she hated. She hated chaos. Underneath, she was a law-abiding citizen. But Ansi had a great desire for power. She was happy only when she was directing others. In rebelling against her teacher, she was trying to make herself more important than the teacher. She hated laws because she hated the power that made laws.

I find such power cases much more difficult to cure than sex cases. One can with comparative ease track down the incidents and teachings that give a child a bad conscience about sex, but to track down the thousands of incidents and teachings that have made a child a sadistic power person is difficult indeed.

The child's desire to be grown-up is a power wish. The mere size of adults will give a child a sense of inferiority. Why should grown-ups be allowed to sit up late? Why do they have the best things – typewriters, cars, good tools, watches?

My boy pupils delight in soaping their faces when I am shaving. The desire to smoke, too, is mainly a wish to be grown-up. Generally, it is the only child whose power is most thwarted; and therefore it is the only child who is most difficult to handle in a school.

I once made the mistake of bringing a young boy to school ten days before the other pupils arrived. He was very happy mixing with the teachers, sitting in the staffroom, having a bedroom to himself. But when the other children came, he became very antisocial. Alone he had helped to make and repair many articles; when the others came he began to destroy things. His pride was injured. He had suddenly to cease being an adult; he had to sleep in a room with four other boys; he had to go to bed early. His violent protest made me decide never again to give a child the opportunity of identifying himself with grown-ups.

It is only thwarted power that works for evil in a child. Human beings are good; they want to do good; they want to love and be loved. Hate and rebellion are only thwarted love and thwarted power.

Once I said to a new pupil, a boy who was being antisocial, 'You are pulling all these silly tricks merely to get me to whack you, for your life has been one long whacking. But you are wasting your time. I won't punish you, whatever you do.' He gave up being destructive. He no longer needed to feel hateful.

Years ago, when I was still a relatively young fellow, a little boy came to us from a school where he had terrorized everyone by throwing things about and even threatening murder. He tried the same game with me. I soon concluded that he was using his temper for the purpose of alarming people and thus getting attention.

One day, on entering the playroom I found the children all clustered together at one end of the room. At the other end stood the little terror with a hammer in his hand. He was threatening to hit anyone who approached him.

'Cut it out, my boy,' I said sharply. 'We aren't afraid of you.'

He dropped the hammer and rushed at me. He bit and kicked me.

'Every time you hit or bite me,' I said quietly, 'I'll hit you back.' And I did. Very soon he gave up the contest and rushed from the room. This was not punishment on my part. It was a necessary lesson: learning that one cannot go about hurting others for one's own gratification.

True, there is difficulty in deciding what is and what is not punishment. One day, a boy borrowed my best saw. The next day I found it lying in the rain. I told him that I should not lend him that saw again. That was not punishment, for punishment always involves the idea of morality. Leaving the saw out in the rain was bad for the saw, but the act was not an immoral one. It is important for a child to learn that one cannot borrow someone else's tools and spoil them, or damage someone else's property or someone else's person. For to let a child have his own way, or do what he wants to at another's expense, is bad for the child. It creates a spoiled child, and the spoiled child is a bad citizen.

In Summerhill, we once had a boy of twelve who had been expelled from many schools for being antisocial. In our school this same boy became a happy, creative, social boy. The authority of a reform school would have finished him. If freedom can save the far-gone problem child, what could freedom do for the millions of so-called 'normal' children who are perverted by coercive authorities?

Love is being on the side of the other person. Love is approval. I know that children learn slowly that freedom is something totally different from licence. But they can learn this truth and do learn it. In the end, it works – nearly every time.

More Problems

The first years in Leiston belong to what I call the problem era. I could not get enough ordinary pupils to make the place pay its way and began to take in all sorts of problems ... thieves, liars, destroyers, hateful brats. The problem era was full of interest and an era of great sacrifice. Coming from Scotland where we sweep up our confetti against a rainy day, or rather a dry day for the next wedding, I had pain in having my books and clothes and watches stolen. Recently, since the early 1960s, because finance forced me to do so, I have had to return to taking in problem children and I don't like it.

I do not want to cure. I hate having to take problems. The joy of discovery has largely gone; I can tell now almost exactly how a problem child will react: he will swear a lot, go unwashed for weeks, be cheeky, steal from tuck-boxes, perhaps sell the workshop tools. It is like a twice-told tale, boring. Boring also because they often come too late. I used to have success by rewarding crooks for stealing, but I question if I could use the method today. Youth is more conscious and less naïve today.

One good thing is that children when free do not lie very much. Our village policeman, calling one day, was much astonished when a boy came into my office saying, 'Hi, Neill, I've broken a lounge window.' Children lie mostly to protect themselves, and lying flourishes in a home with fear. Abolish the fear and the lying will decay.

There has hardly ever been a confirmed or habitual liar among my pupils. When they first come to Summerhill, they lie sometimes because they fear to tell the truth. When they find that the school is a school without an adult boss, they find no use for lies. I cannot say lying disappears entirely. A boy will tell you he has broken a window, but he will not tell you he has raided the fridge or stolen a tool. The complete absence of lying would be too much to hope for.

Freedom will not do away with the fantasy lies in children. Too often parents make a mountain out of this agreeable molehill. When little Jimmy came to me saying that his Daddy had sent him a real Rolls-Bentley I said to him, 'I know. I saw it at the front door. Terrific car.'

'Go on,' he said. 'You know I was really only kidding.'

Now it may seem paradoxical and illogical, but I make a distinction between lying and being dishonest. You can be honest and yet a liar – that is, you can be honest about the big things in life although sometimes dishonest about the lesser things. Thus many of our lies are meant to save others pain. Truth-telling would become an evil if it impelled me to write, 'Dear Sir, your letter was so long and dull that I could not be bothered reading it all.' Or if it forced you to say to a would-be musician, 'Thank you for playing, but you murdered that Étude.' Adults' lying is generally altruistic, but children's lying is always local and personal. The best way to make a child a liar for life is to insist that he speak the truth and nothing but the truth.

One persistent criticism of Summerhill over the years is that the children swear. It is true that they swear – if saying Old English words is swearing. It is true that any new pupil will swear more than is necessary.

Some years ago at our General Meeting a girl of thirteen who came from a convent kept being brought up on charges of shouting out the phrase 'son of a bitch' when she went sea-bathing at a public beach, with strangers around, and that therefore she was showing off. As one boy put it to her, 'You are just a silly little goose. You swear in order to show off in front of people, and you claim to take pride that Summerhill is a free school. But you do just the opposite – you make people look down on the school.'

I explained to her that she was really trying to do the school harm because she hated it. 'But I don't hate Summerhill,' she cried, 'It's a terrific place.'

'Yes,' I said, 'it is, as you say, a terrific place, but you aren't in it. You are still living in your convent, and you have brought all your hate of the convent and your hate of the nuns with you. You still identify Summerhill with the hated convent. It isn't really Summerhill you are trying to damage – it's the convent.' But she went on shouting out her special phrase until Summerhill became a real place to her and not a symbol. After that, she stopped swearing.

Swearing is of three kinds: sexual, religious, excremental. The difference between Summerhill and a prep school is that in the one children swear openly; in the other, secretly.

Our juniors have an interest in the Old English word for faeces. They use it a lot. Children like Anglo-Saxon words. More than one child has asked me why it is wrong to say 'shit' in public, but right to say 'faeces' or 'excrement'. I'm baffled to know.

Children accept swearing as a natural language. Adults condemn it because their own sense of obscenity is greater than that of children. I imagine that if a parent brought up a baby to believe that the nose was dirty and evil, the child would whisper the word 'nose' in dark corners.

With swearing, as with so many other things, it is the law that makes the crime. The law at home voiced by father's forbidding commands curbs the ego of the child and, in curbing that ego, can make the child bad. Suppression awakens defiance, and defiance naturally seeks revenge. Much criminality is revenge. To abolish crime, we must abolish the things that make a child want vengeance. We must show love and respect for that child.

Two kinds of stealing should be distinguished: stealing by a normal child and stealing by a neurotic child. A natural, normal child will steal. He simply wants to satisfy his acquisitive urge; or, with his friends, he wants the adventure. He has not yet made the distinction between mine and thine. Many Summerhill children engage in this kind of stealing up to a certain age. They are free to live out this stage.

School thieving is for the most part a communal affair. The communal theft would suggest that adventure plays an important part in stealing; not only adventure, but showing off, enterprise, leadership.

Only occasionally does one see the lone crook – always a sly boy with an angelic innocence all over his face . . . it is certainly a fact that you can never tell a young thief by his face. However, I have seen many a child who would steal at the age of thirteen grow up to be an honest citizen. The truth seems to be that children take a much longer time to grow up than we have been accustomed to think. By growing up, I mean becoming a social being.

In Summerhill, I cannot leave the fridge or the money box unlocked. At our Tribunal children accuse others of breaking open their trunks. Even one thief can make a community lock and key conscious.

The second kind of stealing – habitual, compulsive stealing – is an evidence of neurosis in the child. Stealing by a neurotic child is generally a sign of lack of love. The motive is unconscious. In almost every case of confirmed juvenile stealing, the child feels unloved. His thieving is a symbolic attempt to get something of great value. Whatever is stolen, the unconscious wish is to steal love. This kind of stealing can be treated only by finding a direct way for giving out love to the child.

I would like to impress upon parents of a habitually dishonest child that they must first examine themselves, trying to find out what treatment of theirs made the child dishonest. Once, in the early days, I had a boy of sixteen sent to my school because he was a bad thief. When he arrived at the station, he gave me the half-fare ticket his father had bought for him in London – a ticket obtained by understating the boy's age.

Some years ago, I had a youth sent to me who was a real crook who stole cleverly. A week after his arrival, I received a telephone message from Liverpool. 'This is Mr X [a well-known man in England] speaking. I have a nephew at your school. He has written to me asking if he can come to Liverpool for a few days. Do you mind?'

'Not a bit,' I answered, 'but he has no money. Who will pay his fare? Better get in touch with his parents.'

The following afternoon the boy's mother called me up and said that she had received a phone call from Uncle Dick. So far as she and her husband were concerned, Arthur could go to Liverpool. They had looked up the fare and it was twenty-eight shillings, and would I give Arthur two pounds ten?

Arthur had put through both calls from a local phone box. His imitation of an old uncle's voice and of his mother's voice was perfect. He had tricked me, and I had given him the money before I was conscious of having been taken in.

I talked it over with my wife. We both agreed that the wrong thing to do would be to demand the money back, for he had been subjected to that kind of treatment for years. My wife suggested rewarding him and I agreed. I went up to his bedroom late at night. 'You're in luck today,' I said cheerfully.

'You bet I am,' he said.

'Yes, but you are in greater luck than you know,' I said.

'What do you mean?'

'Oh, your mother has just telephoned again,' I said easily. 'She says that she made a mistake about the fare: it isn't twenty-eight shillings – it's thirty-eight shillings. So she asked me to give you another ten.' I carelessly threw a ten-shilling note on his bed, and departed before he could say anything.

He went off to Liverpool next morning, leaving a letter to be given to me after the train had gone. It began; 'Dear Neill, you are a greater actor than I am.' For weeks he kept asking me why I had given him that ten-shilling note.

In past days, when I had much more to do with bad delinquents, I again and again rewarded them for stealing. But it was only after a few years, only after the child was cured, that he had any realization of the fact that my approval had helped.

Had I been rich enough I think I should have had two schools – one for easy normal children and a sort of prep school some distance away for those who had much hate and antisocial habits to live out. Mixing the two kinds of kids the way we do does have some advantages: the normal children become more tolerant and more sophisticated. Against this is the fact that the problems often keep back the others, especially the smaller ones. When the young ones might well want to go to lessons or to make a ship or to do something creative, one of our 'gangsters' of – say – thirteen will lead them away to steal or destroy or get bored having nothing to do.

There is no short cut to curing under freedom; it is a long weary time until the problem child turns his or her corner. I am convinced that our characters are formed very early in life, and although they can be modified by environment or therapy, in them remain elements that are beyond change. I can find traces of Calvinism in myself, irrational fears that stem from the first years of my life.

At the moment our self-government is frankly rotten. Partly because of the fact that all the bigger boys are newcomers and not yet Summerhillians; partly because we have too many old pupils who are problems and too egocentric and disturbed to be good citizens. Almost weekly we have special discussions about the lack of community spirit. One or two pupils blame my age: 'Neill is too old now; he doesn't understand us and grouses about us not obeying the laws.' This could have some truth in it. The sudden popularity of Summerhill was possibly too much for a man of my age. I guess that after fifty years of problem children I feel I'd like a rest from them.

Why did I ever call a book *The Problem Child*? The name has appealed as a panacea to a few hundred parents who didn't know what to do with their difficult offspring. Really the curse of the school has been that it never had a chance to show its paces with non-problem pupils. Always we had a sprinkling of antisocial brats who interfered with the freedom of other children. True there was a positive side. The constant dealing with problem children gave the others a charity and an understanding they might never have acquired from living in a normal school. To sit on a jury when you are ten and try an offender, an ordinary occurrence in Summerhill, must give a child something of great value that no other school system could offer.

I have often written and spoken about Summerhill successes. Now let me write about our failures. I think we have followed Homer Lane's beacon too closely, his banner with the words 'On the Side of the Child'. We have kept children in the school who should have been sent to another type of school years before they left us. The worst example is the bully. We have watched a boy bully for years, making other smaller children afraid; we have seen him tried and tried again at Meetings without any improvement on his part. We have held on to a problem girl who led other girls into hate and pure bitchiness.

It wasn't only that we were on the child's side; often we tried to oblige the parents. 'If you send him home what can we do with him? No state school will have a boy of fourteen who can't even read,' or, 'We are moving house and can't have her home.' All the time we knew that we would get no gratitude from parent or child, nay, rather did we guess that they might turn against us and blame the school for the failure. I can think of two old pupils who take up that attitude: 'If I had gone to a decent school where they taught me to learn . . .' We ought to have had a stern rule: if after three terms you still bully, out you go. I don't think it too late to use such a rule.

One mistake we have made again and again is to keep a boy or girl, who has little chance of improving because of a loveless home. It was difficult to put such a child out, for, although vacations were hell and hate, term time was their real home time. Not seldom was the handicap of a loveless home combined with a lack of grey matter. There again we should have acted. The low IQs haven't the guts or the interest to attend lessons when there is no compulsion to attend. They fall behind and later, if they have a vague desire to learn, they are ashamed to go to lessons for they can't read. They again are likely later to blame the school for their lack of education. Nor do they really grasp the meaning of self-government or community living. Freedom works best with those who have enough combined free emotion and free intelligence to absorb it.

One mistake we have been making for years was one we couldn't well avoid. I have more than once written that, if I were rich, I'd take no child over seven. I was never rich and in consequence have had to take too many pupils who were too old for freedom. Every child coming into freedom becomes a problem in some way, and the average boy or girl, thirteen-years-old and over, is certain to go through antisocial stages, wasting material, destroying, loafing without the initiative to make even a mud pie; many have a parent/teacher complex and react with hate to the staff. Ena gets most of this, being the mother who serves out the food and the one who sees and objects to antisocial acts like throwing food about the dining-room. I get a lot of hate from the bigger boys who have fathers they fear, sometimes fathers who hit them. Why such fathers send their boys to Summerhill puzzles me.

These latecomers take years to grasp what it is all about. Already I have had three big boys sent back to America. I told the parents they were getting nothing out of the school, were asocial rather than antisocial, eating and sleeping in the school but spending all day and often late evenings down town with their pals there. Incidentally when a pupil has to find his companionship in the town, it usually denotes a sense of inferiority ... 'I am a nobody in the school, but in the town I am a big guy,' and he proves it by spending a few dollars.

The publication of *Summerhill* in the USA brought us a big influx of pupils from over there, most of them all right; the snag is that you can't interview an American pupil before arrival. Most of our older boys and girls, native and foreign, will be leaving in July, and Ena and I are all for refusing all teenage pupils so that we can have a school of children who grow up with freedom. At the moment our bunch of nine- to eleven-year-olds is a fine bunch of bright and understanding boys and girls. In a couple or so of years they will make a firm foundation for self-government. They are pretty social now.

One mistake, nay, failure of the school has been the failure to keep out fear. We succeeded with the staff who, with one or two exceptions in the past, have inspired no fear. We failed with the pupils. One sadist can make a dozen smaller children unhappy and fearful. It is so difficult to decide in any special case. I see clearly that most cases of hate behaviour are due to a lack of love as a baby. I see that no school treatment can counteract such a beginning or do much against a situation where a mother or stepmother or father gives out hate in the holidays.

What other boarding-schools do with unloved pupils, I don't know. Some, I hear, simply chuck them out, possibly with the recommendation 'Try Summerhill.' I have come to the stage where I'd gladly chuck out, not the unloved child who merely steals, but the child full of hate and aggression. I have long preached that a dozen small children should not be sacrificed for one bully . . . and, like a coward, didn't practise what I preached. I feel like doing so now, and if I hesitate it simply means that I cannot see where to send the misfits.

Private Lessons

In the early days, my main work was not teaching but the giving of 'private lessons'. Most of the children required psychological attention, but there were always some who had just come from other schools, and the private lessons were intended to hasten their adaptation to freedom.

The PLs were informal talks by the fireside. I sat with a pipe in my mouth, and the child could smoke, too, if he liked. The cigarette was often the means of breaking the ice.

Once I asked a boy of fourteen to come and have a chat with me. He had just come to Summerhill from a typical public school. I noticed that his fingers were yellow with nicotine, so I took out my cigarette packet and offered it to him. 'Thanks,' he stammered, 'but I don't smoke, sir.'

'Take one, you damned liar,' I said with a smile, and he took one. I was killing two birds with one stone. Here was a boy to whom headmasters were stern, moral disciplinarians to be cheated every time. By offering him a cigarette, I was showing that I didn't disapprove of his smoking. By calling him a damned liar, I was meeting him on his own level. At the same time, I was attacking his authority complex by showing him that a headmaster could swear easily and cheerfully. I wish I could have photographed his facial expression during that first interview.

He had been expelled from his previous school for stealing. 'I hear you are a bit of a crook,' I said. 'What's your best way of swindling the railway company?'

'I never tried to swindle it, sir.'

'Oh,' I said, 'that won't do. You must have a try. I know lots of ways,' and I told him a few. He gaped. This surely was a madhouse he had come to. The principal of the school telling him how to be a better crook. Years later, he told me that that interview was the biggest shock of his life.

What kind of children needed PLs? The best answer will be a few illustrations.

Lucy, the kindergarten teacher, comes to me and says that Peggy seems very unhappy and antisocial. I say, 'Right oh, tell her to come and have a PL.' Peggy comes to my sitting-room.

'I don't want a PL,' she says, as she sits down. 'They are just silly.'

'Absolutely,' I agree. 'Waste of time. We won't have one.'

She considers this. 'Well,' she says slowly, 'I don't mind a tiny wee one.' By this time she has placed herself on my knee. I ask her about her Daddy and Mummy and especially about her little brother. She says he is a very silly little ass.

'He must be,' I agree. 'Do you think that Mummy likes him better than she likes you?'

'She likes us both the same,' she says quickly, and adds, 'she says that, anyway.'

Sometimes the fit of unhappiness has arisen from a quarrel with another child and sometimes it is a letter from home that has caused the trouble, perhaps a letter saying that a brother or sister has a new doll or a bike. The end of the PL is that Peggy goes out quite happily.

With newcomers it was not so easy. When we got a child of eleven who had been told that babies are brought by the doctor it took hard work to free the child from lies and fears.

Most small children did not require regular PLs. The ideal circumstance under which to have regular sessions is when a child *demands* a PL. Some of the older ones demanded PLs; sometimes, but rarely, a young child did too.

Charlie, aged sixteen, felt much inferior to lads of his own age. I asked him when he felt most inferior, and he said when the kids were bathing, because his penis was much smaller than anybody else's. I explained to him how his fear came about. He was the youngest child in a family of six sisters, all much older than he. There was a gulf of ten years between him and the youngest sister. The household was a feminine one. The father was dead, and the big sisters did all the bossing. Hence, Charlie identified himself with the feminine in life, so that he, too, could have power.

After about ten PLs Charlie stopped coming to me. I asked him why. 'Don't need PLs now,' he said cheerfully; 'my tool is as big as Bert's now.'

But there was more involved than that in the short course of therapy. Charlie had been told that masturbation would make him impotent when he was a man, and his fear of impotence had affected him physically. His cure was also due to the elimination of his guilt complex and of the silly lie about impotence. Charlie left Summerhill a year or two later. He is now a fine, healthy, happy man who will get on in life.

Sylvia had a stern father who never praised her. On the contrary, he criticized and nagged her all day long. Her one desire in life was to get her father's love. She sat in my room and wept bitterly as she told her story. Here was a difficult case to help. Analysis of the daughter could not change the father. There was no solution for Sylvia until she became old enough to get away from home. I warned her that there was a danger that she might marry the wrong man merely to escape from the father.

'What sort of wrong man?' she asked.

'A man like your father, one who will treat you sadistically,' I said.

Sylvia was a sad case. At Summerhill, she was a social, friendly girl who offended no one. At home she was said to be a devil. Obviously, it was the father who needed analysis, not the daughter.

Another insoluble case was that of little Florence. She was illegitimate, and she didn't know it. My experience tells me that every illegitimate child knows unconsciously that he is illegitimate. Florence assuredly knew that there was some mystery behind her. I told the mother that the only cure for her daughter's hate and unhappiness was to tell her the truth.

'But, Neill, I daren't. It wouldn't make any difference to me. But if I tell her, she won't keep it to herself, and my mother will cut her out of her will.'

Well, well, we'll just have to wait till the grandmother's gone before Florence can be helped, I'm afraid. You can do nothing if a vital truth has to be kept dark.

An old boy of twenty came back to stay with us for a time, and he asked me for a few PLs.

'But I gave you dozens when you were here,' I said.

'I know,' he said sadly, 'dozens that I didn't really care for, but now I feel I want them.'

I recall a boy of fifteen whom I tried to help. For weeks he sat silent at our PLs, answering only in monosyllables. I decided to be drastic, and at his next PL I said to him, 'I'm going to tell you what I think of you this morning. You're a lazy, stupid, conceited, spiteful fool.'

'Am I?' he said, red with anger. 'Who do you think you are anyway?' From that moment, he talked easily and to the point.

Then there was George, a boy of eleven. His father was a small tradesman in a village near Glasgow. The boy was sent to me by his doctor. George's problem was one of intense fear. He feared to be away from home, even at the village school. He screamed in terror when he had to leave home. With great difficulty, his father got him to come to Summerhill. He wept, and clung to his father so that the father could not return home. I suggested to the father that he stay for a few days.

I had already had the case history from the doctor, whose comments were, in my estimation, correct and most useful. The question of getting the father to return home was becoming acute. I tried to talk to George, but he wept and sobbed that he wanted to go home. 'This is just a prison,' he sobbed. I went on talking and ignored his tears.

'When you were four,' I said, 'your little brother was taken to the infirmary and they brought him back in a coffin.' (*Increased sobbing.*) 'Your fear of leaving home is that the same thing will happen to you – you'll go home in a coffin.' (*Louder sobs.*) 'But that's not the main point, George, my boy. *You killed your brother!*'

Here he protested violently, and threatened to kick me.

'You didn't *really* kill him, George, but you thought that he got more love from your mother than you got; and sometimes, you wished he would die. When he *did* die, you had a terrible guilty conscience, because you thought that your wishes had killed him, and that God would kill you in punishment for your guilt if you went away from home.'

His sobbing ceased. Next day, although he made a scene at the station, he let his father go home.

George did not get over his homesickness for some time. But the sequel was that in eighteen months he insisted on travelling home for the vacation – alone, crossing London from station to station by himself. He did the same on his way back to Summerhill.

Nowadays, I don't give regular therapy. Curing a neurosis in a child is a matter of the release of emotion, and the cure will not be furthered in any way by expounding psychiatric theories to the child and telling him that he has a complex. More and more I come to the conclusion that therapy is not necessary when children can live out their complexes in freedom. But in a case like that of George, freedom would not have been enough.

In the past I have given PLs to thieves and have seen resulting cures, but I have had thieves who refused to come to PLs. Yet after three years of freedom, these boys were also cured.

At Summerhill, it is love that cures; it is approval and the freedom to be true to oneself. Of our forty-five children, only a small fraction receive PLs. I believe more and more in the therapeutic effect of creative work. I would have the children do more handiwork, dramatics and dancing.

A free school like Summerhill could be run without PLs. They merely speed up the process of re-education by beginning with a good spring-cleaning before the summer of freedom.

A word of warning to amateur would-be therapists. Do not try to use therapy on your friends or, most dangerous of all, on your wife and family. Art teachers are often guilty. 'That picture of yours shows that you hate your mother and want to kill her', the picture being one of a child with an axe trying to chop down a tree.

Interpreting symbolism is like a crossword, a pleasant game. I feel sure that it never helped a patient, and I guess that many analysts have dropped using it. I am told that a lot of Freudian analysts no longer interpret dreams ... the royal road to the unconscious as Freud put it. Anyway a teacher should never touch symbols. If he is going to use psychology he should do so more in action than in words. Hugging a child will often do much more for it than interpreting its dreams.

I am not saying that teachers should not study psychology. Far too few do. When I write a provocative article for an educational journal there is seldom any reply, but if one writes about teaching history there is a sheaf of correspondence. Teachers seem automatically to shy away from anything to do with the emotions.

I know from my own experience the temptation a young teacher has to experiment with the little he knows. Fifty years ago I read a book on hypnotism and thought I should have a go at it. I hypnotized a young woman, and when she was asleep I said to her, 'In two minutes you will wake up and ask me what I paid for my boots.' In two minutes she woke up looking rather confused. It was obvious that she had forgotten about the hypnosis. 'Sorry,' she said, 'I must have fallen asleep.' She sat silent for a little time.

'Oh, Lord!' she cried suddenly. 'When I went to town this morning I quite forgot to get mother's aspirins, and I was in Boots too.' Boots – the chain-store chemists. Her eyes wandered to my feet.

'I have sometimes wondered where you get those broad-toed boots; what did you pay for them?'

I felt I had had success and next time when I put her to sleep said: 'Multiply 3,576,856 by 568.'

She woke up looking dreadful.

'Oh, God, I've got a hell of a headache.'

I never attempted hypnotism again. Only the young dare to play with fire.

A degree does not necessarily teach common sense. I once took a bad problem boy to a psychiatrist in Harley Street. I gave him an account of the boy's behaviour, and then he called the boy in.

'Mr Neill says you are a very bad boy,' he said sternly. Psychology might be termed another word for common sense.

One can argue that the amateur psychologist does no harm. I think that he often does. Adolescents so easily believe what their elders say about them and their motives. One of my girl pupils stole pens and pencils. A man of twenty told her that she was compensating for not being born a boy and having a penis. The poor kid worried about it for weeks. I told her that an equally plausible explanation would be that she wanted to be a writer.

One should study all points of view, all schools of psychology. There is, however, one drawback . . . so many books on education and psychology are such heavy going in style and wordiness. I wonder why learning takes one away from simplicity. Where an uneducated man would write a letter to his local paper about the disturbance of his sleep by a concert of cats, a pedantic teacher might write protesting against a concatenation of raucous sounds emanating from feline wanderers in the night. What is plain should be said plainly.

One disconcerting feature in therapy is the constant undeclared war between the various schools. The Freudians for the most part dismissed Reich as a fake. A Kleinian won't see any truth in what an Adlerian says. They label themselves and when one labels oneself one ceases to grow. Today there is much wrangling among Reich's followers: 'We alone realize what the Master meant.' I am bragging when I say that, although I have been a disciple more than once in my life, I have managed to steer free of idolatry. My motto is: take from each what you want and reject the rest, and never label yourself as one of a school. I'd hate to think that long after I am dead teachers will call themselves Summerhillians. They will thus advertise the fact that they are dead.

Coming back from the psychoanalytic atmosphere of Vienna in the early twenties I thought that analysing was the answer to the problem child. I spent years analysing dreams of such children and was proud when a boy who had been chucked out of, say, Eton for stealing went out of Summerhill cured. It took me a long time to realize that Bill and Mary who had also been expelled for stealing but refused to come to me for analysis also went out cured. I had to accept that it wasn't my therapy that cured; it was freedom to be themselves. A most satisfying realization, for, even if therapy were the answer, the millions of kids in the world cannot all have it.

I think I had more success with the psychology that is not found in textbooks. When I rewarded a bad thief by paying him a shilling for every theft I was not acting on theory – the theory came later and may have been, if not wrong, inadequate. The thief was unloved and was stealing love symbolically. I gave him a token of love in the form of a coin. The point is that the method worked again and again, but I know the situation was complicated. How much did his new freedom in Summerhill help to cure him? How eager was he to be accepted by his peers as a good guy?

The simple explanation of the methods I used may be that I thought of the wrong way to treat a kid and did the opposite. Stealing – the cane or at least a moral talk in conventional schools. I made it non-moral. A boy had run away from three schools. On his arrival I said to him, 'Here is your fare home. I'll put it on the mantelpiece and when you want to run away come and ask for it.' He never ran away from Summerhill, but was it because of my attitude or the pleasure he had in being free for the first time in his life?

I have had successes but also failures. When in Dresden I told a

Yugoslavian girl that she was using too many nails making a box she spat at me, 'You are just like all the bossy teachers I have had.' I couldn't make real contact with her again. When giving out pocket money I said to Raymond, aged nine, 'You are fined six-pence for stealing the front door,' and he burst into tears. I should have seen that he was a mental case before the incident. Telling the nine-year-olds a story about their own adventures I made Martin steal the gold we had found. Later he came to me weeping. 'I never stole the gold.' From then on I made none of them baddies.

True, I laboured under a severe handicap, for I was therapist plus headmaster. At a General Meeting I'd say, 'Who the hell took my twist drill and left it to rust in the rain?' It was Willie, and in his next PL Willie shut up like a clam: I was the nasty policeman. A therapist should have no social connection with a patient, but when a Freudian or a Kleinian walks out of a cocktail party because a patient is present I think him a narrow-minded psy-chological snob.

I was not always the winner in the early days when Summerhill had so many crooks. One asked me for my autograph. I did not notice that the paper was folded until a local shopkeeper showed it to me. 'Please give bearer fifty Players cigarettes – A. S. Neill.' For weeks Dick kept selling me stamps and only the accident of my having stained one with green ink made me aware that he had been robbing my stamp drawer. I gave him five shillings reward for his cleverness, childishly showing him that he couldn't take the old man in. Old man? I was in my forties then.

As I say, I doubt if I could use the reward trick today with a thieving pupil. There is a sophistication in the new generation; it is intangible. The new orientation in youth may stem from the spread of knowledge about psychology. Some of my older pupils, the Americans especially, juggle with terms like inferiority complex, mother fixation, etc. If today at one of our self-government meet-ings a boy were charged for destroying books in the library and I made the proposal that he be appointed chief librarian, I am sure there would be a cry of: 'One of Neill's psychological tricks again.' No child would have said that forty-five years ago.

It is a sad fact that the vast majority of psychologists deal with private patients, and that by and large therapy to them means treating neurotic adults lying on couches. How many Freudians have said, 'The roots of neurosis lie in childhood. I shall deal with children and tell their parents how not to ruin them emotionally'? A meagre few that I know of – Anna Freud, Susan Isaacs.

In a way my staff and I are doing therapy all the time, for being on the side of the child is one of the best assets in therapy. I confess my ignorance of the child clinics that do fine work with play therapy, but I cannot see the point in Melanie Klein's demand that every child should be analysed at four years old. A child brought up freely should not require any analysis at all.

Today the word therapy makes me think of Hermann Goering's: 'When I hear the word *Kultur* I reach for my gun.' In my time I have met dozens of people treated by all schools of psychology, and their therapy had not apparently changed them into active, creative, happy people.

I have often wondered how much psychoanalysis helped me, even Wilhelm Reich's – Reichian vegetotherapy as he called it then. The results cannot be fully assessed. I think it made me capable of seeing the attitude of other people, meaning that it increased my charity. For instance, when I have to sack anyone, my misery is largely due to my asking myself how I would feel if told I wasn't good enough, but an un-analysed person could have similar feelings.

So where do I stand, in my old age, on therapy? I am against it because it is beginning at the wrong end. I do not deny that it can have its merits. A therapist said to me, 'My patients learn to treat their children more sensibly.' That can well be, if the therapist is for freedom. I cannot guess what effect an analysis by an Establishment doctor would have on parents. I am certain that Freud himself did not believe in freedom for children. He remained a paternalist. Remember that most patients seek therapy because of their own complexes, not because they want to rear their families un-neurotically.

Therapy to me is equivalent to drugs for the body. Just as our bodies suffer from all sorts of outside evils like devitalized bread, processed food, maybe artificial manures, atomic rays, insecticides, petrol fumes, so do our psyches suffer from childhood punishment and restraints and fears and character-moulding. The answer in both cases, psychical and somatic, is to prevent complexes, spiritual or bodily, from arising.

Health Issues

In over forty years at Summerhill, we have had very little sickness. I think the reason is that we are on the side of the living process – for we approve of the flesh. We put happiness before diet. Visitors to Summerhill generally remark on how well the children look. I think it is happiness that makes our girls look attractive and our boys handsome.

Eating raw greens may play an important part in curing kidney disease. But all the greens in the world won't affect the sickness of the soul if that sickness is due to repression. A man who eats a balanced diet can warp his children by moralizing, whereas a non-neurotic man will not harm his offspring. My experience leads me to conclude that warped children are less healthy physically than free children.

In Summerhill, we always give even the smallest child complete freedom to choose from the daily menu. There is always a choice of two main-course dishes at dinner. One result is, of course, that there is less waste at Summerhill than at most schools. But that is not our motive, for we want to save the child rather than the food.

As a layman unskilled in dietetics, I am of the opinion that it does not matter whether a child is a meat eater or not. As long as his diet is balanced, his health is likely to be good. We make it a point to always have wholemeal bread. I never hear of diarrhoea in Summerhill, and seldom of constipation. We always have lots of raw greens, but sometimes new children refuse to eat them. Usually, in the course of time, pupils accept them and get to like them. At any rate, Summerhill children are mostly unconscious of the cuisine, which is as it should be. When children are fed a balanced diet, the sweets they buy with their pocket money do no harm.

Because eating provides a great deal of pleasure in childhood, it is too fundamental, too vital, to be marred by table manners. The sad truth is that the children in Summerhill who have the worst table manners are those who have been brought up very genteelly.

The more demanding and rigid the home, the worse the table manners and all other manners – once the child is given the freedom to be himself. There is nothing to do but to let the child live out the repressed tendency until he develops his own natural good manners later on in adolescence.

Oddly enough I find that children sometimes correct each other's table manners. One of my pupils made eating a very loud affair until the others jeered at him. On the other hand, when one little fellow used his knife for eating minced beef, the others were inclined to think it a good plan. They asked each other why you shouldn't eat with a knife. The reply that you might cut your mouth was dismissed on the grounds that most knives are too blunt for anything.

Children should be free to question the rules of etiquette, for eating peas with a knife is a personal thing. They should not be free to question what might be called social manners. If a child enters our drawing-room with muddy boots, we shout at him, for the drawing-room belongs to the adults, and the adults have the right to decree what and who shall enter and what and who shall not.

When a boy was impudent to our butcher, I told the pupils at a General Meeting that the butcher had complained to me. But I think it would have been better if the butcher had boxed the boy's ears. What people generally call manners are not worth teaching. They are at best survivals of customs. Real manners come of themselves. Old Summerhillians have excellent manners – even if some of them licked their plates at the age of twelve.

Most people, parents or otherwise, would be startled at the lack of depth in manners among the usual, character-moulded boys and girls who come to Summerhill. Boys come with beautiful manners and soon drop them completely, realizing no doubt that their insincerity is out of place in Summerhill. The gradual dropping of insincerity in voice, in manner, and in action is the norm.

Food is the most important thing in a child's life, much more important than sex. The stomach is selfish. Selfishness belongs to childhood. The boy of ten is far more possessive about his plate of mutton than the old tribal chief was about his women. When the child is allowed freedom to live out his selfishness as he does at Summerhill, this egoism gradually becomes altruism and natural concern for others.

We strive to give a balanced diet, and we eschew starchy puddings as much as possible. I have already mentioned that we have always had wholemeal bread but nowadays some children will prefer white bread. We find on the whole that new pupils take some time to relish our raw greens, but a lot depends on the food a child has been accustomed to at home.

I find that it is difficult to make up my mind about food. My father died at eighty-five and he had eaten all the wrong food all his life: too much white bread, too many potatoes, not enough fresh fruit, and too many delicious Scottish teacakes. He never had a doctor in until he was on his deathbed. Still, I think we should give our children as much food with vitamin content as possible.

The Summerhill dining-room is a noisy place. Children, like animals, are loud at mealtimes. The teachers do not like too much noise, but the adolescents do not seem to mind the noise of the juniors. And when a senior does bring up the question of the juniors' noise in the dining-room, the juniors quite truthfully roar their protests that the seniors make just as much noise.

Ena looks after sick children in our school. If a child has a temperature she puts it to bed, gives it small portions and lemon or orange juice and water for twenty-four hours, and if the temperature has not gone down she calls in the doctor. Our health record is good. Over thirty-five years ago we built a sanatorium but we have never used it as one; today it is a dormitory for the juniors.

Naturally we carry out parental wishes about illness. In our time we have had children of believers in homoeopathy, in Nature Cure, in drugs and injections, and we try to treat their children in the way parents want us to. American children get more injections than our home ones do. Quite a few pupils are immunized against tetanus, for East Suffolk is notorious for being a dangerous place for tetanus.

The layman is at a great disadvantage in matters of health and sickness. He has not the knowledge to form a scientific opinion. How evil for health are tobacco, alcohol, sugar, pastries? And one can ask on the other hand what dangers lie in drugs. Two generations have taken phenacetin and now reports say that it is a poison. What are the results of a constant intake of aspirin? Not knowing, I think we ought to be chary about introducing drugs to the young. I notice that a couple of my doctor friends hesitate to give their own children drugs of any kind.

Take the matter of milk. For many years our pupils drank milk straight from the cow, in Germany, Austria, Dorset, Wales, and Suffolk, but now it is impossible to get anything but pasteurized milk. Again the layman cannot judge; all I know is that the pasteurized milk has little taste and is incapable of going sour; it only goes bad. It may be that TB, which was attributed to untreated milk, was in fact due to undernourishment among poor children. We are in the hands of the specialists all the time.

Many are objecting to the municipal fluoridization of water supplies. The idea is to stop the decay of children's teeth. A letter in the *Daily Telegraph* today says, 'Dr McLaughlin, Director of Health in Rhode Island, says that he is convinced that the long-term cumulative effect of adding fluoride to the public water supply is to produce chronic fluoride poisoning somewhat similar to lead poisoning.'

If this seems irrelevant to our Summerhill system of feeding I use it only to show how helpless teachers and parents are in the face of expert disagreement about food and water and health. We simply cannot get pure food and water if we want it, for we cannot control the use of insecticides, and artificial manures; we cannot do a thing about the fallout from strontium 90. If I wanted to start a business I should open a health-food store and sell at a profit all the excellent material that is thrown out in the commercial manufacture of food – the wheat germ, the unpolished rice, the molasses, the compost-grown greens.

I lay ill for three months with pyelitis forty years ago and it was then I became interested in Nature Cure. It seemed to fit into my philosophy of education. Raw greens and buttermilk equalled the free child; drugs equalled the outside discipline of the schools – a false analogy of course. I used to make an annual stay in a Nature Cure clinic and certainly felt refreshed and fit after each stay. By and large Nature Cure held that disease comes from within, that the body reacts to its poisons, mainly from bad feeding, by throwing out, so that a skin disease and a cold are methods of getting rid of the poisons, a self-cleaning process. And it sounds rational.

My father and grandfather said that they owed their long lives to the many colds they had had, and some French doctor claimed that his longest-lived patients were those with skin disease. The medical profession laughed what they called this quackery to scorn.

The disease came from infection, outside. The germ was the centre. And the layman really does not know what to think. The Nature Cure practitioners were using oranges and lemons as cures long before vitamin C was discovered.

Emotionally I was all on the Nature Cure side. Yet doubts arose. If diet were so important why did my father die at eighty-five after eating the wrong food all his life? Nature Cure warned against wearing flannel next to the skin. My father wore nothing else, summer and winter. Both sides in the health controversy were narrow and dogmatic. Nature Cure would have no truck with inoculations and few advocates of Nature Cure would accept the fact that tetanus injections had saved thousands of lives in the Great War. My doctor brother told me that after penicillin came in he had not lost one patient with pneumonia. On the other hand the medical men laughed at the idea of fasting, ignoring the fact that an animal fasts when ill. A vet told me that much of the mortality among horses and cattle in his country was due to the farmers forcing food down their throats 'to keep up their strength'.

After my South African tour, after too many drinks and no exercise, I felt like a dying man when I boarded the ship. My urine was like mud. I fasted on water for six days and arrived in Southampton the picture of health. The odd feature of fasting is that one feels so bright mentally. At that point I felt I could tell Einstein where he was wrong.

Doubts increased when people who had lived on a Nature Cure diet all their days died of cancer, proving that diet was not enough. I believed but I did not believe – but then I have the same attitude to doctors who prescribe a salve for a skin disease without asking what is causing it. I have hardly ever seen a doctor who asked what I ate, if I took exercise, if my sex life were satisfactory. The thing was to treat the disease while the Nature Curist tried to build up the whole body. A combination of the two systems might be a solution.

In the matter of personal cleanliness at Summerhill, girls on the whole are tidier than boys. Our boys and girls from about fourteen onwards are concerned about their appearance. On the other hand, girls are no tidier about their rooms than boys are – that is, girls up to thirteen. They dress dolls, make theatre costumes, and leave their floors littered with rubbish, but it is mostly creative rubbish.

Seldom do we have a girl at Summerhill who won't wash. We did have one, aged nine, from a home where her granny had a complex about cleanliness and apparently washed Mildred ten times a day. Her housemother came to me one day, saying, 'Mildred hasn't washed for a couple of weeks. She won't have a bath and she is beginning to smell. What shall I do?'

'Send her in to me,' I said.

Mildred came in presently, her hands and face very dirty.

'Look here,' I said sternly, 'this won't do.'

'But I don't want to wash,' she protested.

'Shut up,' I said. 'Who's talking about washing? Look in the glass.' (She did so.) 'What do you think of your face?'

'It isn't very clean, is it?' she asked, grinning.

'It's *too* clean,' I said. 'I won't have girls with clean faces in this school. Now get out!'

She went straight to the coal cellar and rubbed her face black. She came back to me triumphantly. 'Will that do?' she asked.

I examined her face with due gravity. 'No,' I said. 'There is a patch of white on that cheek.'

Mildred took a bath that night. But I can't fathom just why she did.

I recall years ago the case of an older boy who came to us from a public school. A week after his arrival, he became chummy with the men who filled coal carts at the station, and he began to help them with their loading. His face and hands were black when he came to meals, but no one said a word. No one cared.

It took him several weeks to live down his public-school and home idea of cleanliness. When he gave up his coal-heaving, he once more became clean in person and dress, but with a difference. Cleanliness was something no longer forced on him; he had lived out his dirt complex.

Too often parents attach far too much importance to tidiness. It is one of the seven deadly virtues. The man who prides himself on his tidiness is usually a second-rate fellow who values the second best in life. The tidiest person often has the most untidy mind. I say this with all the detachment of a man whose desk always looks like a heap of papers under a 'No Litter' notice in a public park.

While on the subject of cleanliness . . . some years ago we had a small boy sent to us because he messed his trousers all day long.

His mother had thrashed him for it and, in desperation, she had finally made him eat his faeces. You can imagine the problem we had to cope with. It turned out that this boy had a younger brother, and the trouble began with the birth of the younger child. The reason was obvious enough, the boy reasoned: 'He has taken Mummy's love from me. If I am like him and mess my trousers the way he dirties his nappies, Mummy will love me again.'

I gave him PLs designed to reveal to him his true motive, but cures are seldom sudden and dramatic. For over a year, that boy messed himself three times daily. No one said a bitter word to him. Mrs Corkhill, our nurse, performed the cleaning chores without a word of reproach. But she did protest when I began to reward him every time he made a really big mess. The reward meant that I was giving approval of his behaviour.

During the entire period, the boy was a hateful little devil. No wonder! He had problems and conflicts. But after his cure he became absolutely clean and stayed with us three years. Eventually, he became a very lovable lad. His mother took him away from Summerhill on the grounds that she wanted a school where he would *learn* something. When he came back to see us after a year at the new school, he was a changed boy – insincere, afraid, unhappy. He said he would never forgive his mother for taking him away from Summerhill, and he never will. He is one of the very few examples of trouser messing we have had in all these years.

I remember an incident when I was little boy. My sister Clunie and I followed a band one day to the Market Muir, a long way from home for toddlers' feet. I had a sanitary accident; when I got home, my irate mother marched me down to the outside washhouse, took off the offending pants, and sent me running home with a hearty slap on the bum. I must have been about six, yet I still can recall my fear that someone would meet me in that pantless sprint. Mother seemed to get some amusement out of the incident, for years later she referred to my speed that day as a criterion for swiftness.

Our small boys at Summerhill seem to show no desire to exhibit themselves, and the senior boys and girls hardly ever strip. During the summer, the boys and men wear only shorts without shirts. The girls dress lightly. There is no sense of privacy about taking baths, and only new pupils lock bathroom doors. Although some of the girls take sun-baths in the field, no boys ever think of spying on them.

Many years ago, when we came to Leiston, we had a duck pond. In the morning, I would take a dip. Some of the staff and the older girls and boys used to join me. Then we got a batch of boys from public schools. When the girls took to wearing bathing-suits, I asked one, a pretty Swede, why.

'It's these new boys,' she explained. 'The old boys treated nudity as a natural thing. But these new ones leer and gape and – well, I don't like it.'

I once saw our English teacher digging a ditch in the hockey field, assisted by a group of helpers of both sexes ranging in age from nine to fifteen. It was a hot day and he had stripped. Another time, one of the men of the staff played tennis in the nude. At the General Meeting he was told to put on his shorts in case tradesmen and visitors should happen by. This illustrates Summerhill's down-to-earth attitude towards nudity.

For many years at Summerhill we left smoking alone; any child could smoke, yet at a rough guess I should think about 60 per cent of old pupils are non-smokers. After the lung-cancer scare I felt it right to become an authority and ban it for those under sixteen, knowing that there would be surreptitious smoking in lavatories and bedrooms.

I smoke pipe tobacco and an occasional cigarette. Again and again I have tried to give it up but have always failed in spite of tricks like keeping my pipe in my cottage and my baccy pouch in my office over in the main building. On the positive side, the walking back and forth must have helped my health.

In self-government my wife and I have to be authorities in health matters; for instance we do not allow a child with a temperature to run outside on a cold day. One difficulty about smoking is that some children are allowed to smoke at home. It is a difficult business to make rules about. Strict rules bring in the forbidden-fruit aspect always. And it is hopeless to appeal to reason, hopeless to say to a child that he may later get lung cancer, for no child can see tomorrow, and few adults either, judging from the high sales of cigarettes since cigarette smoking was pronounced dangerous. One encouraging factor is that cigarettes are expensive in Britain and well beyond the pocket money of many children. Some schools prohibit it altogether, and the few staff members who are smokers have to smoke in their own rooms only. At least three quarters of my current staff smoke, including me myself with my pipe.

The problem of children's smoking is especially difficult to solve in view of the vast propaganda for cigarette sales on TV and in papers. I cannot guess what effect the stopping of TV advertising will have, possibly very little. And when millions of parents smoke it will never be easy to persuade their children that smoking is dangerous. But to be logical I should ban all the anti-health rubbish my pupils buy in sweetshops. An iced lolly may be as cancer-producing as a cigarette for all I know. But where should we stop? White bread is bad for health, soft drinks may be dangerous. The question is really most difficult.

Drink I won't have in the school. Drink has not the attraction for children that tobacco has, and few if any would buy it; the trouble is that sometimes a visitor, thrilled to be in a 'free' school, brings in a bottle of whisky or gin and gives it to the children. I have already banned two such seducers from coming again. I have seen too many in my life whose alcoholism dated back to boyhood tippling.

I like a drink but haven't been drunk for many years. Malt whisky is my favourite. When I used to drink rye with Reich I liked it but over here in England it does not appeal to me. Beer I like and some wines. Drugs I have never tried. I know nothing about them and only wonder why to smoke cannabis is a crime while smoking cigarettes is legal, seeing that few die from smoking cannabis while many thousands die of lung cancer. I never used drink as an escape. I drank for the pleasure of drinking.

I can recall only one incident in my drinking life that was unpleasant. In 1936, on my South African lecture tour, I was a guest in the famous Diamond Club in Kimberley. In the bar a merchant stood me a whisky. Six other diamond merchants joined us and I did not notice that each was ordering a double for me. I was in a hole. I had often heard of colonial hospitality and how pained people were if it were rejected. I drank the lot and then rushed to the lavatory and put my finger down my throat. I must have given a lousy lecture that night. Had I been older I would have thanked them and asked them to excuse me in view of my evening lecture.

Then there is the question of sleep. I wonder how much truth there is in the dictum of doctors that so and so much sleep is necessary for a child. With small children, yes. Allow a child of seven to sit up late at night, and he suffers in health because he often cannot go on sleeping late in the morning. Some children resent being sent to bed because they feel they will be missing something.

In a free school, bedtime is the very devil – not with the juniors so much as with the seniors. Youth likes to burn the midnight oil, and I can sympathize, for I hate to go to bed myself.

Work settles the problem for most adults. If you have to be in your job at 8 a.m., you renounce the temptation to stay up until the small hours.

Other factors, such as happiness and good food, may balance any loss of sleep. Summerhill pupils make up their loss of sleep on Sunday mornings, preferring to miss lunch if need be.

As for work in relation to health, much of the work I do has a dual motive. I dig for potatoes, realizing that I could use the time more profitably if I wrote newspaper articles and paid a labourer to dig in the garden. However, I dig because I want to keep healthy – a motive that is more important to me than newspaper income. A friend, who is a car dealer, tells me what a fool I am to dig in an age of mechanics, and I tell him that motors are ruining the health of the nation because no one walks or digs nowadays. He and I are old enough to be conscious of health problems.

A child, however, is completely unconscious of health. No boy digs in order to keep fit. In any work, he has only a single motive – his interest at the time.

The good health that we enjoy at Summerhill is due to freedom, good food, and fresh air – in that order.

Sex and Coeducation

I have never had a pupil who did not bring to Summerhill a diseased attitude towards sexuality and bodily functions. The children of modern parents who were told the truth about where babies come from have much the same hidden attitude towards sex that the children of religious fanatics have. To find a new orientation to sex is the most difficult task of the parent and teacher.

I am quite willing to believe that my unconscious attitude towards sex is the Calvinistic attitude a Scottish village imposed on me in my first years of life. Possibly there is no salvation for adults, but there is every chance of salvation for children, if we do not force on them the awful ideas of sex that were forced on us.

My own earliest memory of sex is a nursery incident when I was six and my sister Clunie was five. We had stripped and were examining each other with great interest and considerable sexual excitement. The door opened, and Mother caught us. She gave us both a severe beating, then made us kneel down to ask God's forgiveness. Later, when Father came home, he took up the cudgels and spanked us again. Then I was locked in the big, dark dining-room. So I learned that of all sins, sex was the most heinous.

The incident affected my life for many years, not only forcing me to associate sex with sin but also giving me a fixation on Clunie, who was connected with the forbidden fruit. It took me decades to get over that early shock; and, indeed, I sometimes wonder if I ever fully got over it.

There were later sexual adventures with Clunie, but she always had a bad conscience afterwards and told Mother, and I got thrashed every time. Only once did I escape a thrashing after Clunie's tale-telling, when my brother Willie was in on it too, indeed, had suggested our wrongdoing. As the oldest, Willie got all the blame. Being the favourite, however, he was never punished for anything.

Naturally, we never had any sexual instruction at home. My

mother went on having babies, and we took it for granted that the doctor was bringing them, for Mother could not tell us lies. Other boys told us the truth, or rather, many half-truths; and by keeping rabbits and seeing farm animals, we knew that the young came out of their mothers. But we never applied this knowledge to Mother. I must have been about eight when I first saw Father go into the privy one day. I stared at him in surprise; I knew he couldn't do dirty things; and finally concluded that he must be going to clean it out. So when we heard the man's part in making a baby, I simply did not believe that, either. My parents were pure and holy; they could never do a thing like that.

Willie went off to school in Edinburgh, and when he came home for holidays he regaled us with dirty stories of all kinds. We thought ourselves very sophisticated but still dared not face the application of sex to our own parents. They were over-modest always; naked-ness was awful. Except for Clunie, I never saw my sisters naked; if anyone came into my bedroom when I was dressing, I hastily covered my body with anything I could seize.

Later, as a twenty-five-year-old student in Edinburgh, I got into the habit of having a cold bath each morning. During the holidays, I got my mother to throw a bucket of cold water over me while I sat in a tub, because our home had no bathroom. Mother did this cheerfully but Clunie told me that my father strongly disapproved.

I cannot recollect our ever mentioning masturbation or, for that matter, practising it. There are a few score slang terms for masturba-tion, but we did not know one of them. I know enough about psychology to realize that there may be some sort of repressive forgetting here, but to the best of my memory we did not mastur-bate either singly or mutually.

We did have a habit that we called 'looking' at each other.

We would lay a smaller boy on his back and open his fly, but that was always a collective practical joke. From the age of seven and a half, I slept in a bed with Willie and Neilie, who resented my presence strongly. This arrangement came about after my ejection from the bed I shared with Clunie by an irate mother, who had again discovered us doing things we shouldn't have. My brothers never let me forget my unwelcome intrusion or the circumstances which led to it.

We know so little of the causes of the sex taboo that we can only hazard guesses as to its origin. Why there is a sex taboo is of no immediate concern to me. That there is a sex taboo is of great concern to a man entrusted to cure repressed children. We adults were corrupted in infancy; we can never be free about sex matters. *Consciously*, we may be free but I fear that *unconsciously* we remain to a large extent what conditioning in infancy made us.

The taboos and fears that fashioned sex behaviour are those same taboos and fears that produce the perverts who rape and strangle small girls in parks, the perverts who torture Jews and Negroes.

In Hitler's Germany, the torture was inflicted by sexual perverts of the Julius Streicher type; his paper *Der Stürmer* was full of vile, perverted sex long before concentration camps were erected. Yet many fathers who berate the sexual perversity of the prison sadist do not apply the same reasoning to their own minor sadisms. To beat a child at home or at school is basically the same thing as torturing a Jew in Belsen. If sadism was sexual in Belsen, it is likely to be sexual in school or family.

To many men, intercourse is polite rape; to many women, a tiresome rite that has to be endured. Thousands of married women have never experienced an orgasm in their lives. In such a system, giving must be minimal; sex relations are bound to be more or less brutalized and obscene. The perverts who require to be scourged with whips or to beat women with rods are merely extreme cases of people who, owing to sex miseducation, are unable to give love except in the disguised form of hate.

I wonder how much impotence and frigidity in adults date from the first interference in a sexual relationship of early childhood. Heterosexual play in childhood is the royal road, I believe, to a healthy, balanced adult sex life. When children have no moralistic training in sex, they reach a healthy adolescence – not an adolescence of promiscuity.

In most schools there is a definite plan to separate boys from girls, especially in their sleeping quarters. Love affairs are not encouraged. They are not encouraged in Summerhill either – but neither are they discouraged.

In Summerhill, boys and girls are left alone. Relations between the sexes appear to be very healthy. One sex will not grow up with any illusions or delusions about the other sex. Not that Summerhill is just one big family, where all the nice little boys and girls are brothers and sisters to one another. If that were so, I would become a rabid anti-coeducationist at once.

Under real coeducation – not the kind where boys and girls sit in class together but live and sleep in separate houses – shameful curiosity is almost eliminated. There are no Peeping Toms in Summerhill. There is far less anxiety about sex than at other schools.

Every now and again an adult comes to the school, and asks, 'But don't they all sleep with each other?' and when I answer that they do not, he or she cries, 'But why not? At their age, I would have had a hell of a good time!'

It is this type of person who assumes that if boys and girls are educated together, they must necessarily indulge in sexual licence. To be sure, such people do not say that this thought underlies their objections. Instead, they rationalize by saying that boys and girls have different capacities for learning, and therefore should not have lessons together.

Schools should be coeducational because life is coeducational. But coeducation is feared by many parents and teachers because of the danger of pregnancy. Indeed, I am told that not a few principals of coed schools spend sleepless nights worrying over that possibility.

Every older pupil at Summerhill knows from my conversation and my books that I approve of a full sex life for all who wish one. I have often been asked in my lectures if I provide contraceptives at Summerhill, and if not, why not? This is an old and a vexed question that touches deep emotions in all of us. That I do not provide contraceptives is a matter of bad conscience with me, for to compromise in any way is to me difficult and alarming. On the other hand, to provide contraceptives to children either over or under the age of consent would be a sure way of closing down my school. One cannot advance in practice too much ahead of the law.

Yet of course adolescents in Summerhill must have slept together in a school in which there is no teacher going round with a flashlight of evenings. How we have escaped pregnancies in all these years I do not know. One explanation may be the strong feeling the pupils have about the fate of the school. There may have been pregnancies that I never heard of, but I cannot believe that any parents would have hidden the news from me.

At Summerhill, the sex question has always been a pain in the neck. For many years I have advocated a sex life for adolescents, for any couple who are ready for it, but I have had to discourage it in the school because even Summerhill cannot be free of the establishment with its Victorian morality. The only thing I could do was to tell the kids frankly what my position was, and they realized that I was not taking a moral standpoint.

Two adolescents of fifteen fell in love. They came to me to ask if they could have a bedroom to themselves. I said, 'I'd gladly give you one but I daren't.'

'Why not? This is a free school.'

'Yes, but it isn't a free civilization. Suppose I gave you one and the Ministry of Education heard of it. They would close my school.'

I said to the girl, 'You know that your mother is scared of sex. Suppose you got pregnant? What a stink that would make. Also,' I said, 'you can't afford contraceptives and I dare not give you any.'

They accepted the situation. I can see no other attitude to take since I don't believe that sex is a sin or bad or dirty. One advantage of this attitude is that I can sleep soundly at night without worrying.

In one of my books I tell of a time when a few adolescent girls asked me if they could be fitted with Dutch caps. I told them that I couldn't do anything without the consent of their mothers. I wrote to the mothers. Only two in six agreed and all six had been in the school from the age of seven or eight. That was forty years ago; I wonder how many mothers today would say yes. What I was preaching fifty years ago, he said proudly, is now accepted as normal by many parents.

Reich wrote about the sexual misery of adolescents but I think that was an exaggeration, at least with the middle classes I have dealt with. We did manage to destroy the shattering belief that many children have that they alone are guilty of the awful deed of masturbation. Some American psychologist wrote many years ago: 'Ninety-nine out of a hundred masturbate ... the hundredth won't tell.'

The reason that I entertain no fears that the older pupils at Summerhill who have been here since early childhood might indulge in sexual licence is because I know that I am not dealing with children who have a repressed, and therefore unnatural, interest in sex.

Some years ago, we had two pupils arrive at the same time: a boy of seventeen from a boys' private school and a girl of sixteen from a girls' private school. They fell in love with each other and were always together. I met them late one night and I stopped them. 'I don't know what you two are doing,' I said, 'and morally I don't care, for it isn't a moral question at all. But economically I do care. If you, Kate, have a baby, my school will be ruined.'

I went on to expand upon this theme. 'You see,' I said, 'you have just come to Summerhill. To you it means freedom to do what you like. Naturally, you have no special feeling for the school. If you had been here from the age of seven, I'd never have had to mention the matter. You would have such a strong attachment to the school that you *would* think of the consequences to Summerhill.' It was the only possible way to deal with the problem. Fortunately, I never had to speak to them again on the subject.

Most of my pupils have had a good start in life. They were not lectured to, nor punished, for masturbation; many are accustomed to nakedness at home. In the main their attitude to sex is healthy and natural. I do not know what attitude a school can take when the parents do not choose the school. Thousands of parents of children in state schools ignore sex in the bringing up of the children, or they frown on it.

When I asked a few adolescents from a famous private coed school if there were any love affairs in their school, the answer was no. Upon expressing surprise, I was told, 'We sometimes have a friendship between a boy and a girl, but it is never a love affair.' Since I saw some handsome lads and some pretty girls on the campus, I knew that the school was imposing an anti-love ideal on the pupils and that its highly moral atmosphere was inhibiting sex.

I once asked the principal of a progressive school, 'Have you any love affairs in the school?'

'No,' he replied gravely. 'But then, we never take problem children.'

Conditioned children of both sexes are often incapable of loving. This news may be comforting to those who fear sex; but to youth in general, the inability to love is a great human tragedy.

Those who are against coeducation may object that the system makes boys effeminate and girls masculine. But deep down is the moral fear, actually a jealous fear. Sex with love is the greatest pleasure in the world, and it is repressed because it is the greatest pleasure. All else is evasion.

This brings up the question of sex without love. A young couple can have sex together with much pleasure even though they are not in love with each other, but if they go on looking for casual chances of intercourse, their sex lives must lack something of value, call it love or tenderness, call it what you will. There can be no permanent pleasure in promiscuity. The happiest love affairs I have seen were those which had some permanency. The Casanovas and the Don Juans are not likely to give a girl anything like full enjoyment.

A girl or boy should be free to have a sex life when she or he wants it. Without parental approval it will be apt to be a guilty one, and without contraceptives, a dangerous one. On the other hand no parents should make up for a poor sex life by advising their daughters to have a sex life when one is not wished for.

The invention of contraceptives must in the long run lead to a new sexual morality, seeing that fear of consequences is perhaps the strongest factor in sexual morality. To be free, love must feel itself safe.

Personally I don't see the point in teaching sex. Sex instruction in a school must be a pale affair; the parents would never stand for a lesson that told of the emotional part of sex, of the bliss of sexual intercourse. The lessons are compelled to be purely physical because parental opinion would not tolerate any other kind.

Most children get their sex information from other children, and it is all wrong and pornographic and often sadistic. From the safety angle a girl has only to learn that intercourse without contraceptives can lead to pregnancy, and both sexes should be told again and again that venereal disease is real and dangerous.

I know of no argument against youth's love life that holds water. Nearly every argument is based on repressed emotion or hate of life – the religious, the moral, the expedient, the arbitrary, the pornographic. None answers the question why nature gave man a strong sex instinct, if youth is to be forbidden to use it unless sanctioned by the elders of society.

Youth today has little opportunity for loving in the true sense.

Parents will not allow sons or daughters to live in sin as they call it, so that young lovers have to seek damp woods or parks or motor cars. Thus everything is loaded heavily against our young people. Circumstances compel them to convert what should be lovely and joyful into something sinister and sinful, into smut and leers, and shameful laughter.

I know that adolescent sex life is not practical today. But my opinion is that it is the right way to tomorrow's health. I can *write* this, but if at Summerhill I approved of my adolescent pupils sleeping together, my school would be suppressed by the authorities. I am thinking of the long tomorrow when society will have realized how dangerous sex repression is.

Theatre and Music

I saw my first play, *A Night of Pleasure*, at the age of twelve in Edinburgh's Theatre Royal. For me it certainly was a night of bliss, for I had never seen such visions of radiant loveliness in my life. I had never imagined any woman could be so beautiful as the heroine. What the story was about I do not remember, save that the lovely damsel was wronged in some way. But it all came right in the end.

Years later as a student teacher I had the joy of becoming a regular theatre-goer. Dundee had a theatre and touring companies came every week. Musical-comedy successes came from London, and we saw Martin Harvey, a popular actor of the period, in *The Only Way*, *The Breed of the Treshams*, even *Hamlet*. My cultural standards those days may be better understood if I say that *The Only Way* seemed a much better play than *Hamlet*.

Sometimes, in Dundee, I took my sister Clunie to my favourite plays. She was just as ignorant of the theatre as I, but my slight advancement made me laugh in a very superior way when the curtain fell on the first act of *The Only Way*, and she, with memories of local shows in the village school, remarked, 'Martin Harvey will be helping to shift the furniture, won't he?'

My strong interest in plays began when I first read Ibsen, and he is the only dramatist who has tempted me to travel a hundred miles to London to see one of his plays. Ibsen himself I could never get interested in. All I read about him made me feel that I wouldn't have liked the grumpy remote man, so critical of society but so pleased to receive society's titles and honours. But how great a dramatist that man was: his technique is almost beyond criticism.

In my student days I played with the idea of becoming an actor. I knew that I had little chance of success; for one thing I could not have got rid of my Scottish accent, and few Scots are required in the play world. I know I had some talent but not enough to make me reach the stars; also, I am sure I would have balked at being told how to act by a director. My face was not of the brand that gets laughs and to be a comedian was out of the question.

Whatever the cause, I renounced any ambition to go on the stage and I have never regretted it. In a way I did become an actor, speaking to thousands of students and parents and teachers. At first I had stage fright and had a phobia that I would stick and not be able to go on speaking; hence I used notes, but for many years have never needed them.

The trick in lecturing is to hold your audience. One of mine was to tell a funny story if people looked bored or rustled. Once in Scotland I faced a grim crowd with set faces.

'What's wrong with you lot?' I said. 'You all look dead, so I take it you are all teachers.' Laughter and they were with me. On another occasion I began, 'I feel guilty. When I knew I was to speak to teachers with all their respectability I did a cowardly thing – I put on a tie.' I took my tie off, and again the ice was broken. So I did become an actor after all.

During the winter, Sunday night at Summerhill is acting night. The plays are always well attended. I have seen six successive Sunday nights with a full dramatic programme. But sometimes after a wave of dramatics there will not be a performance for a few weeks.

At the end-of-term celebrations we always have a triple-bill programme. I always write the Cottage play myself, and one day I may publish a volume of these plays . . . if the general public would stand their 'vulgarity'. The audience is not too critical. It behaves well – much better than some London audiences do. We seldom have catcalls or feet thumping or whistling.

The Summerhill theatre is a converted squash-rackets court, which holds about a hundred people. It has a movable stage; that is, it is made of boxes that can be piled up into steps and platforms. It has proper lighting with elaborate dimming devices and spotlights. There is no scenery – only grey curtains. When the cue is *'Enter villagers through gap in hedge'*, the actors push the curtain aside.

The tradition of the school is that only plays written in Summerhill are performed. The cast makes its own costumes, too, and these are usually exceptionally well done. Our school dramas tend towards comedy and farce rather than tragedy; but when we have a tragedy, it is well done – sometimes beautifully done.

Once a visitor suggested a Shaw play. A parent of a boy at the school said, 'No, no, if I want to see Shaw I go to a play produced by professionals. In Summerhill I want to see plays written and produced in the school.'

Girls write plays more than boys do. Small boys often produce their own plays; but usually the parts are not written out. They hardly need to be, for the main line of each character is always 'Stick 'em up!' In these plays the curtain is always rung down on a set of corpses, for small boys are by nature thorough and un-compromising.

Daphne, a girl of thirteen, used to give us Sherlock Holmes plays. I remember one about a constable who ran away with the sergeant's wife. With the aid of the sleuth and, of course, 'My Dear Watson' the sergeant tracked the wife to the constable's lodgings. There a remarkable sight met their eyes. The constable lay on a sofa with his arm around the faithless wife, while a bevy of loose-looking women danced sinuous dances in the middle of the room. *The constable was in evening dress*. Daphne always brought high life into her dramas.

Girls of fourteen or so sometimes write plays in verse, and these are often good. Of course, not all the staff and children write plays. There is a strong aversion to plagiarism. When, some time ago, a play was dropped from the programme and I had to write one hastily as a stopgap, I wrote on the theme of one of W. W. Jacobs's stories. There was an outcry of 'Copycat! Swindler!'

Summerhill children do not like dramatized stories. Nor do they want the usual highbrow stuff so common in other schools. I myself think that Shakespeare is too difficult for children, at least pre-adolescent ones. Years ago we staged *A Midsummer Night's Dream* and our most gifted actress of twelve made a mess of Puck. 'I didn't understand the language,' she said.

Our crowd never acts Shakespeare; but sometimes I write a Shakespearean skit as, for example, Julius Caesar with an American gangster setting – the language a mixture of Shakespeare and the *Black Mask* magazine. Mary brought the house down when as Cleopatra she stabbed everyone on the stage, and then, looking at the blade of her knife, read aloud the words 'stainless steel', and plunged the knife into her breast.

I also did *Hamlet* as rewritten by Shakespeare and the mystery writer Edgar Wallace in collaboration . . . and with Freud as psychological advisor. So it came about that in one of my comic exams later a small boy in answer to the question, 'Who was Hamlet?', answered, 'A chap in Neill's play.'

The acting ability of the pupils is of a high standard. Among Summerhill pupils there is no such thing as stage fright. The Cottage kids are a delight to see; they live their parts with complete sincerity. The girls act more readily than the boys. Indeed, boys under ten seldom act at all except in their own gangster plays; and some children never get up to act nor have any desire to do so.

We discovered in our long experience that the worst actor is he who acts in life. Such a child can never get away from himself and is self-conscious on the stage. Perhaps self-conscious is the wrong term, for it means being conscious that others are conscious of you.

Acting is a necessary part of education. It is largely exhibitionism; but at Summerhill when acting becomes only exhibitionism, an actor is not admired. I used to think that either one is born an actor or not; I am not quite so sure now. There is Virginia who is a born actress, but there is Edna who was a bad actress and is getting better and better each performance. As a comedy actress she is great.

As an actor, one must have a strong power of identifying oneself with others. With adults, this identification is never unconscious; adults know they are play-acting. But I question if small children really do know. Quite often, when a child enters and his cue is, 'Who are you?' instead of answering, 'I am the abbey ghost!' he will answer, 'I'm Peter.'

In one of the Cottage plays there was a dinner scene with real food. It took the prompter some time and concern to get the actors to move on to the next scene. The children went on tucking in the food with complete indifference to the audience.

Acting is one method of acquiring self-confidence. But some children who never act tell me that they hate the performances because they feel so inferior. That is a difficulty for which I have found no solution. The child generally finds another line in which he can show superiority. The difficult case is that of the child who loves acting but can't act. It says much for the good manners of the school that such a child is seldom left out of a cast.

Often I have had stammerers in the school, but every time one acted in a play he or she spoke fluently and well. I suppose the reason was that by taking on another personality he or she became a normal vocal child.

Boys and girls of thirteen and fourteen refuse to take any part that involves making love, but the small children will play any part easily and gladly. The seniors who are over fifteen will play love parts if they are comedy parts. Only one or two seniors will take a serious love part. Love parts cannot be played until one has experienced love. Yet children who have never known grief in real life may act splendidly in a sorrowful part. I have seen Virginia break down at rehearsals and weep while playing a sad part. That is accounted for by the fact that every child has known grief in imagination. In fact, death enters early into every child's fantasies.

Plays for children ought to be at the level of the children. It is wrong to make children do classical plays which are far away from their real fantasy life. Their plays, like their reading, should be for their age. They also prefer a story of their own environment. Although Summerhill children perform the plays that they themselves write, they nevertheless, when given the opportunity, respond enthusiastically to really fine drama.

Often in the winter I read a play to the seniors once a week. I read all of Barrie, Ibsen, Strindberg, Chekhov, some of Shaw and Galsworthy, and some modern plays like *The Silver Cord* and *The Vortex*. Our best actors and actresses liked Ibsen.

The seniors are interested in stage technique and take an original view of it. There is a time-honoured trick in playwriting of never allowing a character to leave the stage without his making an excuse for doing so. When a dramatist wanted to get rid of the father so that the wife and daughter could tell each other what an ass he was, old father obligingly got up, and remarking, 'Well, I'd better go and see if the gardener has planted those cabbages,' he shuffled out. Our young Summerhill playwrights have a more direct technique. As one girl said to me, 'In real life you go out of a room without saying anything about why you are going.' You do, and you do on the Summerhill stage too.

For many years every programme included dances. These are always arranged and performed by the girls, and they do them well. They do not dance to classical music; it is always jazz. We had one ballet to Gershwin's *An American in Paris* music. I wrote the story and the girls interpreted it in dance.

I have a vague notion that in one of my books I described my experience of dance in Germany. In our international school in Hellerau we had a division devoted only to eurythmics and dance, girls from sixteen upwards. We often had a solo dance evening. Too many chose a *Totentanz*, and I began to wonder why girls who expressed their emotions all day long in movement chose a Dance of Death. That experience knocked on the head a belief I had previously held, that movement was curative.

I don't think that dance or art or music in themselves are curative. I wonder how really relaxed girls are in an opera chorus or an art school or a music school. One must remember that there is no real freedom in most schools of music, art, dance. The girls and boys are under a strict discipline. The wonderful Russian dancers must be drilled like soldiers, I fancy. Perhaps the least disciplined are the art students who stand or sit and paint.

Given freedom to live freely all children will benefit from movement and rhythm. For years I have seen that our children learn to dance, but not by taking lessons in foxtrot, tango, twist; they tend to invent as they go along.

In the early years nearly every night our private living-room filled with children. We often played records and here disagreements arose. The children wanted Duke Ellington and boogie-woogie and I hate the stuff. I like Ravel and Stravinsky and Bix Beiderbecke.

In *Young Man with a Horn* by Dorothy Baker, a vivid characterization of a trumpeter whose life was said to be founded on the life of the early jazz musician Bix Beiderbecke, the author makes her hero so real that we almost hear him playing his horn. I have read the book four times.

Actually, it does not matter to one's happiness in life whether one loves Beethoven or Beiderbecke. Schools would have more success if they included jazz or rock and roll in the curriculum and left out Beethoven.

At Summerhill, three boys, inspired by jazz bands, took up musical instruments. Two of them bought clarinets and one chose a trumpet. On leaving school, they all went to study at the Royal Academy of Music. Today, they are all playing in orchestras which play classical music exclusively. I like to think that the reason for this advance in musical taste is that when they were at Summerhill each was permitted to hear Duke Ellington *and* Bach, or any other composer for that matter.

Summerhill specializes in a certain branch of dramatic art which we call spontaneous acting. I begin with easy situations: *Put on an imaginary overcoat; take it off again and hang it on a peg. – Step in dog dung in the street. – Pick up a bunch of flowers and find a thistle among them. – Open a telegram that tells you your father (or mother) is dead. – Wheel a heavy barrow. – Be a blind man crossing the road. – Take a hasty meal at a station restaurant and be on tenterhooks lest the train leave without you.*

Then I go on to speaking parts. I give only the skeleton. 'You are a father, you a mother, and you have been expelled from school. Carry on.' We have a rule that two heads cannot get together first to decide about the situation and the dialogue.

Another time I asked the children to telephone the doctor and get the butcher by mistake. One boy carried on a confused conversation about liver and heart.

One can imagine many situations. *Ask a London bobby the way. – Strike up a conversation with a fellow in a train. – Burgle a safe and the owner comes in.*

'What the devil do you think you are doing?'

A bright boy of twelve: 'Are you the owner of the house? Good, glad you came.'

'But you are robbing my safe.'

'Ah, you have got it all wrong. I am from the safe company and we go round testing our safes.'

'And come in by the window instead of ringing the front door bell. It won't do. I'll call the police.'

'Got me wrong again. We have to test to see if your windows are burglar proof.'

Sometimes the acting is a 'talkie'. For example, I sit down at a table and announce that I am an immigration officer at Harwich. Each child has to have an imaginary passport and must be prepared to answer my questions. That is good fun.

Again, I am a film producer interviewing a prospective cast, or a businessman seeking a secretary. Once I was a man who had advertised for an amanuensis. None of the children knew what the word meant. One girl acted as if it meant a manicurist and this afforded some good comedy.

I find that children shy away from serious situations. I can think of only one in which they are always deadly serious. *Alf has done seven years for robbery. He was framed by the gang leader. Released, he gets a gun and sets out to kill the leader. Slowly he realizes that the man he is to kill is blind.* The last attempt went thus.

'Hullo, Spike.'

'That's Alf's voice. Hallo, Alf, so you're out at last.'

'Nice place you've got here, Spike. That grand piano must have cost a packet. In the money, ain't you? Get up. Put your hands up, you dirty swine. Move over there.'

Spike stumbles over a chair and Alf moves forward to look at him.

'My God, you are blind!'

I have tried this one out many times but no one ever shot the gangster.

Spontaneous acting is the most exciting side of our school acting – it is the vital side. Perhaps the fun and wit seem to be of more value to the children than the acting. One result of this kind of acting is the complete absence of nervousness; you have no lines to forget. But I fancy it is best done by children who are free. A few state-school teachers have told me it is difficult to get their pupils to lose their self-consciousness and their fear of failing.

Some children who act well in plays cannot act spontaneously. Only older children can act a honeymoon Channel crossing on a rough sea. One difficulty is the young exhibitionist, the boy or girl of nine who wants to try every part.

How much should acting be taught? In spontaneous acting never, but when a play is being produced the producer, adult or child, must have the right to give directions as to position, movement, etc.

Our theatre has done more for creativity than anything else in Summerhill. Anyone can act in a play, but everyone cannot write a play. The children must realize, even if dimly, that their tradition of performing only original, home-grown plays encourages creativity rather than reproduction and imitation.

Some time ago the Summerhill Society offered to present a TV set to the school. I put it to the general meeting, and to my surprise the meeting refused the offer by a large majority. Some of the older ones said that it would ruin the social programme ... games, debates, country dances, etc. The younger ones said that a TV set would mean constant squabbling about which station to switch on to. I had been anxious lest I should have a school of inactive screen watchers. At the meeting the staff expressed no opinion and did not vote.

Television has come to stay, and there is no point in regretting its advent. I fear it from an educational viewpoint, for it must emphasize passivity, absorption of facts, sensationalism and too often brutality. Even the pictures of police action against agitators or Negroes are bad for young children, who often show fear when they see them.

However there are many features on the screen that are not violent or brutal. Charlie Chaplin's *The Great Dictator* would be much more salutary for children than a textbook on Hitler and Mussolini. A good Western is not brutal, with all its shooting – wonderful how often the hero misses – and the reason may be that in a Western, as in most thrillers, no one lives; they are all stick figures, and children apparently cannot attach any emotion to them. The villain dies and no one sheds a tear.

Yet many a tear has been shed at the death of a Hamlet, a Lear, an Othello or a Garbo in *The Lady of the Camellias*. I always shed a few at that most poignant ending of *City Lights*. I spend, or should I say, waste a lot of time watching TV, although I think it is geared to a mental age of ten in every country. I am bored stiff with the old films so often presented in Britain, even those of Garbo, yet I would walk a long way to see Chaplin's *City Lights* and *Modern Times*.

There is a mystery about Charlie Chaplin. I asked our local cinema to get both films and the distributors said that they were not in circulation. I wrote to Charlie in Switzerland asking why, and saying it wasn't fair that the young generation should miss his greatest work and see only the old bottom-kicking, pastry-throwing shorts. I got no reply. A man who knows him tells me that Charlie does not answer letters – a talent I wish I had when my postal delivery adds up to twenty at a time.

It sounds odd that children should reject TV but odder still is the fact that they are not at all keen on being photographed for TV. Like myself they get tired of the techniques ... long waits until the cameras are set up, longer ones until the lighting is arranged. One would think that all children would like to see themselves on the screen, but I admit that one programme in which every child saw itself was appreciated. The idea that children are all exhibitionists is a doubtful one; the opposite is shown in our art room, where a child seldom signs a picture.

I sympathize with their weariness in being televised. In the few times I have been on TV I have found it most tiresome. You go to the studio at six and you hang about until midnight: nothing seems to be ready, or else some other programme has to be filmed during your stay.

Commercial folks pay big money to have their advertisements on TV. When we were screened some years ago by ITV the producer said to me: 'You are getting £7,000 worth of publicity for nothing.' The film was seen by millions . . . and not a soul wrote asking for a school prospectus. But how many wrote and protested against the showing I do not know.

On alternate Sunday nights, I tell the younger children a story about their own adventures. I have done it for years. I have taken them to Darkest Africa, under the sea, and over the clouds. Some time ago, I made myself die. Summerhill was taken over by a strict man called Muggins. He made lessons compulsory. If you even said 'dash', you got caned. I pictured how they all meekly obeyed his orders.

Those three- to eight-year-olds got furious with me. 'We didn't. We all ran away. We killed him with a hammer. Think we would stand a man like that?'

In the end, I found I could satisfy them only by coming to life again and kicking Mr Muggins to the front door. These were mostly small children who had never known a strict school, and their reaction of fury was spontaneous and natural. A world in which the schoolmaster was not on their side was an appalling one for them to think of – not only because of their experience of Summerhill but also because of their experience at home where Mummy and Daddy were also on their side.

Teachers and Teaching

Several writers have tried to assess my work, too often assuming that I am a teacher. I am criticized because I do nothing to help teachers practically, because I have no solution to overcrowded and often violent schools, because I am not interested in organization or exams or methods of teaching. And the criticisms would be just if I were a teacher – that is an imparter of knowledge, a moulder of character, a guide to the young.

I refuse to be classified as a teacher. Think what a tin god a teacher really is. He is the centre of the picture; he commands and he is obeyed; he metes out justice; he does nearly all the talking.

I might define myself as a true believer in humanity. My message has been this one; a child's emotions are infinitely more important than his intellectual progress. I have tried, with I fear little success, to show that schools, by ignoring emotions, leave them to outside influences, the press, the kitsch of radio and TV, commercial TV ads, a plethora of magazines geared to a mentality of ten. Teachers cannot see the wood behind the trees, the wood that means life abundant, freedom from character moulding.

When I lecture to a group of teachers, I commence by saying that I am not going to speak about school subjects or discipline or classes. For an hour my audience listens in rapt silence; and after the sincere applause, the chairman announces that I am ready to answer questions. At least three quarters of the questions deal with subjects and teaching.

I do not tell this in any superior way. I tell it sadly, to show how the classroom walls and the prison-like buildings narrow the teacher's outlook and prevent him from seeing the true essentials of education. His work deals with the part of a child that is above the neck and, perforce, the emotional, vital part of the child is foreign territory to him.

Parents also are slow in realizing how unimportant the learning side of school is. Children, like adults, learn what they want to

learn. All prize-giving and marks and exams sidetrack proper personality development. Only pedants claim that learning from books
is education.

Books are the least important apparatus in a school. All that any
child needs is the three Rs; the rest should be tools and clay and
sports and theatre and paint and freedom.

It is time that we were challenging the school's notion of work.
It is taken for granted that every child should learn mathematics,
history, geography, some science, a little art, and certainly literature. It is time we realized that the average young child is not much
interested in any of these subjects.

I prove this with every new pupil. When told that the school is
free, every new pupil cries, 'Hurrah! You won't catch me doing
dull arithmetic and things!'

I am not decrying learning. But learning should come after play.
And learning should not be deliberately seasoned with play to
make it palatable.

In the home, the child is always being taught. In almost every
home, there is always at least one un-grown-up grown-up who
rushes to show Tommy how his new engine works. There is always
someone to lift the baby up on a chair when baby wants to examine
something on the wall. Every time we show Tommy how his engine
works we are stealing from that child the joy of life – the joy of
discovery, the joy of overcoming an obstacle. Worse! We make
that child come to believe that he is inferior, and must depend on
help.

Freedom works best with clever children. I should like to be able
to say that since freedom primarily touches the emotions, all kinds
of children – intelligent and dull – react equally to freedom. I
cannot say it.

One sees the difference in the matter of lessons. Every child
under freedom plays most of the time for years; but when the time
comes, the bright ones will sit down and tackle the work necessary
to master the subjects covered by government exams. In a little
over two years, a boy or girl will cover the work that disciplined
children take eight years to cover.

The orthodox teacher holds that exams will be passed only if
discipline keeps the candidate's nose to the grindstone. Our results
prove that with bright pupils that is a fallacy. Under freedom, it is

only the bright ones who can concentrate on intensive study, a most difficult thing to do in a community in which so many counter-attractions are going on.

I know that under discipline comparatively poor scholars pass exams, but I wonder what becomes of the passers later on in life. If all schools were free and all lessons were optional, I believe that children would find their own level.

Indifferent scholars who, under discipline, scrape through college or university and become unimaginative teachers, mediocre doctors, and incompetent lawyers would possibly be happier as good mechanics or excellent bricklayers or first-rate policemen.

In our educational policy as a nation, we refuse to let live. We persuade through fear. But there is a great difference between compelling a child to cease throwing stones and compelling him to learn Latin. Throwing stones involves others; but learning Latin involves only the boy. The community has the right to restrain the antisocial boy because he is interfering with the rights of others; but the community has no right to compel a boy to learn Latin – for learning Latin is a matter for the individual. Forcing a child to learn is on a par with forcing a man to adopt a religion by act of Parliament. And it is equally foolish.

I learned Latin as a boy – rather I was given Latin books to learn from. As a boy, I could never learn the stuff because my interests were elsewhere. At the age of twenty-one, I found that I could not enter the university without Latin. In less than a year, I learned enough Latin to pass the entrance exam. Self-interest made me learn Latin.

I got a high mark in history at the university, but today I couldn't tell what the Long Parliament did, and I am uncertain about who won the Wars of the Roses. I once studied both Latin and Greek; today I doubt if I could say the Greek alphabet, and I am sure that I couldn't read the Latin inscription on a gravestone.

How many copies of Shakespeare or Tennyson would one find in the homes of a Cup Final crowd? The criterion is all wrong. As Michael Duane said recently, the problem is largely a social one, a question of class education, the social assumption being that a grammar-school boy with five A levels is better educated than a potter or a skilled toolmaker.

Most of the school work that adolescents do is simply a waste of time, of energy, of patience. It robs youth of its right to play and play and play; it puts old heads on young shoulders. 'Education' does not consider the motives of children, their desire to play, their longing to be free, to escape moulding by adults who do not know how to live themselves.

In all countries, capitalist, socialist, or communist, elaborate schools are built to educate the young. But all the wonderful labs and workshops do nothing to help John or Peter or Ivan surmount the emotional damage and the social evils bred by the pressure on him from his parents and his schoolteachers, or the pressure of the coercive quality of our civilization.

Why school subjects ever came to be standardized I cannot guess. Why history and not botany? Geography and not geology? Maths and not civics? I think the answer may lie in the words of the old public-school headmaster: 'It doesn't matter what you teach a boy so long as he dislikes it.'

At Summerhill I never ask one of my teachers how he teaches. I know that there are new methods of teaching – say – maths, and some of them are excellent, especially in the early stages. I cannot visualize any modern way of teaching quadratic equations or factors; if there is a new way of drawing a tangent to a circle from a point outside it, I do not know it.

The snag about teaching is that it is ruled by the university exams, and the exam papers look to me to be the same ones that were set when I was a youth. Pupils are supposed to learn about how to do square roots. Apart from my job I have never done a square root in my life, not even a long division of money.

Dickens, Hardy, Shaw, Hemingway . . . it is a sobering thought that probably not one of these men could have told you the difference between a noun clause and an adverbial clause of time. Hence I am not really interested in making subjects interesting by modern methods; rather, I am desirous of scrapping the lot of useless, boring subjects.

Mind you I am all for teachers who can make their subjects interesting, who can make them live, although I cannot even visualize a history teacher who would make his class excited over the repeal of the Corn Laws.

I think that a teacher is born, and that all the training in all the colleges will not make one a good teacher. Without boasting, I say

I was a good teacher, although not an ideal one from an examination point of view. My teaching dwelt too much on imagination, so that when I set an essay it was not 'How I spent my holidays' but 'My false teeth fell out on my plate' or 'Give a snail's description of its journey from the front door to the school gate.' Nearly fifty years ago I said to a class: 'I am going to give you the first sentence of an essay or story or what not. Here it is: "Hell and buggery, said the bishop!" Carry on.'

A boy of thirteen wrote, 'The bishop leaned over his pulpit. "Brethren," he said solemnly, "as I entered the cathedral this morning I heard one of you use these dreadful words. I shall take them as my text."' I certainly could not have risen to that standard; I'd have made the bishop foozle at golf. At one time I had to give up teaching the older pupils because they protested that my method would not help them to pass the external examinations; a valid criticism, condemning, not me, but the dead ones who set English papers. I could tell a child's standard in English in a half hour's talk plus a blank book in which he could write anything he liked.

My personal opinion is that English should not be a school subject. We learn by reading, talking, writing, but the authorities decree that we must study grammar. To adapt old Henry Ford: 'Grammar is bunk.' I grant that it is bad English to say '*these* sort of people', or '*who* did you see?' But what is the point of all the parsing and analysis, the breaking up a sentence into separate clauses? Grammar used to make a good exercise for country dominies before the days of crosswords.

Some time ago, I met a girl of fourteen in Copenhagen who had spent three years in Summerhill and had spoken perfect English here. 'I suppose you are at the top of your class in English,' I said.

She grimaced ruefully. 'No, I'm at the bottom of my class, because I don't know English grammar,' she said. I think that disclosure is about the best commentary on what adults consider education to be.

But, says one, a child must learn to spell. I am convinced after a long career as a teacher that spelling cannot be taught. It comes mainly via reading and is therefore primarily visual. This theory does not always work. I have a boy of fifteen who reads all day and late into the night. He cannot write a line without a misspelling. My American pupils write 'travelling' with one l, 'plough' as 'plow';

New York has electric signs like 'Nite Club'. In this day and age spelling is local, or rather national.

Some think that a teacher can give children a good taste in literature. It may be, but I never succeeded myself. My favourite novel is *The House with the Green Shutters*, but I have never managed to interest a pupil in George Douglas Brown. I suppose that there are teachers of English who manage to inspire the children's reading more successfully than I can.

Style cannot be taught, it is you. One of my greatest pleasures is writing, or rather typing. By and large I write as I speak, without purple patches, without an involved prose style. How much I was influenced by my teacher George Saintsbury, with his aversion to artificial elegance of language, I cannot guess. His own style was bad, full of parentheses and digressions – a fault I have myself but I did not learn it from him.

At Summerhill we have French and German for those pupils who want them. The difficulty is that the learning is apt to stop too soon. I was just beginning to appreciate the language of the *Aeneid* when I passed an exam in Latin and never looked at a Latin book again. Thousands who pass their exams in French never go to France, never read a French book, and, two years after the exam, if they visited Paris, they might be able to ask a gendarme the way, but most probably they would not be able to understand his reply.

The ideal way to learn a language is to live in the country when one is young. My foreign pupils are speaking English in a way in three weeks. They learn the swear words first. If a child sees no immediate end in view any language is heavy and dull. A few of us on the staff used to say private things in German, and the keenness to learn the language grew so fast that we found it unwise to carry on our private conversations in that language.

I get scores of letters from schoolchildren complaining about their homework. One girl said it took her four hours each evening. This martyrdom of children is criminal. I am all for homework when it is sought by the pupils, but when it is enforced by teachers and parents I am strongly against it. When children are free to direct their own lives they can tackle the dirty work demanded by the examiners, and they do not require to sit up late at night to master a subject. Nearly fifty years ago I taught in King Alfred's School in Hampstead. Homework was never given and yet quite a few pupils did well later in universities and the arts. But the school now has introduced homework.

When I was a student in my father's school he gave us homework every evening. The rural scholars in our Scottish village, destined to be hewers of wood and drawers of water, had none. But we were different. Every night at a certain hour, our games with the village lads were sadly and roughly interrupted by a dog whistle my father blew at the back door.

'Time for the dogs to ging hame,' cried our chums, and the dogs went home with their tails between their legs – Neilie and Clunie and me. Our brother Willie, a law unto himself, required neither driving nor coaching. The rest of us trooped into the nursery and attempted to turn our thoughts from 'smuggle the gig' to Allen's *Latin Grammar*.

How I hated that book! Tags from it still linger in my memory. 'A dative put with show and give, tell, envy, spare, permit, believe: to these add succour, pardon, please.' Neilie and Clunie had no great difficulty in learning such things, but I never could; and often I had to sit poring over the stuff when they had been allowed to go back to the village lads and their play.

There *are* skills that have to be taught – hence the good old apprenticeships, even if the first year consisted of making tea for the journeyman – but my contention is that school exams, by and large, deal with things that do not matter.

Teachers become as narrow as their subjects. Maybe that is why I have so often found university professors and lecturers rather dull men. Bacon, if he lived today, might say that specialization maketh a narrow man. This applies not only to teachers but to doctors: I have seldom met a doctor who had a wide interest or a wide area of conversation.

When I lecture to students at teacher training colleges and universities, I am often shocked at the ungrownupness of these lads and lasses stuffed with useless knowledge. They know a lot; they shine in dialectics; they can quote the classics – but in their outlook on life many of them are infants. For they have been taught *to know*, but have not been allowed *to feel*. These students are friendly, pleasant, eager, but something is lacking – the emotional factor, the power to subordinate thinking to feeling. I talk to them of a world they have missed and go on missing. Their textbooks do not deal with human character, or with love, or with freedom, or with self-determination. And so the system goes on, aiming only at standards of book learning – goes on separating the head from the heart.

I wish I could see a bigger movement of rebellion among our younger teachers. Higher education and university degrees do not make a scrap of difference in confronting the evils of society. A learned neurotic is no better than an unlearned neurotic.

How much of our education is real doing, real self-expression? Handwork is too often the making of a pin tray under the eye of an expert. Even the Montessori system, well-known as a system of directed play, is an artificial way of making the child learn by doing. It has nothing creative about it.

Creators learn what they want to learn in order to have the tools that their originality and genius demand. We do not know how much creation is killed in the classroom with its emphasis on learning.

I have seen a girl weep nightly over her geometry. Her mother wanted her to go to the university, but the girl's whole soul was artistic. I was delighted when I heard that she had failed her college entrance exams for the seventh time. Possibly, the mother would now allow her to go on the stage as she longed to do.

Learning is important – but not to everyone. Nijinsky could not pass his school exams in St Petersburg, and he could not enter the State Ballet without passing those exams. He simply could not learn school subjects – his mind was elsewhere. They faked an exam for him, giving him the answers with the papers, so a biography says. What a loss to the world if Nijinsky had really had to pass those exams!

Summerhill Staff

I have suggested more than once that the adults in Summerhill are no paragons of virtue. We are human like everyone else, and our human frailties often come into conflict with our theories. In the average home, if a child breaks a plate, father or mother makes a fuss – the plate becoming more important than the child. In Summerhill, if a child breaks a plate, I say nothing and my wife says nothing. Accidents are accidents. But if a child borrows a book and leaves it out in the rain, my wife gets angry because books mean much to her. In such a case, I am personally indifferent, for books have little value for me. On the other hand, my wife seems vaguely surprised when I make a fuss about a ruined chisel. I value tools, but tools mean little to her.

In Summerhill, our life is one of giving all the time. Visitors wear us out more than the children do, for they also want us to give. It may be more blessed to give than to receive, but it is certainly more exhausting.

Our Saturday night General Meetings, alas, show the conflict between children and adults. That is natural, for to have a community of mixed ages and for everyone to sacrifice all to the young children would be to spoil these children completely. The adults make complaints if a gang of seniors keeps them awake by laughing and talking after all have gone to bed. Harry complains that he spent an hour planing a panel for the front door, went to lunch, and came back to find that Billy had converted it into a shelf. I make accusations against the boys who borrowed my soldering outfit and didn't return it. My wife makes a fuss because three small children came after supper and said they were hungry and got bread and jam, and the pieces of bread were found lying in the hallway the next morning. Peter reports sadly that a gang threw his precious clay at each other in the pottery room. So it goes on, the fight between the adult point of view and the juvenile lack of awareness. But the fight never degenerates into personalities; there is no feeling of bitterness against the individual. This conflict keeps Summerhill very much alive. There is always something happening, and there isn't a dull day in the whole year.

Luckily, the staff is not too possessive, though I admit it hurts me when I have bought a special tin of paint at £3 a gallon and then find that a girl has taken the precious stuff to paint an old bedstead. I am possessive about my car and my typewriter and my workshop tools, but I have no feeling of possession about people. If you are possessive about people, you ought not to be a schoolmaster.

I do not say that we are a crowd of angels. There are times when we adults make a fuss. If I should be painting a door and Robert came along and threw mud on my fresh paint, I would swear at him heartily, because he has been one of us for a long time and what I say to him does not matter. But suppose Robert had just come from a hateful school and his mud-slinging was his attempt to fight authority, I would be tempted to overlook his mud-slinging because his salvation is more important than the door. I know that I must stay on his side while he lives out his hate in order for him to become social again. It isn't easy. I have stood by and seen a boy treat my precious lathe badly. I knew that if I protested he would at once identify me with his stern father, who always threatened to beat him if he touched his tools.

The strange thing is that you can be on the child's side even though you sometimes swear at him. If you are on the side of the child, the child realizes it. Any minor disagreement you may have about potatoes or scratched tools does not disturb the fundamental relationship. When you treat a child without bringing in authority and morality, the child feels that you are on his side. In his previous life, authority and morality were like policemen who restricted his activities.

When a girl of eight passes me and says in passing, 'Neill is a silly fool,' I know that that is just her negative way of expressing her love, of telling me that she feels at ease. Children do not so much love as they want to be loved. To every child, adult approval means love; whereas disapproval means hate. The attitude of the children to the Summerhill staff is quite like the attitude of the children to me. The children feel that the staff is on their side all the time.

The wear and tear of materials in Summerhill is a natural process. It could be prevented only by the introduction of fear. The wear and tear of psychic forces cannot be prevented in any way, for children ask and must be given. Fifty times a day my office door opens again and a child asks a question: 'Is this cinema night?' 'Why don't I get a PL?' 'Have you seen Pam?' 'Where's Ena?' It is all in a day's work, and I do not feel the strain at the time, though we have no real private life. This is partly because the house is not a good one for a school – not from the adult's point of view, for the children are always on top of us. But by the end of term, my wife and I are thoroughly fatigued.

One noteworthy fact is that members of the staff seldom lose their tempers. That says as much for the children as for the staff. Really, they are delightful children to live with, and the occasions for losing one's temper are very few. If a child is free to approve of himself, he will not usually be hateful. He will not see any fun in trying to make an adult lose his temper.

We had one woman teacher who was over-sensitive to criticism, and the girls teased her. They could not tease any other member of the staff, because no other member would react. You can only tease people who have dignity. Years ago, in one of my books, I wrote that when interviewing a prospective teacher, my test was: 'What would you do if a child called you a bloody fool?' It is my test today, except that *bloody* – never a real swearword outside British realms – has been changed to a more popular expletive.

When lessons are not compulsory you have to be a very good teacher if you are to have any pupils attending your classes. Of course what I want are teachers with some humour and with no dignity; they must not inspire fear and they must not be moralists.

Without humour you are a positive danger to children. Humour to a child means friendliness, lack of respect, and the absence of fear; it means affection from the adult. Humour is usually kept out of the classroom because it is a leveller. It would kill the respect the teacher demands because his laughter mingling with that of his pupils would make him too human. The best teachers are those who laugh *with* their children, and the worst are those who laugh *at* their children.

Schoolchildren are so unaccustomed to humour from teachers that when I say to a new boy of ten: 'I'm looking for Neill. Do you know where he is?' he stares at me as if I were mad. I tried it on a girl of eleven who had been with us for three years.

'Dunno,' she said casually. 'He went round that corner two minutes ago.' Humour is one of the most priceless gifts and it is almost completely left out of a child's education.

Small children have a sense of fun rather than a sense of humour. Ask a girl of ten how many feet are in a yard. She will tell you. Then ask her how many feet are in Scotland Yard and she may stare at you. One of my pupils, accustomed to fun, immediately replied: 'Depends on the number of cops and typists in the building.'

The greatest insult one can offer to a man is to say he has no sense of humour. Such a verdict is unforgivable. One of the most humourless men I know often sums up others – 'What is wrong with that man is that he has no sense of humour.'

I wonder why humour is suspect in so many walks of life. They say that Adlai Stevenson failed to become President of the United States because he was prone to make jokes. I make the guess that any British minister studies his speeches most carefully in case he should be accused of being a funny fellow.

When I first lectured in the USA in 1947 I discovered that the Americans had a humour different from that of the English. A joke I made that would have raised laughter in London fell flat in New York, and more than once laughter arose when I could not see why. Every nation has its own kind of humour, which is therefore apt to become hackneyed, like the stories of Scottish meanness. When I lived in Germany the only Germans who seemed able to laugh at themselves were the Jews.

I think that humour has been of great assistance to me in my work. I speak to every child lightly unless he or she seeks my help. Joking with a child means to it friendliness, equality, brotherhood. When someone asked me who would run Summerhill after my death I replied, 'No idea, but if he or she has no humour the school will go fut.'

A school that is not a funfair is a bad school. Alas the dignity of teachers too often kills all the fun. One of my teachers was offended because a pupil called him a damned fool.

'Man,' I said, 'half a dozen kids have been following me around all morning crying, "Neill, Neill, Banana Peel." Do you expect me to stand on my dignity and get annoyed?'

I begin to think that my success at Summerhill has been due, at least in part, to this ability to be a fun kid among other fun kids. Fun is of far greater importance than mathematics or history and all the other soon-to-be-forgotten subjects. Humour is a kind of emotional safety-valve and if a man cannot laugh at himself he is dead before his death. Someone once wrote that most men die when they are forty but aren't buried until they are seventy. He must have meant the humourless men.

There is another difficulty for teachers at Summerhill. I have had teachers who came because consciously they believed in freedom for children, but after a few weeks they showed that they were really seeking freedom for themselves, and they behaved very much as unfree children do when they come to Summerhill. To live in freedom is far from easy for adult or child.

I sometimes think that I have had more trouble with staff than I have had with pupils. I have had some odd bods in my time, the science man who let a boy of eight handle a bottle of cyanide and a girl of the same age pour fuming nitric acid into a tube so that she burned herself.

There are no duties for our teachers barring being in their classrooms at teaching periods. Neurotic ones have taught their classes all morning and slept or read all the rest of the day. For the most part they have a strong community sense and feel that apart from teaching their whole interest is in living actively in the community.

Once I saw a queue for a toilet on the ground floor. I went upstairs and there was another queue. A bright boy got in by the window and found that someone had locked all the doors and got out by the window. I went into the staffroom and told the staff what had happened.

'I did that,' said a young teacher fresh from college.

'Oh,' I said. 'Why?'

He grinned. 'I've been longing to do that all my life and this is the first time I have had a chance to do it.' I hasten to say that not all new teachers react in this way.

I have been lucky with my staff all these years. I can remember only one occasion on which I had to say to a teacher, 'You mustn't treat a kid in that way.' Naturally I have never appointed teachers who could not possibly fit into the system, he-men types with much muscle and little understanding. My pupils reject such. When we had an ex-scout master with his 'Come on, lads, we'll build a boat!', they turned away in scorn. Free children will not follow a suggesting leader.

One feature has appeared again and again – the teacher who seeks popularity by being on the side of the child for the wrong reason. Children soon see through such a teacher. Too many new teachers and houseparents have difficulty in discriminating between freedom and licence. One housemother let her crowd smash a lot of furniture because 'I thought I wasn't ever supposed to say no.'

Once a young man thought he could run the school better than I could. He agitated among the staff and made some converts so that the atmosphere was one you could cut with a knife. I should give up being the boss; the staff should handle everything, finance, enrolment of pupils, salaries. Naturally I got rid of the rebels as soon as I could, reluctantly, for they were good teachers. I fancy that, instead of challenging father at fourteen, they delayed the challenge until they found a father substitute, even a non-authoritarian one. I doubt if Summerhill could be run by a committee, for the progress of a committee is too often the pace of the more conservative members.

I have a complex about being a boss that is almost morbid. I hate telling anyone what to do, rationalizing perhaps . . . if he does it only because I tell him to he isn't original enough. I hate being God, and when I have to send a kid away, say, for terrorizing smaller children, I always feel miserable and slightly guilty. But I never feel guilty when I tell an unsuccessful teacher to leave, not guilty, just embarrassed. The most painful task in my work is to say to a teacher, 'The kids say your lessons are so dull that they won't go to them, so you'll have to leave.'

I expect I identify myself with him and think: 'How would I feel if I were told I am no good?' My first wife had a sort of genius in cases of this kind; she managed to sack – say – a cook and give her the impression that she was paying her a great compliment.

It is simply not easy to get a good staff and, in spite of Summerhill's fame, I find it hard to get new teachers. If I advertise I get letters like this: 'I am not a teacher, I am a bank clerk (or a librarian or what not) but I know I can teach.' Many think that teaching is an unskilled job. Why so few apply I do not know. It may be a question of money; yet now we pay as near the state standard as we can. It may be that teachers fear to teach in a school where lessons are voluntary.

By law I have to have qualified teachers, not that training makes much difference; I have had trained and untrained teachers with good and bad in both categories. Teaching is an art, not a science. But the law is there, and a Picasso would not be able get a job as an art teacher in England if he had not been trained.

I have had some excellent teachers – no, not teachers but community-minded people. George Corkhill (Corkie), our science master for nearly thirty years, good stolid old George, never ruffled, always the centre of a group of little ones whose criterion of chemistry was making lemonade and fireworks. George followed their interests. He was a great loss to the school when he retired.

Never once have I told a teacher what to do, how to teach. One or two complained that I did not come to their classrooms often enough. But my chief difficulty was when there was a disagreement between a teacher and a pupil.

Once a boy wanted to make a banjo. The woodwork teacher refused to let him, saying that it was too difficult a task. Both came to me to arbitrate. I said, 'If he wants to make a banjo that is his affair, his wish; if he makes a mess of it it is his affair. Give him the wood.' The teacher was furious, accusing me of siding with a pupil against the staff. He resigned on the spot. I thought too late that it should have been a matter for the General Meeting to decide.

It is sad that old pupils do not become teachers and return as members of the staff. Perhaps they are too well-balanced to teach, but I have had housemothers who were ex-pupils and they did this work well – partly because they did not require a period of living out their complexes when coming to a non-authoritarian atmosphere.

The most dangerous teaching applicant we ever have is the one who cries or writes, 'I simply must come and work in Summerhill. It is my idea of Paradise. I'd give my right hand to be a teacher in your wonderful school.'

Such a teacher will usually show signs of discontent in a few weeks. The dream was too vivid, too heavenly. Always there is disillusionment. In fact two of our best teachers came without ever having heard of the school before.

Personally I incline to favour the man who can use his hands. I have had teachers who had been educated at public schools. Hardly one of them could hammer in a nail. I like young men who will see something damaged or broken and proceed to mend it, men who will see a hollow in the front drive and fill it up with broken bricks, but, alas, most of my staff seem to have a complex about the front drive and for many years I have filled in the holes myself. Why not? They have no cars and I have. Yes, I like chaps who can use tools . . . and then I curse them for borrowing mine and not returning them. But tools should never be communal, never. Ask any garage proprietor about that.

Once a big stone was knocked off a wall by some kids. It lay on the path. I stopped to lift it and then paused . . . leave it and see what happens. Staff and pupils walked round it for six weeks and then I lifted it back to its place. But here a factor comes in. I have a feeling of possession about the house and grounds. They are my property. My staff do not have this feeling that the place is theirs and I understand.

Fifty years ago Sir William Osler said that a man is too old at forty. I say he is too young at forty; I have found in long years that the men on my staff who will take on an unpleasant job like carting bricks are usually the over-forties. But I have had exceptions under forty. Under compulsion of course the under-forties would have to do the work.

It is easy to live in Summerhill and it is difficult at the same time. We usually live together without wrangling. I have seen so many staffrooms that were filled with jealousies . . . 'The geography man has seven periods a week and I have only five for maths.' Dogs fighting over bones, dry bones in this case. No, we have none of that rivalry; freedom gives peace even to staffs, and that may be why so many visitors ask, 'Which are pupils and which are staff?'

Religious Freedom

Religion says: 'Be good and you will be happy', but the adage is truer the other way round: 'Be happy and you will be good.' Forty-five years of Summerhill has convinced me that the latter version is the true one. Happiness is the right of all children, and it is evil to give them a hard life in order to prepare them for a life that may not contain much to make them happy. For too many parents still believe that a child is born in sin and has no right to happiness, only to mercy – when it repents. One cannot be bound and happy at the same time. The necessity for a child's happiness should be the first tenet of all educational systems. A school should be judged by the faces of its pupils, not by its academic successes.

A recent woman visitor said to me, 'Why don't you teach your pupils about the life of Jesus, so that they will be inspired to follow in his steps?' I answered that one learns to live, not by *hearing* of other lives, but by *living*; for words are infinitely less important than acts. Many have called Summerhill a religious place because it gives out love to children.

That may be true; only I dislike the adjective as long as religion means what it generally means today – antagonism to natural life. Religion as I remember it in my childhood is nothing I wish to be identified with.

Religion to a child almost always means only fear. And to introduce fear into a child's life is the worst of all crimes. God is a mighty man with holes in his eyelids: he can see you wherever you are. To a child, this often means that God can see what is being done under the bedclothes. No one who in childhood has been threatened with fear of an afterlife in hell can possibly be free from a neurotic anxiety about security in *this* life.

In my boyhood, faith was easy to accept. The earth was the centre of the universe and a kindly God had put the sun and moon and stars there to light our footsteps. He was a very personal God; he knew us all individually and when we died rewarded us with a harp or punished us with a fire. We had no idea that our earth was a minnow in an ocean of stars and planets. Because our earth was the centre of the universe, man was the supreme subject of creation, and like the stars immortal.

My Granny Sinclair lived with us until her death when I was fourteen. As her favourite grandchild, I think I must have loved her as much as a boy can love an old woman. She used to suck peppermints, and her way of showing her love was to kiss me while shoving a peppermint from her mouth into mine. She was very religious, read much in the family Bible, and liked to tell us that as a girl she had walked nine miles to church every Sunday and nine miles back. Her faith was a simple one with no doubts or scepticism whatsoever. I remember discovering the word 'bugger' when I was about seven, and Granny making me kneel down beside her to ask God for forgiveness. My early fear of hell must have come from her.

She made us read aloud to her from various books of sermons, including Boston's *Fourfold State*. Boston, apparently, had no doubts either. For me, the most terrifying passage of that book was one in which the Man of God, as Granny called him, gave a minute description of the pains of hell. It began in this fashion: 'If you want to know what the torments of hell are like, just light a candle and hold your finger in the flame.' And because Granny and Boston had no doubts about what was going to happen to sinners, I also had no doubts, but I knew, as if by instinct, that hell was my destination. Yet there was no hate in Granny. She was a very human, loving old woman, and one of her joys was to listen to the often obscene gossip of the woman from the cottage over the road.

My sister Clunie, an early atheist, threatened as a child to commit the unforgivable sin – blasphemy against the Holy Ghost. She never did, but when my oldest brother Willie, at the age of thirteen, stood out in a thunderstorm and invited the Almighty to strike *him* down dead for asking God to perform an unnatural act on the Holy Ghost, I was terrorstruck. As the thunder crashed, I shut my eyes tight. It is of interest to note here that Willie became a minister.

The Bible says, 'The fear of the Lord is the beginning of wisdom.' It is much more often the beginning of psychic disorder. For to invest a child with fear in any form is harmful.

Many people believe deep down 'If children have nothing to fear, how can they be good?' Goodness that depends on fear of hell or fear of the policeman or fear of punishment is not goodness at all – it is simply cowardice. Goodness that depends on hope of reward or hope of praise or hope of heaven depends on bribery.

Children may fear us and then accept our values. And what values we adults have! One week I bought a dog for three pounds, tools for my turning lathe for ten pounds, and tobacco for five guineas. Although I reflect on and deplore our social evils, it did not occur to me to give all that money to the poor. Therefore, I don't preach to children that slums are an abomination unto the world. I used to – before I realized what a humbug I was about it.

There is no case whatever for the moral instruction of children. It is psychologically wrong. To ask a little child to be unselfish is wrong. Every child is an egoist. The world belongs to him. His power of wishing is strong; he has only to wish and he is king of the earth. When he is given an apple his one wish is to eat that apple. And the chief result of mother's encouraging him to share his very own apple with his little brother is to make him hate the little brother.

Altruism comes later, comes naturally if the child is *not* taught to be unselfish; probably never comes at all when the child is taught to be unselfish. The young altruist is merely the child who likes to please others while he is satisfying his own selfishness.

By suppressing the child's selfishness the selfishness becomes fixed. An unfulfilled wish lives on in the unconscious. The child who is taught to be unselfish will remain stuck being selfish through life. Moral instruction thus defeats its own purpose.

Many a time a parent has said to me, 'I do not understand why my boy has gone bad. I have punished him severely, and I am sure we never set a bad example in our home.' My work too often has been with damaged children who have been educated through fear of the strap or fear of the Lord – children who have been coerced into being good.

The happiest homes I know are those in which the parents are frankly honest with their children without moralizing. Fear does not enter into these homes. Love can thrive. In other homes, love is crushed by fear. Pretentious dignity and demanded respect hold love aloof. Compelled respect *always* implies fear.

It was Wilhelm Reich who pointed out that in sudden fear we all catch our breath for the moment, and that the child who lives in fear has a life of catching its breath . . . and holding it. The sign of a well-reared child is his free, uninhibited breathing. It shows that he is not afraid of life.

Here at Summerhill, children who fear their parents haunt the teachers' rooms. The children are always testing us out. One boy of eleven, whose father is a strict man, opens my door twenty times a day. He looks in, saying nothing, and shuts the door again. I sometimes cry out to him, 'No, I'm not dead yet.' The boy has given me the love that his own father would not accept, and he has a fear that his ideal new father may disappear.

I find hardly any fear of thunder among our small children. They will sleep out in small tents through the most violent storm. Nor do I find much fear of the dark. Sometimes a boy of eight will pitch his tent right at the far end of the field, and he will sleep there alone for nights. Freedom encourages fearlessness. I have often seen timid little chaps grow into sturdy, fearless youths.

I find that most children are not really afraid of death. Every child sees death – a beetle, a sparrow, carcases in butchers' shops. Death arouses more curiosity than shock . . . when I was headmaster of a village school in Scotland I rang the bell after break and not a child came into the school; the playground too was empty. A farmer was shooting an old horse in a nearby field. As little children my sister, Clunie, and I longed for the tide to ebb so that we could find the corpse of a drowned mariner in a pool. But then we had all the morbidity of a Calvinist upbringing.

If a child is taught that certain things are sinful, his love of life must be changed to fear and hate. When children are free, they never think of another child as being a sinner. In Summerhill, if a child steals and is tried by a tribunal of his fellows, he is rarely punished for the theft. All that happens is that he is made to pay back the debt. Children unconsciously realize that stealing is sickness. They are little realists, and are far too sensible to postulate an angry God and a tempting devil.

Religion cannot reach a boy's unconscious through preaching. But if some night his minister went out stealing with him, that action would begin to dissolve the self-hatred responsible for the antisocial behaviour. That sympathetic kinship would start the boy thinking in different terms. Action touches the unconscious where words can't. This is why love and approval will so often cure a child's problems. I have proved in action that freedom and the absence of moral discipline have cured many children whose future had appeared to be a life in prison.

An incident that occurred at Summerhill during a spontaneous acting class one night emphasizes a child's natural sense of reality if his reactions have not been warped by fear.

One night, I sat down on a chair and said; 'I am St Peter at the Golden Gate. You are to be folks trying to get in. Carry on.'

They came up with all sorts of reasons for getting in. One girl even came from the opposite direction and pleaded to get out! But the star turned out to be a boy of fourteen who went by me whistling, hands in pockets.

'Hi,' I cried, 'you can't go in there.'

He turned and looked at me. 'Oh,' he said, 'you are a new man on the job, aren't you?'

'What do you mean?' I asked.

'You don't know who I am, do you?'

'Who are you?' I asked.

'God,' he said, and went whistling into heaven.

I personally have nothing against the man who believes in god – no matter what god. What I object to is the man who claims that *his* god is the authority for his imposing restrictions on human growth and happiness. The battle is not between believers in theology and non-believers in theology; it is between believers in human freedom and believers in the suppression of human freedom.

This battle for our youth is one with the gloves off. None of us can be neutral. We must take one side or the other: authority or freedom; discipline or self-government. No half measures will do, the situation is too urgent.

When the psychologists say that our early experiences rule our lives, one is apt to question it. But I have had no doubts about this since my dearly loved sister Clunie died of pneumonia at the age of thirty-four. In all her years, she had never compromised her atheism. To her the Christian religion was both superstition and a cruel humbug. Yet on her deathbed she kept muttering the prayers she had learned as a baby, imploring God to save her soul. In the weakness of dying, she returned to emotions that had slumbered for thirty years. To me, that was convincing proof that the feelings of early childhood live on for a lifetime.

To be a free soul, happy in work, happy in friendship, and happy in love, or to be a miserable bundle of conflicts, hating one's self and hating humanity – one or the other is the legacy that parents and teachers give to every child.

Why have not more Christians followed the path of their master? Roman Catholic and Protestant schools have long been beating boys as if Jesus had said, 'Suffer little children to come unto me and be beaten.' Can anyone imagine Christ's beating a child? Catholics and Protestants give tacit support to our inhuman prisons and our cruel laws. I often wonder how much juvenile crime stems from the disillusionment of children taught scripture at home and in schools. They are told that lying and stealing and adultery are sins. Then they find their parents lying or swindling the income tax office; they get to know when their fathers go to other women. They do not know but they feel that religion is only words.

Once I took on a Catholic boy against my better judgement; the experiment failed. The boy lived in a school that does not believe in sin or punishment, and he had to go to a priest and confess his sins, so that the poor lad simply did not know where he stood.

I am not going to argue about religion. I could tolerate it if its adherents lived their religion and turned the other cheek and sold all they had and gave to the poor. I could admire it if the Vatican and Canterbury symbolized the poverty of the life of Jesus instead of parading their golden images and their capital investments. And I just sit and wonder why Christ's followers became so anti-life, for they are disciples of the man who asked if any man was pure enough to cast the first stone at a woman of easy virtue. Jesus gave out much love and charity and understanding but among his followers were John Calvin, who had his rival Servetus roasted over a slow fire, and St Paul, who hated women. In fairness I must grant that many a Christian *has* given out love and charity, however.

One questioner at a recent lecture said, 'You are a Humanist. Why don't you teach Humanism?' I replied that it is as bad to teach Humanism as it is to teach Christianity. We do not mould children in any way; we do not try to convert them to anything. If there is such a thing as sin it is the propensity of adults to tell the young how to live, a preposterous propensity seeing that adults do not know themselves how to live.

I am quite aware of the limitations of rationalism. To the Humanist, as to the believer, life is a mystery that cannot be solved. How did the universe begin? I look at my granddaughter, three weeks old, and marvel at her being. When she raises her hand she does something that no computer, no Rolls-Royce engine can do. We simply have to accept the mystery of life knowing that it will remain a mystery.

In later life my parents gave up their Calvinism for Spiritualism. When my sister, Clunie, died in 1919 they asked me if I could get in touch with a medium. I was then in London. With great difficulty I arranged to have an interview with Sir Oliver Lodge's medium, Mrs Leonard. She went into a trance and said things that astonished me, that Clunie had been a teacher, that she had died of lung trouble, both correct. I began to wonder if there was something in Spiritualism after all and then – 'Have you any questions for your sister?'

'Yes, ask her if she ever thinks of Spott.'

'She says, yes; she loved Spot but then she loved all animals.'

Alas, my question had meant the village she had taught in – Spott. I did not tell my parents that part of the interview.

I am an earthy fellow even if my head is sometimes in the clouds. I'm afraid I am personally indifferent to what is called the spiritual in life. I was not one of Wordsworth's little ones who came to the world trailing clouds of glory. I could not take the higher life, nor think the beautiful thoughts of the theosophists I worked with on *New Era*, nor, later, could I accept the uplift of the German teachers in Dresden. I wonder if this absence of the so-called spiritual has anything to do with my inability to appreciate poetry. Nay, I am a prosy fellow, unable to fly and having no desire to take wing.

Here is a sad thought: as an atheist, death means for me the end of fun. If the Bible had even one joke in it I'd be inclined to believe in a heaven. Heaven for holiness, hell for company, said Bernard Shaw. Might be some fun in hell after all. If there is one, I know who are in it – Shaw, Wilde, O. Henry, Damon Runyan, Mark Twain. But their light style may be cramped by the presence of St Paul, Calvin, John Knox – and of course most politicians.

What a shock I shall get if I find a devil with a fork waiting for me – 'Down those steps, Mr Neill.' But it could be worse. An angel might point a holy finger upwards. 'You will find your harp upstairs, Mr Neill.'

To postulate a god who was the architect of the grand design seems to me pure childish superstition. Even if we call god cosmic energy we are not solving anything.

Some day we will have a new religion. Religions are no more eternal than nations are eternal. A religion – *any* religion – has a birth, a youth, an old age and a death. Hundreds of religions have come and gone. For all the millions of Egyptians who believed in Amon Ra through the better part of four thousand years, not a single adherent of that religion can be found today.

Faith and religion are geographical. Had I been born in Arabia my religion would have forbidden alcohol, and permitted me three wives. Born in Dublin I could have been a sadistic teacher in a Catholic school, though not necessarily, for I was born in Calvinist Scotland and grew out of that anti-life religion. But in the main most people accept their home religion. My pupils live without it and of our many old pupils I know of only a few who sought religion later.

The idea of God changes as culture changes: in a pastoral land, God was the Gentle Shepherd; in warlike times, he was the God of Battles; when trade flourished, he was the God of Justice, weighing out equity and mercy. Today, when man is so mechanically creative, God is H. G. Wells's 'Great Absentee', for a creative God is not wanted in an age that can make its own atom bombs.

Some day a new generation will not accept the obsolete religions and myths of today. When the new religion comes, it will refute the idea of man's being born in sin. It will refuse the antithesis of body and spirit. It will recognize that the flesh is not sinful. The new religion will be based on knowledge of self and acceptance of self. And finally, the new religion will praise God by making men happy. 'He prayeth best who loveth best all things both great and small' – thus Coleridge, the poet, expressed the new religion.

Old Summerhillians

A parent's fear of the future affords a poor prognosis for the health of his children. This fear, oddly enough, shows itself in the desire that his children should learn more than he has learned. This kind of parent is not content to leave Willie to learn to read when he wants to, but nervously fears that Willie will be a failure in life unless he is pushed. Such parents cannot wait for the child to go at his own rate. They ask, 'If my son cannot read at twelve, what chance has he of success in life? If he cannot pass college entrance exams at eighteen, what is there for him but an unskilled job?' But I have learned to wait and watch a child make little or no progress. I never doubt that in the end, if not molested or damaged, he will succeed in life.

Of course, the philistine can say, 'Humph, so you call a lorry driver a success in life!' My own criterion of success is the *ability to work joyfully and to live positively*. Under that definition, most pupils in Summerhill turn out to be successes in life.

Tom came to Summerhill at the age of five. He left at seventeen, without having in all those years gone to a single lesson. He spent much time in the workshop making things. His father and mother trembled with apprehension about his future. He never showed any desire to learn to read. But one night when he was nine, I found him in bed reading *David Copperfield*.

'Hullo,' I said. 'Who taught you to read?'

'I taught myself.'

Some years later, he came to me to ask, 'How do you add a half and two fifths?' and I told him. I asked if he wanted to know any more. 'No thanks,' he said.

Later on, he got work in a film studio as a camera boy. When he was learning his job, I happened to meet his boss at a dinner party, and I asked how Tom was doing.

'The best boy we ever had,' the employer said. 'He never walks – he runs. And at weekends, he is a damned nuisance, for on Saturdays and Sundays he won't stay away from the studio.'

There was Jack, a boy who could not learn to read. No one could teach Jack. Even when he asked for a reading lesson, there was some hidden obstruction that kept him from distinguishing between b and p, l and k. He left school at seventeen without the ability to read.

Today, Jack is an expert toolmaker. He loves to talk about metalwork. He can read now; but so far as I know, he mainly reads articles about mechanical things – and sometimes he reads works on psychology. I do not think he has ever read a novel; yet he speaks perfectly grammatical English, and his general knowledge is remarkable. An American visitor, knowing nothing of his story, said to me, 'What a clever lad Jack is!'

Diane was a pleasant girl who went to lessons without much interest. Her mind was not academic. For a long time, I wondered what she would do. When she left at sixteen, any inspector of schools would have pronounced her a poorly educated girl. Today, Diane is demonstrating a new kind of cookery in London. She is highly skilled at her work; and more important, she is happy in it.

One firm demanded that its employees should have at least passed the standard college entrance exams. I wrote to the head of the firm concerning Robert, 'This lad did not pass any exams, for he hasn't got an academic head. But he has got guts.' Robert got the job.

Winifred, aged thirteen, a new pupil, told me that she hated all subjects, and shouted with joy when I told her she was free to do exactly as she liked. 'You don't have to go to any lessons if you don't want to,' I said.

She set herself to have a good time, and she had one – for a few weeks. Then I noticed that she was bored.

'Teach me something,' she said to me one day; 'I'm bored stiff.'

'Righto!' I said cheerfully. 'What do you want to learn?'

'I don't know,' she said.

'And I don't either,' said I, and left her.

Months passed. Then she came to me again. 'I am going to pass the college entrance exams,' she said, 'and I want lessons from you.'

Every morning she worked with me and other teachers, and she worked well. She confided that the subjects did not interest her much, but the aim *did* interest her. Winifred found herself by being allowed to be herself.

It is interesting to know that free children take to mathematics. They find joy in geography and in history. Free children cull from the offered subjects only those which interest them. Free children spend most time at other interests – woodwork, metalwork, painting, reading fiction, acting, playing out fantasies, listening to rock and roll.

Tom, aged eight, was continually opening my door and asking, 'By the way, what'll I do now?' No one would tell him what to do.

Six months later, if you wanted to find Tom you went to his room. There you always found him in a sea of paper sheets. He spent hours making maps. One day a professor from the University of Vienna visited Summerhill. He ran across Tom and asked him many questions. Later the professor came to me and said, 'I tried to examine that boy on geography, and he talked of places I never heard of.'

But I must also mention the failures. Barbel, Swedish, fifteen, was with us for about a year. During all that time, she found no work that interested her. She had come to Summerhill too late. For ten years of her life, teachers had been making up her mind for her. When she came to Summerhill, she had already lost all initiative. She was bored. Fortunately, she was rich and had the promise of a lady's life.

I had two Yugoslavian sisters, eleven and fourteen. The school failed to interest them. They spent most of their time making rude remarks about me in Croatian. An unkind friend used to translate these for me. Success would have been miraculous in this case, for the only common speech we had was art and music. I was very glad when their mother came for them.

Over the years we have found that Summerhill boys who are going in for engineering do not bother to take the matriculation exams. They go straight to practical training centres. They have a tendency to see the world before they settle down to university work. One went around the world as a ship's steward. Two boys took up coffee farming in Kenya. One boy went to Australia, and one even went to remote Guyana.

Derrick Boyd is typical of the adventurous spirit that a free education encourages. He came to Summerhill at the age of eight and left after passing his university exams at eighteen. He wanted to be a doctor, but his father could not afford to send him to the university at the time. Derrick thought he would fill in the waiting time by seeing the world. He went to the London docks and spent two days trying to get a job – any job – even as a stoker. He was told that too many real sailors were unemployed, and he went home sadly.

Soon a schoolmate told him of an English lady in Spain who wanted a chauffeur. Derrick seized the chance, went to Spain, built the lady a house or enlarged her existing house, drove her all over Europe, and then went to the university. The lady decided to help him with his university fees. After two years, the lady asked him to take a year off to drive her to Kenya and build her a house there. Derrick finished his medical studies in Capetown.

Larry, who came to us about the age of twelve, passed university exams at sixteen and went out to Tahiti to grow fruit. Finding this a poorly paid occupation, he took to driving a taxi. Later he went to New Zealand, where I understand he did all sorts of jobs, including driving another taxi. He then entered Brisbane University. Some time ago, I had a visit from the dean of that university, who gave an admiring account of Larry's doings. 'When we had vacation and the students went home,' he said, 'Larry went out to work as a labourer at a sawmill.' He is now a practising doctor in Essex.

Some old boys, it is true, have not shown enterprise. For obvious reasons, I cannot describe them. Our successes are always those whose homes were good. Derrick and Jack and Larry had parents who were completely in sympathy with the school, so that the boys never had that most tiresome of conflicts: which is right, home or school?

An American, Max Bernstein, published a survey of old pupils who lived near London. I shall take up those pupils who said they did not get enough from the system. Among others Bernstein gives these criticisms:

four said there wasn't enough protection against bullies;
three mentioned a too rapid turnover of staff;
one said he was too much influenced by other children
who were irresponsible with regard to academic work.

Bernstein added, 'These persons tend to be the less verbal ones, the shy or withdrawn ones, both before and after the Summerhill experience.'

Not knowing who they were I cannot even guess about them, their home backgrounds, their mental alertness; I do not know which might have a chip on their shoulders; I cannot tell how long they were at the school. However I can take up their criticisms:

Bullying. In disciplined schools a boy is afraid to bully but in a free school in which punishment by staff is out, to deal with a bully is not easy. Most bullies are rather stupid. The bright lad hits back with repartee, but the dunce can only use his fists. I have time and again felt that a boy who makes smaller boys afraid should not be in the school, but I did nothing about it, mainly because I could not think of a school to which he could go without being harshly treated. Of course there are lots of coed boarding schools where a child is not treated harshly, but they do not want to take problem children. We do our best to curb the bully by charging him in meetings and tribunals, showing him what public opinion thinks of him. In some of the worst cases I have had to send a bully out.

The rapid turnover in staff has been bad for the children. The situation is much better now that we can pay them a decent salary, whereas a few years back teachers could not afford to stay with us.

One ex-pupil had something when he said he was influenced by *other children who were irresponsible with regard to academic work.* Yes, that situation arises sometimes. A vigorous boy or girl who hates all lessons, usually because of past experience, can keep other children from lessons.

That raises the question that I have never been able to answer: is Summerhill better for the more intelligent children? Thinking about the pupils we have had who loafed for all their time at the school (and generally bullied), I know that most of them had a chip on their shoulders. Most of them had had homes that did not give enough love, broken homes. It is usually the not-so-bright ones who are easily led by a gang; those who skip lessons are often those children who feel that they are not good at lessons. I fancy that the failures Bernstein interviewed were those who blamed the school for their lack of education.

I had one girl many years ago who came back to see me when she was married. She complained that Summerhill had ruined her life, that she had had no education. I asked her who were in her class. Two doctors, two lecturers, two artists. I then said, 'Why did they get an education in Summerhill and you didn't?' She was not dull, indeed she was a clever lass.

We do not shut our eyes to the boys or girls who persuade others to stay away from lessons. Sometimes they are brought up in a meeting – sometimes by a member of the staff, sometimes by an older pupil – charged with going against the rule of the school that lessons must be voluntary. No staff will ever ask a child to attend lessons, and no pupil should therefore ask another not to go.

I don't want to paint the picture too black. More than one pupil went to no lessons in ten years but made good later. I don't think that many old pupils consider themselves failures. Summerhill has not solved the problem of the child who needs a shove in life. But it is comforting to know that so few pupils have wanted a shove, seeing that the whole world is composed of folks who have been shoved all the way from cradlehood.

On the positive side Bernstein found that the majority of past pupils felt good about their education. A few of his examples:

> eight felt that the school had given them a healthy attitude to sex;
>
> seven said they were unafraid of authority (five in relation to teachers in subsequent schools);
>
> five felt that it helped them to understand their own children better, and to raise them in a healthy way;
>
> five felt that it helped them to grow out of the need to play continuously and thus to settle down into academic or more serious pursuits;
>
> three said that it led them to have an active interest in the world around them;
>
> two felt that it enabled them to work through hostility and other antisocial feelings.

Bernstein's study of old Summerhillians is a piece of good but of limited research. For one factor is completely ignored – the home factor. It does not surprise me that some ex-pupils are critical of the school. Our parents have always been of two types, those who brought up their children in freedom and wanted the school to carry on this freedom, and those who felt that they had failed with their family and thought that Summerhill would undo the damage.

Summerhill has always been a dumping place for problem children, and very often we were not told beforehand that they were problems. Today we have at least half a dozen difficult children who arrived as normal children 'who don't like lessons'.

At a recent Summerhill Society meeting, a former parent, answering someone who asked why old pupils didn't send their children to Summerhill, said, 'Lack of money isn't the main answer. We sent our kids because we felt we had failed with them, because we were inadequate. Now they are parents they don't feel that way; they feel they can bring up their kids freely even if they have to attend the local state school.' Some truth there.

Every time I lecture I get: 'Mr Neill, why have you never inspired any of your old pupils to start a Summerhill? From all accounts they never seem to challenge anything, never march in protests, never take up social work like local government, etc.' Implying that we produce a lot of selfish buggers. I get a mild satisfaction in replying that we haven't produced an LBJ or a Reagan.

There is a regrettable belief among some people that Summerhill can work miracles. We are supposed to remake as little saints boys and girls who come at twelve after having been treated without love in home or school for years. No child can advance farther than its character and ability decree. But perhaps some ex-pupils feel that, because they have gone to Summerhill, they should succeed and be better than those from conventional schools.

Every school has failures. Yet I know of only one old pupil so far who has not been able to hold down a job. We have had quite a few boys and girls who could not read at fourteen. The psychology of the fact I do not know. The lessons are there every day for those who want them. One pupil will attend regularly for years and pass the English exams in the end, but a boy or girl of the same age will scorn all lessons and be content to remain illiterate. Two boys who left at sixteen barely able to read and write, are now in their fifties in good jobs; I never despair of any backward pupil, but that may have a personal side, for at school I was always at the bottom of the class.

Some of the cases can be guessed at as to their causes. An adopted girl, obsessed with her origins, could not concentrate on reading or writing. The son of an ambitious teacher, who wanted his family to be scholars, had possibly so strong a negative attitude that he was damned if he would do what his father wanted him to do. Another boy had a father who was always down on him ... 'You can't do anything right. Now when I was your age ...' The boy was convinced that he could never do anything right, so why try? It looks as if a deep sense of inferiority keeps some children from learning even the elements. Parents should be very careful never to give children the idea that they are no good. True, in some cases it works the other way: 'Father thinks I am a dud; I'll show him that I am not,' but I fancy such cases are in the minority.

And we must also consider ability. Some people hold that everyone is as clever as the next person, just as some musicians hold that everyone is equally musical. I cannot believe it. There are pupils who are dull and slow in thinking and grasping, very often the type that is good mechanically; indeed, when I come to think of our failures who could not read, the boys at least, were all good with their hands and keen on woodwork and metalwork. Some are now successful engineers.

Oddly enough girls seldom remain unable to read and write – at least that is our experience in Summerhill. Again I do not know why; it cannot be because they are not absorbed by nuts and bolts as the boys are.

So much for failure in lessons. Do we have failures psychologically? Does a young thief go on stealing after a few years in the school? Not if he comes early enough, say by eleven. Does a bully remain a bully? Alas, a few bullies do up to the age of leaving, fifteen or sixteen. Does a child who comes full of hate go on hating all during his school life in Summerhill? Seldom, if ever, so that I repeat what I have so often said, that freedom cures most things. And, as I have said before, it cannot completely cure the child who has had no love as a baby, but it cures those children who have been conditioned into hate and fear by a few years of strict discipline at home and in school.

Who is to judge failure? A boy or girl may be a failure in school and shine forth later in life. History gives instances, but the only ones I can think of at the moment are Einstein, Conan Doyle, Churchill. We must also ask ourselves how much the curriculum does to produce academic failures. I am ever optimistic about my pupils, partly because I am not interested in their careers as such; I am pleased to see unhappy children full of hate and fear grow into happy children with heads that are held high. Whether they become professors or plumbers is all the same to me, for I think that whatever their job, they have acquired some balance and zest in their lives.

Has Summerhill produced any geniuses? No, so far no geniuses; perhaps a few creators, not famous as yet; a few bright artists; some clever musicians; no successful writer that I know of; an excellent furniture designer and cabinet-maker; some actors and actresses; some scientists and mathematicians who may yet do original work.

However, I have often said that a generation or two of free children does not prove anything much. Even in Summerhill some children get a guilty conscience about not learning enough lessons. It could not be otherwise in a world in which examinations are the gateways to some professions. And also, there is usually an Aunt Mary who exclaims, 'Eleven years old and you can't read properly!' The child feels vaguely that the whole outside environment is anti-play and pro-work.

One comforting thing about Bernstein's survey is that old pupils have definite opinions about the system, pro and con. I have often asked old Etonians and Harrovians how many old boys ever challenged the public-school system, and the biggest percentage I ever got was 4 per cent. I like challengers even when they challenge my life-work. I have never liked yes-men.

Speaking generally, the method of freedom is almost sure with children under twelve, but children over twelve take a long time to recover from a spoon-fed education. I am not trying to defend Summerhill. I like to think it requires no defence, but it does require objective criticism. Personally I am quite content to know that Summerhill must be one of the few schools in the world where a child weeps at having to leave, one of the few boarding-schools where pupils go home gladly and return as gladly after each vacation. Success to me does not mean degrees and good jobs and fame; success means seeing a child come with a face full of hate and fear and in two years have a face full of life and happiness.

Our Inspectors

Britain is the freest country in the world. In no other country could I have had Summerhill. When I think of the authoritative interest taken by the state in Continental private schools, I am glad I live and work in a country that allows so much scope to the private venture.

But all schools are under the control of the Ministry of Education, now the Department of Education and Science (DES), and all schools, public and private, are inspected by Her Majesty's Inspectors. Our first big inspection was in 1939. Then after a gap of ten years came another inspection and report.

With one exception Summerhill has never been inspected by HMIs who seemed to have any understanding of what the system stands for – living first, learning second. I have always had the feeling that the DES if not hostile, was indifferent. It was inspecting Summerhill from an angle that is not ours. We think beyond lessons. In fifty years our pupils have been successes in their careers; even the many problem children we have had turned out well for the most part.

The inspection report by John Blackie in 1949 is the only proof that at least one man in the Ministry has had any inkling of what Summerhill was doing. Since then we have been badgered by inspectors judging the school only by its lessons and teaching, and every report in essence said: 'The school does not come up to our standard and we give you a year to pull your socks up if you want to remain on our list of registered schools.'

Our frank and free pupils found the inspectors policemen, stiff, unsmiling, unapproachable ... even by myself and the staff. Little people with a narrow vision. When one inspector said, 'Mr Neill, we are not interested in your system of education,' I was too shocked to answer him. Actually, he need not have said it: his whole attitude betrayed the fact. Everything they said was a criticism, and they seemed to find nothing good in Summerhill whatever. It was hopeless to try to explain that our criterion is living and not learning.

Their chief job is to inspect domestic arrangements and lessons. I told John Blackie, a broad-minded man, that he could inspect progress in maths and French but he could not inspect happiness, sincerity, balance, tolerance. 'I'll have a try,' said John, and he made a good try.

He and his colleague made a remarkable adaptation, and obviously enjoyed themselves in the process. Odd things struck them. Said one, 'What a delightful shock it is to enter a classroom and find the children not taking any notice of you, after years of seeing classes jump up to attention.' Yes, we were lucky to have the two of them.

I said to another HMI, 'Your criterion is learning but ours is living. You take a short view – concern because Willie cannot read at twelve – but we take a long view. I can think of only one old pupil who can't hold down a job.' The answer: 'Maybe, but I don't see them, do I?'

It puzzles me why Summerhill is appreciated by thousands of teachers and parents all over the world, and yet the DES seem to rank it with the conventional schools and apply the usual tests. For years we often had a hundred visitors a week but they never asked about lessons; they wanted to see what free children were like.

The DES officials are the Establishment, conservative whatever political party is in power, fearful of change especially if the demand for change comes from the believers in freedom for children, freedom that could be dangerous later on, challenging the whole idea of paternalism and rule from outside authority. I have noticed that to the inspectors our self-government seemed of little moment. I could see the pained looks they had when they saw free children milling around without attending classes. Their narrow vision did not see that every child who comes to Summerhill rejects all lessons, for weeks, for months, sometimes for years. One boy who attended no lessons for ten years is now in East Pakistan helping fight starvation and writing dispatches to our press about it.

The inspectors are blind to the fact that Summerhill runs on the principle that if the emotions are free our intellect will look after itself. One cannot teach anything of importance – to love, to have charity – and one cannot inspect anything of importance.

The DES is, must be, the Establishment. It represents education as it is generally accepted by the majority of parents and teachers. If, today in 1971, a Secretary of State for Education were to make a decree that corporal punishment be banned, the outcry from parents and teachers would make the ban impossible. If he or she ruled that there be no religious instruction in schools there would be public meetings of protest all over the country, attended, I fancy, by a majority who make no attempt to live as Christians. The Department is tolerant of schools like Summerhill but could not officially approve of them.

The little bureaucrats turn a blind eye to world opinion. No use telling the DES that since my book *Summerhill* was published in the USA in 1960 scores of new schools have sprung up there claiming to be free. The book was a bestseller in the USA and in a year the German translation sold about a million copies. It has been translated into fourteen languages and my mail from abroad is more than I can cope with. I shouldn't be the one to say it, but Summerhill has had an enormous influence on world educational thinking. This is a fact, not boasting.

Yet the DES has ignored us when it wasn't needling us, and I don't think it has anything to do with party politics. Labour wants to abolish all private schools and if that were done there could never be another school like Summerhill; in a state school one can experiment with methods of teaching history but not with methods' of living. Or in a public school for that matter. No head of Eton could abolish chapel or introduce self-government.

In England every private school is registered, but to be 'recognized as efficient' it has to apply for recognition which is or is not granted after an inspection. I have never applied, partly because, to me, recognition means something bestowed. I also had a good notion that Summerhill would not qualify for recognition because of its failure to meet the normal standard in book learning. Indeed, the fact that every new pupil, when told that lessons are optional, immediately drops all school subjects barring the creative ones like art and woodwork proves to me that lessons are forced on children against all their natural wishes. So that Summerhill pupils often bloom late from an academic point of view. One old boy, an engineer, seldom attended any lessons. Today he has half a dozen letters after his name. To a visiting inspector that boy would probably have been classed as a failure.

Recognition means nothing to me personally, but if I had it poor parents could send their children to Summerhill. A poor widow wanted to send her boy, saying that her county council had offered to pay half the fees. Then the council discovered that we were not recognized and therefore they could not pay the fees. So I have to continue being ashamed that I have to take middle-class pupils only.

I am not trying to sell my school when I say that it is 'recognized' in a dozen countries. What pains me is this: if I had a private school with ideal premises and teaching plus fear and the cane I would be recognized. It would be great if Mrs Thatcher, the new Education Secretary, would begin her reign by abolishing the barbarity and cowardliness of corporal punishment in all schools, but, if she tried to she would have many teachers against her. I hear that Mrs Thatcher voted to keep hanging so I doubt if she is a Neill fan.

To most folks a child's playing is a waste of time. It would be impossible to have a DES that did not think work of more importance than play.

HMI reports always mention the poor academic performance of the ten-to-twelve-year-olds. Even with an excellent teacher it is difficult for these children to get through the ordinary state school work. If children in a state school at the age of ten or twelve were free to climb trees or dig holes instead of going to lessons, their standard would be similar to ours. We accept this period of a lower standard of learning because we think that play is of greater importance.

The handicap of not being up to a state-school standard when a junior in Summerhill does not necessarily mean being of a low standard as a senior. For my part I have always liked late starters, perhaps for subjective reasons because at the age of nineteen, in a competitive examination for entrance to a Normal Teachers' Training College, I was something like 104th on the list of 106 candidates. Of course I did not manage to become a Normal student.

More objectively, I like late starters because I have seen a few bright children who could recite Milton at four blossom forth as drunkards and loafers. I like to meet the man who, at the age of fifty-three, says he doesn't quite know what he is to be in life.

When I was a boy my father's salary was based on the inspection reports, and Her Majesty's Inspector at that time was a sour, unfriendly man who begrudged my father any praise for his work. My poor father had a splitting headache on inspection day, knowing that his salary depended on the number of passes of Standard V, which always seemed to consist of morons. This man would give glowing reports of the neighbouring school of Inverarity – a school in which my father had his first appointment as assistant – but Elder of Inverarity was no better a teacher than Father.

Inspection day was an agony for my father. I see him yet, his white, strained face looking out of the window to watch the HMI and his assistant come down from the station in the morning. Father's obvious fear infected us, and we also trembled before the mighty authorities. The inspector was a bad examiner, who attempted to find out what we did not know, rather than draw out from us what we did know. He kept writing notes in a pocket diary, and all of us, including my father, believed them to be notes of damnation.

Afterwards, the stern inspector softened a little when he came over for lunch at the schoolhouse. Mother was a good cook, and on inspection day she always gave the guest his favourite pudding. We children were never at table. To this day I cannot meet an HMI easily, although I realize that the modern ones are different from the old, and much less powerful.

Inspectors had special arithmetical test cards on pink cardboard, and the only piece of dishonesty I can ever remember in my father occurred when test cards were once purloined from Dominie Deas's inspection the week before ours. Father worked out the tests on our blackboard, but dishonesty had its own reward, for the inspector brought a new edition when he came to us. I conjecture that he had missed a few cards when he left the dominie's school and was taking no risks.

To this day I have an inspector complex. The very name inspector is an insult. In education the word advisor would be better, and today that is what an inspector is, even if his advice is limited to irrelevancies like methods of teaching. I have said it many times and say it again, that you cannot teach anything of importance. Maths, English, French, yes, but not charity, love, sincerity, balance, or tolerance.

Inspection makes Summerhill insincere. The kids tidy up, rub out the shits and fucks on the walls; they feel self-conscious and unhappy. Some time ago when an HMI inspected the school he got a hostile reception and was troubled, and so was I. I knew what was behind it. A sensational daily paper had had an article alleging that the DES was gunning for Summerhill, and the kids looked on the harmless inspector as a dangerous spy who might close the school. The Ministry, of course, can close an independent school but I fancy that this seldom happens unless in cases where a headmaster is a practising homosexual or for that matter a practising heterosexual (with schoolgirls).

What puzzles me is why the teaching profession should tolerate inspection. The doctors and the lawyers, with their powerful trade unions, would not. True, they are not state servants as the teachers are, but since National Health began most doctors are paid by the state and I am sure would fight any attempt to make medicine an inspected profession. But the National Union of Teachers accepts its low, bus-conductor status. I belong to a profession that has no guts. I am gutless myself; I should take a stand against inspection; I should reject it on the grounds that my old pupils are nearly all successful in life; I should say to the DES: 'For fifty years educated and intelligent parents have sent their children to Summerhill, believing in its system, pleased with its results. Why should I have to have my school judged by an official standard that is not mine? Summerhill is primarily for living and it refuses to be judged by a body of people who think only of learning and teaching methods and discipline. Let them rule about the number of toilets and baths and fire extinguishers. Summerhill accepts that ruling.'

Alas, I am not brave enough to defy the powers above, so I compromise; I employ eight teachers for sixty children, some the wrong teachers from my viewpoint – those who teach the exam subjects which I find most pupils look upon as necessary dull grinds. Not that children dislike all exam subjects. Some of our teachers are good, some not so good, as in any state school. If they have good methods I am pleased and the children attend their lessons. But I can't teach teachers to teach and it is difficult to get good teachers in any school.

In 1967 we had two inspectors, typical dead officials. Everything wrong, not one word of praise. They wanted me to retire and close the school. 'Even if you get your premises up to standard I doubt if your teaching would allow you to continue. Your pupils at most take five O levels, but grammar schools take ten.' My reply, a question, did not register . . . 'Why do hundreds come to see Summerhill and not the local grammar school?' You can't talk to people who speak a different language. The wrong men, little officials with small minds. I think the whole set-up of freedom shocked their little souls.

In 1968 it turned out that the Department was not trying to close us, only saying that we had to make a hell of a lot of improvements to pass their muster. Once again the local HMI hadn't the faintest idea what Summerhill is about, he was a typical bureaucrat, stiff, formal . . . I called him Keeney; he replied Neill.

England is the land of independent schools. There are few on the Continent, and, until the 'new school' rage in the USA, I think that the private school there was usually a military academy. Scotland never had the tradition; there are four public schools there but they are English schools with the English tradition of Eton and Harrow, and at a venture I should say English speech. John Aitkenhead's Kilquhanity is the only free boarding-school I know of in Scotland. It has also had its troubles with the inspectorate.

When the HMIs advised our scrapping a few buildings we did not have the money to rebuild, so, much against the grain, I sent out an appeal. Friends helped a lot, the money poured in, and we used every penny of it erecting new teaching huts and dormitories. For many years I poured all my book royalties and article fees into keeping the school afloat.

I have mentioned the inspection of buildings, etc. I had strict orders about how many toilets I must have for so many children; then I read in the press about many state schools with earth closets, some a hundred yards away, and it made me wonder if the demands made on me had behind them the motive of making me close down.

Too often Summerhill has been in the red, mainly because of bad debts. Had all the debts been paid up during the last fifty years I could have lorded it in a Rolls-Royce, chauffeur driven. (No, that would have meant wearing a tie.)

We have been unable to do all we wanted to do because of poor finance. We have art and handwork teachers but cannot afford a dance or a music teacher, to me of much more importance than a maths or history teacher. We long to have a fine library, a well-equipped physics and chemistry lab, a cookery department. State schools can afford all these things, which are seen as luxuries by some parents and teachers but as necessities by us, who cannot afford them. And I wish I could pay my staff more than I do. Our fees have always been among the lowest in England and yet our inability to take poor children has been a sadness for fifty years.

Today (1971) Summerhill is perfect so far as buildings are concerned, with its central heating, modern dormitories, tarred paths, swimming-pool, riding stable, etc.

Ah, well, I should not complain. The DES has left me very much alone and will probably do so until I die. What will happen then I cannot guess. I prophesy that when I am gone the DES will make demands that will kill the principles of Summerhill – for example, making lessons compulsory; this would knock the basis out of Summerhill's freedom. Some Secretary of State may say, 'We tolerated that school until the old man died but we cannot go on allowing a school in which children can play all day without learning lessons.'

The Future of Summerhill

I have written so much about Summerhill that I have no great desire to describe it again now. One thing that people often mention is that the school looks untidy. The furniture is not sumptuous, the chairs are mostly hard ones; scraps of paper lie about the bedroom floors . . . and no one cares except the tidy-minded visitors. But I am not the one to talk for I am most untidy myself; I never clean up my office or workshop until I have lost something, and I console myself with the thought that Van Gogh's studio was a most untidy place.

Children are untidy because they usually are doing something with a purpose. Our girls make dresses and dolls in their bedrooms and the floors are strewn with clippings and the girls never notice them. I had my first lesson about tidiness when I was headmaster of a Scottish school. The charwoman came to me in anger.

'How can I clean up the mess these brats make?'

'Leave it,' I said. 'They will soon become conscious of the disorder and clean it up themselves.'

She and I waited for two weeks . . . and then got brooms out and cleaned the classroom up. The pupils had never noticed the mess.

But, one may say, they will be untidy for life. They are not. At the moment their inner life is to them infinitely more important than any external trappings. Yet I notice that our boys and girls dress up in their best bibs and tuckers for the end-of-term parties, the girls more than the boys.

Today Summerhill is not well known in Britain. Many Americans say to me, 'We talked of Summerhill to people in London and they had never heard of it, whereas in New York or Los Angeles many know it.' I do not know the answer. Not claiming to be a seer I hesitate to quote the Bible saying that a prophet is not without honour save in his own country.

Summerhill has never been patronized by the élite – the rich, the stage, the TV folks. I doubt if Princess Anne would have fitted in,

not after her first school holiday, when Buckingham Palace would
have learned a few four-letter words. We get many Americans but I
do not know who is famous there.

Interestingly enough, small children have no class feeling at all.
If one of our pupils were driven to school in a Rolls-Royce the
others would have no reaction whatever. So with colour. When we
get black pupils even the smallest child does not notice their colour.
We have Jewish pupils and no one knows or cares – though it
might be a different matter with children of Orthodox parents. I
had one forty years ago. He had to tell some beads every morning
and wrote home saying he had lost them. His father drove up to
the school, said nothing to me, took his boy by the collar, shoved
him into the car and drove off. I was concerned, for he had paid a
term's fees.

When I returned to England in 1924 I was almost broke, and our
stay in Lyme Regis was one long financial struggle. But we had one
stroke of luck there. An Australian called Cooper sent me a cheque
payable to the New Education Fellowship to which I belonged. I
wrote saying that I was the wrong guy and should I forward it to
the Fellowship? No, he said, keep it. It was a godsend then and
may have saved us from bankruptcy.

For many years we had no gifts. In 1950 a friend of the school
made a deed of covenant giving me £1,000 per annum for seven
years. He was a retiring, modest lad and I felt that he did not want
his generosity to be a public matter and so I did not broadcast his
gift. More recently, Joan Baez gave a special concert for Summerhill
in London and gave me the proceeds, £1,400; after singing at a pop
concert in the Isle of Wight she sent £2,000.

Twice I have had men who wanted to finance the school. Twice I
asked, 'You would want a say in the running, wouldn't you?' and
to the answer, 'Of course,' I said, 'Nothing doing.' The situation
was different when money came from Henry Miller, Joan Baez and
many other kind Americans, for then there were no strings
attached.

In recent years we have been swamped by visitors. I really don't
know what to do about them; I'd hate to make Summerhill a
closed shop, an island that does not want to be visited. I am not
boasting when I say that in the late sixties it became a Mecca for
the faithful. They come not as single spies, but in battalions. The

children complain that few visitors have anything to give them, but when someone out of the ordinary comes they are glad – a man who has travelled in Africa, a musician.

I am a social sort of man but at the end of the summer term I am just exhausted; the same questions crop up again and again. Seldom is a visitor anti-freedom, at least verbally; most of those who come are genuinely interested in seeing how children can govern themselves in community meetings. After the Saturday night meeting I always take the visitors to a classroom and answer their questions. Some take notes. An Indian lady asked me a string of questions. She flicked back her pages.

'But, Mr Neill, ten minutes ago you gave the very opposite reply.'

'I grow quickly,' I said. 'You can't expect me to stand still, can you?' She did not even smile.

I really ought to prohibit visits from teachers. So many come from disciplined schools in which they have no freedom at all . . . not even to wear jeans. They see how happy, free children behave, and then return to their dreary task of drilling facts into unwilling heads. The alarming thing is that as a body teachers do not demand change in the system. A young teacher is in danger if he or she challenges the system and the reasons for not challenging are deep down. So few can ever overcome their conditioning.

In the last crowd of visitors, 170 or so, a woman teacher said, 'I don't agree about freedom to stay away from lessons. If I hadn't had to go to maths I'd never have learned any.'

I asked her, 'Can you solve a quadratic equation?' She said no. I asked for a show of hands – three went up, maths teachers.

Parents often puzzle me. I do not know how much I have lost in bad debts in these last fifty years, but the sum must run into thousands. I think that in most cases the children were hated – 'Why should I pay for kids I don't love?' – and the term 'free school' may have had something to do with it. One or two have even shown some indignation when asked to pay up. I can't understand their meanness – to let Summerhill hold the baby for years, paying out fare money, pocket money, clothes money. No, such folks are outside my comprehension. One factor is troubling; if a child knows (and he usually does) that his fees haven't been paid for years he can be antisocial and hateful to us.

I have usually found that the poorer the parents the more punctual they are in paying the fees. At a time when I badly needed the money I wrote four letters to ex-parents who each owed my school nearly £1,000. 'Please,' I wrote, 'when are you going to start paying your debt? Summerhill needs every penny if it is to keep going.' I did not get a single reply. Long and bitter experience has told me that once another school is found, my bills are seldom if ever paid.

But I cannot see how we can avoid being taken in by dishonest parents. We aren't a business; we can't say: 'If you don't pay your milk bill we'll stop the supply.' I am glad to say that today Ena sees they pay up. Most of them do.

I have noticed that it is chiefly in the matter of clothes that a parent shows his money complex. We once had a very bad young thief in Summerhill who was cured after four years of hard work and infinite patience on the part of his teachers. This boy left at seventeen. His mother wrote, 'Bill has arrived home. Two pairs of his socks are missing. Can you please see that they are returned to us.'

At times, parents exhibit jealousy of the housemother who looks after their children in Summerhill. I have had visiting mothers go straight to their children's clothes closets with many a frown and a *tut tut*, suggesting that the housemother was inadequate.

Unfortunately, when a child loves Summerhill too much some parents get jealous. New pupils are not always tactful at home, and I have had complaints from parents that too often a child is bored at home during vacations and tactlessly says so. Of course many get bored at home. They may be confined to a flat; being from a boarding-school they go home and know no local children who they can make their companions. Many have necessary restrictions at home . . . a doctor has to tell his boys that they can't make a row outside his surgery. Children can usually accept such limitations, realizing that they are necessary.

Recently a girl of fifteen said to me, 'If you have good parents Summerhill makes you love them more, but if they are bad ones Summerhill makes you see through them, and then you can't stand them.' She had difficult parents. I asked her why she thought them bad. 'Because they only believe in freedom with their heads. They sent me here to be free but when they saw that I was getting too independent they turned against the school. They knew that the system left a kid to go to lessons because it wanted to and not because it was advised to, but they keep nagging me about lessons. I know of course why they are worried; they fear that I won't ever get anywhere without some O levels at least. I know that, but why did they send me in the first place? I think I've got brains enough to pass exams when I am ready for them.'

The ideal parents – and I have had many of them – are those who wholeheartedly support the school. They never worry about progress in lessons, or the untidiness of rooms; they never ask why we don't inspire the children by putting up reproductions of Cezanne or Rembrandt on the walls; they never ask us to give the children Bach and Beethoven. They never worry about inessentials like teaching children manners. In short they believe what we believe – that children must grow at their own pace. Such parents are a delight to me and my staff.

I am always a little nervous in writing to parents about their children, fearing that they may leave my letter lying around when the child is home in the holidays. Even more, I fear that they will write to their children, saying, 'Neill says you are not going to classes and are being a general nuisance this term.' If that happens, the child will never have any trust in me. So, usually, I tell as little as possible, unless I know the parents are absolutely trustworthy and aware.

Most of my work seems to consist of correcting parental mistakes. I feel both sympathy and admiration for the parents who honestly see the mistakes they have made in the past and who try to learn how best to treat their child. But other parents, strangely enough, would rather stick to a code that is useless and dangerous than to try to adapt themselves to the child. Even stranger, they seem to be jealous of their child's love for me.

The children do not love me so much as they love my non-interference in their affairs. I am the father they daydreamed about when their real father shouted 'Stop that row!' I never demand good manners or polite language. I never ask if faces have been washed. I never ask for obedience or respect or honour.

I realize, after all, that there can be no real competition between the father and me. His work is to earn an income for his family. My work is to study children and to give all my time and interest to children. If parents refuse to become more aware of their children's development, they must expect to be left behind. And parents often are left behind.

I have had a parent write to a child in my school, 'If you can't spell better than you do, I'd rather you did not write to me.' That was written to a girl of whom we were not quite sure whether she was mentally defective or not.

More than once I have had to cry to a complaining parent, 'Your boy is a thief, a bedwetter; he is antisocial, unhappy, inferior – and you come to me and grouse because he met you at the station with a dirty face and dirty hands!' I am a man slow to wrath, but when I meet a father or mother who will not or cannot acquire a sense of values about what is important and what is trifling in a child's nature and behaviour, I do get angry. Perhaps that is why I have been thought to be anti-parent. On the other hand, what a joy it is when a mother comes for a visit, meets her muddy, tattered child in the garden, beams, and says to me, 'Isn't he looking well and happy?'

When I come to think of it, at Summerhill we treat children really as equals, in that by and large we treat them as if they were adults, knowing that they are different from adults and yet have some points in common. We do not demand that Uncle Bill must clear his plate when he dislikes carrots or that father must wash his hands before he sits down to a meal. In heaven's name what does it matter if Tommy sits down to a meal with unwashed hands? It matters in America where the nation is germ mad; it matters in suburbs where cleanliness is considered to be quite a long way ahead of godliness. By continually correcting children we must make them feel inferior and we injure their natural dignity.

A question that is often put to me is, 'But isn't Summerhill a one-man show? Could it carry on without you?' Summerhill is by no means a one-man show. It never really has been. True, the idea was mine, but without help it would have remained just an idea. In the day-by-day working of the school my wife Ena and the teachers are just as important as I am. It is the idea of non-interference with the growth of the child and non-pressure on the child that has made the school what it is.

My first wife helped me to build up the school, sacrificing just as much as I did. We differed in opinion about how the children should be treated. Her background – Australia, Leipzig Music

Schools, her residence in Germany – was quite alien to the life she lived in the school. On the other hand she had been a militant suffragette and had done time. She was in the rebel movement.

My second wife, Ena, with another kind of background, fitted into the system from the moment she entered it. She has always backed me up in upholding the principles of freedom, and has slaved and still slaves for the school. She is easily the hardest worker in Summerhill.

Both women had a difficult time. They got all the hate from girls who were up against their mothers. They looked after the domestic side and served out the meals and often had to be firm with children who tried to use licence instead of freedom. I think that anyone dealing out food must get a lot of hate from children. Both women had to complain about food wastage and damage to furniture. This was inevitable if they were not to allow the children to take advantage.

Back to the question of whether Summerhill is a one-man show. Was the Little Commonwealth (p. 208) a one-man show? Was Albert Schweitzer's hospital a one-man show? I expect that Eton and Harrow started as one-man shows, but they have not been so for a long time. Tradition takes the place of the founder. Put it this way: Does it matter much who is head of a great public school? I suspect that no single headmaster can make any fundamental change, for example no head could make Eton coeducational or self-governing. Organization kills pioneering.

The young devil in hell rushed to his master in great perturbation.

'Master, master, something awful has happened; they have discovered truth on earth!'

The devil smiled. 'That's all right, boy. I'll send someone up to organize it.'

Well, so far Summerhill is not organized, nor has it become a tradition. I cannot deny the fact that Summerhill was me, but I am not so sure whether it is still me. Today the system seems to run by itself. When I was off for three months with sciatica I knew that the school was running as usual, but here it can be said that Ena my wife is part of the two-person show, for she knows and feels about the school in the same way as I do. And the staff is with us. How much my personality (let me boast a bit), my patience, my humour, my absence of fussiness, my refusal to be a positive guide to any child, how much these qualities have to do with the success of the school I cannot assess. Nor can anyone else. It is like asking how much Homer Lane's smile did for his immediate disciples.

I dislike the idea of one-man-ness, for it is not the man that matters; it is the idea. The personality cult was rightly condemned in Russia. I cannot for the life of me understand why a thousand teachers cannot have schools that are free and happy. It takes no genius; one does not have to be a superman, only a man or woman without the wish to tell others how to live.

Communism was to do away with the one-man show . . . and it gave us Lenin and then Stalin. It looks as if one-man-ness is a branch of religion. Most people want a god to lean on and follow; most Britishers want a monarch to bow before. The question arises: can humanity ever do without leaders?

I am not a leader. I am a member of a community government. All I can say here is that I dislike leaders of any kind. I should define a leader as a man who is primarily self-centred, seeking power for its own sake. My reward is not praise, not a title, not followers, it is the simple one – joy in having done a job with all my heart and energy.

Any society that follows after a leader will tend to stagnate: 'Our founder didn't do this, so we mustn't.' Steiner was a very bright laddie, but in Stockholm after a lecture the head of the Rudolf Steiner school there said to me, 'I didn't agree with anything you said tonight. You educate for this life, while we educate for the lives to come.' I don't think Steiner himself would have said that.

Some have said that my work has been negative, and to me that is a compliment, for the other side is too damn positive with its disciplines and mouldings. If you do not know what a child should be you have to be negative, a looker-on, and that is what the Establishment will not, cannot do. It knows what a child should be. Montessori and Rudolf Steiner knew, but Homer Lane didn't. And I don't know; on the other hand I have never despaired when a child seems to stand still for years. One such, a boy who in Summerhill never went to a lesson, left school barely able to read. Today he is a bright young man who has hiked all over the world. He worked for the starving in Bangladesh and is now on his way to south-east Africa to see what he can do to help the natives. But he can't spell well and has never heard of the Long Parliament. This brings up again the vexed question: What is education? I say it is, among other things, forming character from the inside, not the dictated character of Eton and Harrow and the grammar schools.

Another frequent question is: When you die who will carry on Summerhill? I have often wondered if I could find someone on the outside who would carry on my work, but I have never found anyone. This implies a gigantic conceit, an exaggerated ego, yet does the man exist who thinks that another could do his job? In my school I do many an odd job that I could delegate to someone else – mending locks, repairing chairs, painting doors – simply because of my conviction that the other fellow will not do it so well. I did not succeed Homer Lane: I only learnt from him, and if he were still alive I know that we should differ strongly on many points. Reich did not succeed Freud: he went on building on the foundation that Freud had laid, and then extended the structure with completely new foundations. Disciples are dangerous and too often inferior.

No, Summerhill will probably die when I die or retire, and I say that it won't matter very much. I am no prophet and any guess I make about the future of education has no special value. It may be that when the present East–West tension and fear and hate are resolved, by war or compromise or the victory of one political and ideological side or the other, that world education will accept more freedom for children.

I can imagine a student at a training college some day in the future reading in his textbook: 'In the middle of the century there was quite a lot of experiment in education, and freedom was the watchword. The most famous, or perhaps we should say notorious, of these experimenters was a Scot named McNeill who founded a private school called Summerhill in Sussex. We can look back and smile at his extreme views today – complete freedom to learn or play, government by the children themselves, no moral moulding – but as we smile we must admit that he did some good by preaching against the futile worship of lessons. Our generation, of course, rejects the idea of complete freedom. Since religious instruction was abolished twenty years ago we have not given up our sacred right to guide children by kindly giving them the benefits of our adult experience. At the same time we must give credit to our

McNeills for helping to do away with ancient pestilences like punishment and strict discipline and unnecessary fear in our schools.'

My sadness is that I shall soon have to leave all these new buildings the HMIs have made me put up, for at eighty-eight I cannot expect to live long. I hope my family will be able to carry it on when I am dead, but, without my name, I do not know if it will continue to attract pupils. But even if it has to die with me it has been an honest bit of work for the last fifty years.

Part Two

Scottish Boyhood[1]

It cannot be easy for younger generations to imagine village life at the end of the last century. Every village boy of today is within reach of a cinema; he has, or he can hear, a radio; he watches television, and he sees lorries, vans, and buses going by. In my childhood, life went by slowly, in gigs and on bicycles. Once a year, we had a school picnic. That was a swell affair. We went in farmers' carts, and the ploughmen spent nights polishing their harnesses and grooming their horses. Of all the days in the year, that one was nearest heaven; the day following was the deepest hell. On the day after the school picnic, I invariably plumbed the depths of bitter despair, weeping in sheer misery. The glory had departed and would never come again.

On the other 364 days of the year nothing happened in Kingsmuir. This monotony of life was broken only by an occasional wedding or funeral. We welcomed both but preferred marriages. They were often forced ceremonies, the couple having 'cut the wedding cake before the marriage', as the saying went.

Death was no stranger to me. I had been at the burial of little members of the family more than once, and knew the trappings of death and the tears – yes, and the airy relief after the body was left in the grave. I must have attended three funerals before I was ten. Counting a still-born infant, my mother had thirteen children in all. Years later, when we used to criticize her for having so many, she indignantly told us that it was God's will, and she got furious with my sister Clunie for saying, 'That's all very well, but you had no right to have me eleven months after Allie; and if you call that God's will, he is to blame for my poor health.'

Like most children, we did not appear to be conscious of the changing seasons. My haziest memories are of the winters, when there seemed to be more snow than now, and we made slides on

1. A. S. Neill was born in Forfar, Angus, Scotland, on 17 October 1883, and died in Aldeburgh, Suffolk, on 22 September 1973.

the roads, skating as clumsily as frogs. Sometimes when the frost was good, we tried to skate on a local pond, but never efficiently. Our skates were partly to blame, being so blunted by cart tracks that they would not grip the ice.

Games had their special periods: marbles when the March dust was blowing, tops later in the spring. We all had marbles and tops, and iron hoops which we called girds, but I never knew how we got them. Marbles in the shops were expensive – ten a penny at one time – yet when the season began, poor ragged boys would appear suddenly with their 'pooches full of bools'. I was feeble at organized games and, at football, always had the dishonour of being the last chosen when sides were tossed for. Yet I cannot recall ever making an athlete my hero.

To us – first of all – spring meant dust, blowing with the March winds, and then the joy of bird-nesting. We all had egg collections, but harried every nest we came across, no matter how many specimens we already possessed. This search for nests was exciting because it led us into forbidden areas where gamekeepers were savage and terrifying in voice. I can still feel the agony of hearing a voice cry, as I prepared to climb a tree, 'What the hell are you doing there?' We had all heard tales of gamekeepers beating boys up, but these tales must have been legends, for these men never touched us. As a timid lad, I often had to stand guard for the others; that was far worse than actually taking part in a raid.

Examination day was the last day of school and one of the brightest of the year to us. It meant the prelude to weeks of freedom, when we could catch minnows all day long in the Back Ditch, or go farther afield to the Vinney where we tried to 'guddle', to catch trout with our hands – but never got any. We never attempted to use a line and hook, no doubt because they were too expensive.

Many years later when cycling Vinney way as a student, I looked over the bridge and saw my youngest brother Percy with rod and line. I asked him how long he had been standing there. 'Two hours,' he said, 'and not even a nibble.'

'I'll show you how to fish,' I said, with all the superiority of an elder brother, casting the line. A trout jumped at it, and I whisked it out.

'That's how to catch fish,' I said, and left him. It was the only fish I ever caught in my life, but to his dying day I am sure Percy considered me an expert angler.

In late summer, we also came up against the gamekeepers when we went gathering raspberries. Here we were slightly fortified by the knowledge that we were poaching with parental approval. It was an economic necessity for my mother to make as many pots of raspberry jam as possible, and there were berries in the woods for the taking. The local squires did not prohibit the gathering of berries out of arrogance; their defence was that pickers disturbed the pheasants and partridges.

My mother slaved during the berry season. The jam pot was seldom off the fire, and we loved the delicious smell of the skimmings. She was really a wonderful housekeeper; how she managed to make just the right amount of jam to supply us for the whole year makes me marvel, even now. She was proud of her jam-making, especially as she was the only woman in the village who could get her strawberry jam firm. Equally satisfying to her was her washing and ironing. She slaved at the washtub and ironing-board, using a charcoal iron, and I fear her criterion of whiteness in linen has made me consider most steam laundries inferior ever since.

During the years when I was a boy, she suffered extreme pain – often agony – from gallstones, but she never made her illness an excuse for shirking her housework. I think her proudest moments were on Sunday mornings when she stood at the garden gate and watched us troop off to the kirk: my father in his chimney hat and starched shirt; the boys in their well-brushed clothes and stiff pockets; the girls with their well-ironed dresses. She had become stout, and seldom made the long walk to town herself, only on special occasions like the sacrament days.

To us children Sundays always seemed a depressing time, when we were rigged up in Sabbath clothes with starched collars and cuffs. We were accustomed to the collars, because Mother prided herself on the fact that her boys wore genuine stiff collars even on weekdays. Getting ready for the kirk was hateful to us. We struggled with clumsy cufflinks: we resentfully stood to have oil rubbed in our hair. We were all dressed up with nowhere to go – nowhere, at any rate, that we wanted to go. We knew there lay before us an hour and a half of extreme boredom, of sitting on a

hard pew with upright back – only the rich had cushions – or
listening to dull psalms and hymns and a seemingly interminable
sermon by Dr Caie.

The Scots religion of my boyhood was a modified Calvinism. I
cannot remember ever being taught that the doctrine of predestina-
tion separated us for ever as sheep and goats, without our having
any say in the matter at all. No, we had free will. We could choose
heaven or hell, but might reach heaven only after praying to God
or Jesus and getting sanction. The road to hell was easy enough.
You only had to be a sinner to go there.

I got my emotional religion from the home, not from the kirk. It
was Granny, I think now, who kept my parents up to the mark in
religion. To her, everything was so simple. Since God's word was
inspired – true from first to last – you had only to 'believe' and you
were safe for heaven. My mother and father stuck to this religion
until mellowed by age. Then they lapsed for many years, finding
their salvation at last in Spiritualism.

We were not specifically taught religion; it was in the air, an
atmosphere of negation of life. My father said grace before each
meal, but only when my mother was there. It was she who paused
after she had served us all with soup. 'Now, George,' she would
say, and he would thank the Lord for his mercies. I can still hear
her voice change when she said; 'Now, George.' It makes me think
of the BBC announcer who, after cheerfully telling us about floods
in China, suddenly hushes his voice to report: 'It is with great
regret that we announce the death of . . .'

Sunday was a holy day; only necessary work could be done. Our
reading was censored, and we had to read our penny dreadfuls
within the protective pages of a 'good' book. Granny, with her
sharp nose for deception, sometimes caught us. All games were
taboo; our walks were not much joy. Village boys played football
with tin cans on the road, but even these heathens did not play an
organized game with a real ball.

Without being told, we knew precisely the milestones on the
broad road 'that leadeth to destruction'. They were sex, stealing,
lying, swearing, and profaning God's day. (The last named included
nearly everything that was enjoyable.) I cannot remember that such
virtues as obedience and respect were milestones on the other way
– the straight and narrow path that 'leadeth unto life'. At any rate,

disobedience did not come into our line of vision; we were too well trained to attempt it.

My sister Clunie had less timidity and faith than I had. She wouldn't have hell at any price; and when she took the next step and wouldn't have God and his heaven, I actually feared that she might be struck down dead on the spot. My fright was caused by a grim story in Granny's annotated *Shorter Catechism* about a servant girl accused of stealing a silver spoon. 'May God strike me down dead if I stole the spoon!' she cried; and, of course, she fell down dead there and then, the silver spoon tinkling on the floor. I reminded the atheistic Clunie of this tale more than once, but she merely laughed me to scorn.

My Granny was psychic. She had none of that second sight so often mentioned in the Scottish tales I heard all my youth – tales like the one about Old Tamson touching Mrs Broon on the shoulder in the kirk, and whispering: 'Better go home, for your laddie has just broken his neck'; after which Mrs Broon drives the seven miles home to discover that exact calamity. Many such stories were told in my boyhood, but it was always a case of 'I know a man who heard about it from a man'. No, Granny contented herself with more simple phenomena: her special department was knocks. 'I'm no' long for this life,' she would say, coming down from her room of a morning, very, very depressed. 'I heard three warning knocks loud and clear. My Maker has called me.' And she would go upstairs again to get her death linen in order. Naturally, we grew accustomed to her premonitions, but suffered some remorse in the end when she died after hearing her knocks.

When a boy, I seldom read a book. I can't remember my brother Neilie reading much then either. Any book I did read was one recommended by my brother Willie or my sister Clunie. Willie read everything he could find, and at an early age had a fine taste in books. Clunie also was an omnivorous reader, and although a year younger than I, read Dickens and Thackeray and *Jane Eyre* when my level was the penny dreadful. It was through them that I discovered H. G. Wells, W. W. Jacobs, Anthony Hope – *The Prisoner of Zenda* delighted me – and Rider Haggard. After reading *She*, I knew that my future lay in central Africa. I also read Marie Corelli. Clunie and I agreed that she was the greatest writer who had ever lived; and together, we wrote her a letter to this effect. If she would only send us her signature, we should cherish it until death. She never replied, and soon we grew critical of her work.

Today, when I get letters telling me that I am easily the greatest man alive, I always answer them, hypocritically disclaiming the compliment but wishing the senders all luck in their own futures. Marie Corelli lost two earnest admirers by not answering them; I have so few that I dare not lose any. If any youth thinks that I am greater than Shakespeare and Shaw rolled into one, it would be brutally unkind for me to contradict him. The heroes of my youth often let me down, but perhaps my tactics were all wrong. Had I written, 'Dear Miss Corelli, You can't write for nuts, your characters are dead sticks, and your philosophy is tripe,' I am sure I should have had an answer.

My father did not care for me when I was a boy. Often he was cruel to me, and I acquired a definite fear of him, a fear that I never quite overcame in manhood. I see now that Father did not like *any* children; even though he was the village teacher he had no real contact with them. He did not know how to play, and he never understood the child's mind. The boy he admired was the boy who could beat the others in lessons; and since I never had any interest in lessons and could not learn, I had no hope of gaining Father's interest or affection.

Father's school was on one side of the road; our dwelling, the schoolhouse, on the opposite side. The house had a parlour, dining-room, kitchen, and five bedrooms. Our toilet was an earth closet far up the garden. I simply had to cross the road to go to school but my brothers had to go to Forfar Academy and walk two miles, morning and evening.

Forfar Academy was the stepping-stone to a university education. To my father, advancement in life meant advancement in learning. We were to be scholars, and Willie led the way. In the Academy, he topped his class in most subjects. Without visibly doing any work, he managed to go to university at sixteen. His brilliance as a scholar seemed remarkable. His method was to sit up for three nights before the exam with a wet towel around his head; his memory was prodigious.

When it came to my turn to go to the Academy, I was not sent. I was the only one of the family who never went to the Academy. The sad truth is that it would have been useless and hopeless to send me there, for I could not learn. My father still did not care much for me and little wonder: I was obviously the inferior article, the misfit in a tradition of academic success, and automatically I accepted an inferior status. If there was a particularly hard and unappetizing heel to a loaf, my father would cut it off with a flourish; with another flourish, he would toss it over the table in my direction, saying, 'It'll do for Allie.'

My father's school was a two-roomed building divided into the 'big' and 'little' rooms. It was in the main a happy school. Sometimes my father used the strap a lot, especially when exasperated by the dunces, for his salary depended on the number of Standard V students he passed. For some obscure reason, Standard V came to be the parking place of dunces; as inspection day approached, and my father got more and more irritable, the blows of the strap grew many and hard.

Lest he be accused of favouritism, he punished his family as severely as the others, and I came in for more than my fair share when the strappings were given for noise or mischief: as a Neill, I ought to have kept away from the bad boys.

It must have been about the age of fourteen that I began to seek importance as a wag, and I have a faint recollection of making my schoolmates laugh easily. Their standard was not high; in geography, the River Po – 'po' was toilet slang to us – kept them sniggering guiltily for the whole lesson.

For any sexual offence in school, my father always gave a savage punishment. I remember his giving Jock Ross six with the belt, on his hand held down on the desk, for pretending to drop his slate pencil while taking the occasion to put his hand up a girl's petticoats.

I feared my father much at that time. He had a nasty habit of taking me by the cheek and pinching me hard between thumb and forefinger. Often he pinched my arm painfully. There must have been something very unlikable about me then, for the other members of the family received fairer treatment. I was clumsy and my unprepossessing appearance did not help. My stuck-out ears earned me the nickname Saucers, and my feet grew suddenly to the size they are now. I was much ashamed of the enormous boots I wore. Because my toes turned in, I clattered along the road with those great boots hitting each other, sometimes tripping me up. I was certainly not the kind of son desired by a father who sought high academic distinction for his family.

Willie and my second sister, May, prospered, simply because they went their own ways, whereas we timid ones, fearful of discipline, did what we were told. I was obedience personified, although in the long run, my passive obedience backfired. Obedience made me stare at Allen's *Grammar*, but something inside me negated my passive response by refusing to allow me to learn anything.

I know that my ability as a teacher came from watching my father's methods. My father certainly had the knack of drawing out his pupils. Long before modern methods in teaching geography, he kept telling them to ask why ... Why is Glasgow where it is? Why London? Why is there more rain on the west coast of Scotland than on the east?

He used to have a class which he called Intelligence. We formed a half-circle and if the boy or girl at the top did not know the answer the one who did went up top. His method certainly gave us a vocabulary. And my father gave us a sound training in grammar, so that, even today, I have a mild shock when someone says, 'He spoke to Jim and I' or 'These sort of things are useless.' In teaching us Latin he showed us how it helped spelling; we knew that committee had two 'm's' because it came from *con* ('with') and *mitto* ('I send'). That was all I ever got from Latin. I had just got to an appreciation of the lines of Virgil when I passed an examination and never opened a Latin book again.

That is the absurd feature about learning the classics. One spends dreary years over the grammar and unless one takes classics at the university the whole subject disappears from memory.

My failure to learn Latin angered my father, but my inability to learn even two lines of a psalm gave my mother more sorrow than anger. What did anger her was my forgetting 'messages' when sent to town. As the only child who didn't go to the Academy, my job of a morning was to walk to Forfar with the Academy lot and fetch household supplies.

'Now are you sure you can remember the list?' my mother would ask. 'Pound of flank and a marrowbone, two pounds of sugar, mustard, and a bottle of vinegar.'

So off I'd trudge to town in my big boots. When I got to the

East Port, however, I had completely forgotten the items. Sometimes I made wild guesses, but the result of bringing home sugar when I had been told to get salt was too painful, and I took to telling feeble lies about Lindsay and Low being out of sugar at the moment. Then I was given a written list, though sometimes I lost even that.

Working Youth

As a boy I loved my mother deeply – loved her too much – but at that age I could not love my father. He was too stern, too far away from me. As a model for us children, he used to hold up a frail little chap with glasses, who never played a game in his life but was an earnest student, actually weeping if he weren't at the top of the class. We hated that lad; he became a railway porter.

Many years later, I came to love the old man. His ambitions for us had long since gone, and he accepted us as we were. But in the times of which I speak, he held himself aloof from us boys and would never talk about his childhood. It was only before his death at the age of eighty-four that he told me of his first great tragedy, his mother's death of cholera when he was a boy. 'I grat [wept] for weeks,' he said, as the tears came to his eyes and my own.

I do not know why he was so strained and unhappy when we were young. True enough, he was trying to do all he could for his family with very inadequate means. I am convinced, however, that economic circumstances never go deep enough to affect individuals fundamentally. I am sure, for instance, that no man ever killed himself because of loss of fortune, the reason given so often in the newspapers. For many, money comes too late in life to have any deep significance. My father's youngest brother, who never had a bean, was always cheerful. Father's pessimism must have sprung from an abnormal fear of life and a sense of its disappointment. But how his fear arose cannot be known. Certainly his ambitions for us must have been a transfer of his own.

When I was fourteen, my father decided to send Neilie and me out to work. Neilie was doing no good at the Academy, and I had been learning nothing at Kingsmuir School. When Father asked us what we wanted to be in life, Neilie replied, 'A sheep farmer,' and I, 'An engine driver.' 'Ugh,' said my father in disgust, 'you'll both go into offices.'

Neilie got a job as a clerk in a Leith flour-mill; three months later, I received a reply to one of my many letters replying to advertisements in the *Scotsman*. My handwriting was good at that time, and I had penned my applications in a slow hand that attempted to be copperplate.

The letter in answer to my application informed me that I had been appointed a very junior clerk in the office of W. & B. Cowan, Ltd, gas-meter manufacturers in Edinburgh. My feelings were mixed.

I was now to be freed for ever from studying Latin grammar, but against that weighed the knowledge that I also was to be freed from play and bird-nesting and catching minnows. However, I set off boldly enough. I was to lodge with Neilie in Leith. Neilie earned fifteen shillings a week, and I was to earn six.

W. & B. Cowan's was one long misery to me. I did not labour in the central office, but in a dark, evil-smelling hole of an office in the middle of the works. There I lived in a stink of solder and paint and gas. My happiest moments were those in which I was sent to find someone in the works. I loitered with the workmen, and then got sworn at when I returned to the office.

Neilie lost his job. It proved too difficult for a boy of sixteen, and he went home, leaving me alone. For the first time in my life, I experienced homesickness. I kept writing miserable letters to the family until finally my mother came to see me for two days. I clung to her in bitter tears and implored her to take me home with her. She told me that that was impossible, and when she left, my homesickness was almost unbearable.

After being in Edinburgh three months, I was allowed to go home at New Year's for four days. After seven months, I was allowed to return home permanently. I still remember the embarrassment of that homecoming, a shame at not having been able to stick it out. When one farmer remarked in company that 'Thae Neills canna bide at nithing,' Neilie and I blushed.

Why was I taken back? I do not know. No doubt my parents had tired of my despairing letters, though there might have been another reason, too. I had written to my father, telling him that the chances of promotion were very poor in Cowan's, and that my future would be much brighter if I came home and studied hard for the Civil Service. From the hell that was Edinburgh, sitting in Kingsmuir schoolhouse all day long seemed like paradise. And I think I truly believed that once home, I should study all the time.

Neilie and I were set down again to study for the Civil Service –
men clerks this time. But history repeated itself; we could not
concentrate. One night in despair, my father threw our textbooks
at us and said he gave up. 'They're just fit for nothing, Mary.'

But Johnston the chemist needed an apprentice, and my father
fixed things up that I should begin work there on the following
Monday. During the week, however, another local firm advertised
for an apprentice – Anderson & Sturrock, drapers – and my father's
plans rapidly altered: Neilie would be the chemist, and I the draper.
So early on the Monday morning we walked to Forfar to our new
jobs.

I hated the drapery business. I was on my feet from seven-thirty
in the morning to eight in the evening, and then had the two-mile
walk home. Since I wore heavy boots, my big toe joints got inflamed
and gradually stiffened – their condition to this day. My toes got
so bad in fact that I had to give up the job. This I did gladly,
vowing to my father that now I had acquired sense, I would slave
at the Civil Service exam. Poor Neilie had no excuse for giving up
his chemist's apprenticeship; and for four long years he went back
and forth, hating it all the time.

The old problem had arisen again. My concentration was no
better than it had ever been, and for the third time my father
despaired of me. This time he really gave me up, he said, and I
stared gloomily into the future, seeing myself as a good-for-nothing
tramp, wondering whether I would fail as an ordinary ploughman.

'The boy's just hopeless,' said my father gloomily.

'He might be a teacher,' ventured my mother.

'It's about all he's fit for,' said my father grimly, and without a
smile.

Now that Father had given me up, Mother stepped in. She
pointed out that no other teacher had as many classes as he had,
and 'Really, George, you need a pupil teacher.' I knew that my
father wasn't keen about it, but somehow she got him to broach
the subject to the school-board clerk, and in due time I was appointed PT, a student teacher, in Kingsmuir School. There I served
an apprenticeship of four years.

Though it is hard to recall my days in the school, I must have
taken classes to relieve my father, for I do remember teaching small
boys and girls to read by the look-and-say method. I found that

the best way to learn anything is to teach it, and soon I could string off nearly every town, cape and river in the whole world, as well as the exports of Peru or the imports of China. I think I learned my profession well, for I copied my father, and he was a good teacher – good in the sense that he could draw out rather than stuff in.

My student-teacher days are mostly a blank to me now, though photographs of school groups show me standing stiffly with a very high choker collar. I look back on my position as a difficult one, for I had to be on the side of authority before my own desire to play had been lived out. It was the role of a boy pretending to be a man.

During my student-teaching days, I met a man who made mathematics live for me. He was Ben Thomson, the maths master at the Academy, and later its rector. When I went to him for private tuition, he gave me a genuine love for the subject, which explains why I belong to that rare breed of people able to while away a railway journey doing algebraic and geometrical problems. Ben was a staunch friend. He gave me most of the lessons free of charge, and years later would help me by post when I had difficulties with the subject. I regret that he never wrote a textbook, for his way of presenting maths was unique. I kept telling him he should do this, and my last request reached him shortly before his sudden death. Forfar Academy in his time turned out many brilliant mathematicians.

I have said that I was not a reader. Nevertheless, I must have read quite a lot in the practice-teaching period, and recall borrowing many books from the Meffan Library, mostly fiction. I revelled in the whimsical sentimentality of J. M. Barrie's novels, identifying myself with his Sentimental Tommy. Again and again I cycled to his Thrums (Kirremuir, seven miles away), and, sitting in the den, tried, not very successfully, to people it with his characters.

My ambitions seem to have been latent at this time. The future did not exist for me, possibly because I dared not contemplate a future as an unsuccessful teacher with no hope of promotion. What I daydreamed about is long forgotten. By this time, religion had become an empty, outside thing, and my church-going had only one object; to see the girls.

When my apprenticeship ended, I applied for jobs, and finally got one in Bonnyrigg near Edinburgh at fifty pounds a year. The school was run by an old lady called Miss MacKinley, who looked like an eagle and was a very stern disciplinarian. After the laxity of my father's school, it was a great shock to find myself suddenly in a school where the children were not allowed to talk in class. I was ordered to thrash any child who even whispered, and did so because I was really scared of the old woman. I stood it for two months and then got a better job at sixty pounds a year in Kingskettle in Fife.

If anything, the discipline of Kettle school was worse than that of Bonnyrigg. For three years, I had to be the sternest of taskmasters. The room used by Calder, the headmaster, was separated from mine by a glass partition, and his sharp eye could see everything that went on. For three years, I did my work with fear in my heart. Calder never relaxed; he kept me at arm's length, and all my attempts to approach the human side of him were frozen by his stony stare.

Yet, in a queer sort of way, I felt that he liked me; and also in a queer sort of way, I liked him in spite of my fear. Calder's teaching methods were surprising to me. When he gave his class a test in arithmetic, he slowly worked out every problem on the blackboard first; then the children worked out the same problems in their books. Only the very stupid ones got the answers wrong under such a system, and God help them when they did, for the headmaster wielded a fierce strap and laid on heavily. The HMI gave Calder excellent reports – because he kept excellent whisky, the cynics said.

Kingskettle remained a horror to me. There must have been times during those three years when I was happy, but the main memory is one of fear; fear of being late in the mornings, fear of having my class examined by Calder, fear of him when he leathered the poor ones who could not learn. I realized that if I had been his pupil, I would have been strapped every day. My father had never been that strict. True, he had strapped often and sometimes hard, but there was in his school a certain freedom, freedom to laugh and chat and carve your name on the desk. We never had to march in or out like soldiers.

Kettle school was like a new world to me. There was no laughter in the school save when Calder made one of his oft-repeated jokes at the expense of a pupil. All pupils moved in military style; and everyone, including myself, was insincere, inhuman, fearful. Calder was my first contact with a real army disciplinarian. I had heard of the type – a few notorious ones existed in Forfar – and they all had a common characteristic: they were all men of small stature.

One interesting point about Calder was his habit of always writing very slowly in copperplate. Even if he made a pencil note, it was beautifully written. Practically every pupil in the school could write well, too.

Once I took Calder's senior drawing class in his room, while he stood doing his registers at the desk. The lesson was given in dead silence, but when he went over to his house, hell broke loose, and I could hardly keep the pretence of discipline. But I never reported the ringleaders to Calder when he returned. I tried to teach designing, with flowers and leaves as bases, and some pupils brought forth rather good, balanced patterns of the wallpaper type. These designs were the only original work ever allowed in the school, for even an essay was first written on the blackboard by Calder and then copied by the class.

Calder was unhealthy, kept having painful boils on the back of his neck, and was quite unable to carry on his work for weeks at a time. During such periods, I was in complete charge of the school. I enjoyed these times, even though it was not an easy matter to keep order; not that I tried very much, knowing well that the moment Calder came back, his army discipline would grip the pupils automatically.

It was during my stay in Kettle that I became ambitious to enter the ministry. The man who encouraged this desire was the local minister, the Revd Aeneas Gunn Gordon. He was a Canadian, tall, straight, distinguished, with a strong beard and a nose like an eagle's beak. He took me under his wing, and I told him of my wish. 'You need Greek,' he said. 'Come down to my house every morning at eight and I'll teach you.'

He knew his Homer, almost by heart, and taught me so well that I could read the first two books of the *Odyssey* and a part of Herodotus. (Today I cannot read a word of Greek.) Gordon had one failing, which never affected my admiration – sometimes he drank too much, and I recall seeing him of a morning holding Homer upside down, while quoting it correctly. He was a man who read everything but appeared to absorb little and gave out less. Though liberal in the way of charity and human kindness, he delivered dull sermons, and his conversation seemed commonplace. Yet he gave me a certain interest in literature.

He used to read aloud from *Paradise Lost*, and I learned to appreciate 'the organ music of Milton'. On his advice I read Dante and Tasso, and then the essays of Macaulay. The latter gripped me, making me conscious of literary style for the first time in my life; I was then in love with a girl in Glasgow, and used our correspondence to improve my own style. How far beyond her those purple passages and that noble diction must have been. My present attitude towards style, with few exceptions, can be stated simply: the important thing is *what* is said, not *how*.

Having reached by stages a teaching salary of seventy-five pounds a year, I applied for a job in Newport at a hundred pounds. About four o'clock one day, two strange men called at the Kettle school to take me to tea. One of them was H. M. Willsher, the Newport headmaster. They offered me the job, and I packed my little trunk. Actually, I had passed my final exam and was now the possessor of an Acting Teacher's Certificate. That, of course explains why I now earned a hundred pounds a year.

I was determined to go to the university by hook or by crook. During my time in Kettle, I had worked hard, and one morning cycled over to St Andrews for the first part of my preliminary exams – two subjects, English and maths. I made a bad mess of the first maths paper; it was far too difficult for me, even though Ben Thomson had been coaching me once again by post. I came out in despair, half thinking that I should give the whole thing up, without attempting the second paper in the afternoon.

At lunch, I ran into a lecturer, an old pal of Willie's, and told him of my failure; he patted me on the back cheerfully. 'What you want is a brandy and soda,' he said, and led me to the Cross Keys. I had never tasted brandy before but liked the taste and had another double. If not singing as I entered the exam hall, no doubt I felt like it. My memory of the paper is nil, but I did pass in both subjects. Thus, when I went to Newport, I was already a semi-matriculated student. Now I studied Latin and physics for the second portion of the exam.

Harry Willsher, the school's headmaster, could not have been more unlike Calder. His discipline was easygoing – he did not care how much the children talked – and from the first day I loved the school. My two years in that southern suburb of Dundee were perhaps the happiest of my life thus far.

Willsher became my musical mentor. Apart from his personal talents, he was a music critic for the Dundee paper. One evening, hearing me remark that I liked Elgar's 'Salut d'Amour', he sat down and played it. Then, without a word, he repeated the composition. 'Shall I play it again?' he asked, but I said no. He smiled. 'The lesson is this, Neill. Good music you can hear again and again: inferior music bores you stiff if you get it more than once.' I was much impressed; yet today, if I had to listen ten times in succession to something I really like – the trio from *Der Rosenkavalier*, for instance – I should feel like drawing a gun on the singers.

Newport is one of the few places I still return to with strong feelings. It gave me peace, and helped me to carry on my teaching work without fear. I shall always have a tender spot in my heart for Harry Willsher, who was a companion rather than a master.

University Life

The door to the university was now open, and I said a sad farewell to Newport in the summer of 1908. Since Edinburgh University did not open until October, I went back to Kingsmuir. I had saved enough to carry me over a year, or maybe two – heaven knows how.

Neilie was in his final year of medical study, and I went to lodge with him. It was a cheap place off Clerk Street; the better-off students all lived over Marchmont way. Mrs Sutherland, our landlady, was a gem; a dear, kind woman who looked after me for four years. I was now really hard up and had to look twice at every penny spent, for there was no means of earning more. Luckily I came under the Carnegie Trust and had my university fees paid by that grant, although matriculation and exam payments were not included.

Neilie and I could only allow ourselves threepence a day for lunch. The Students' Union had a restaurant; also a lunch counter, where every day we each had a glass of milk and two penny buns. Other students had the same but they dined well at night. We could only afford high tea in our lodgings, and our only good meal of the week was the Sunday midday dinner. We always quarrelled about the division of it until we evolved a sound plan: Neilie divided the main dish between two plates and then I chose one.

Though my approach to higher education may have been casual, I took seriously my first-year classes in chemistry and natural philosophy – at least in the beginning. Every morning we had a lecture by Sir James Walker, the chemistry professor, and I took voluminous notes. I thought it a waste of talent, however, for Walker to spend his precious time teaching raw students the elements of this subject; and in 1936, when I dined with the principal of Johannesburg University, I made such a remark at table. The professors present were up in arms at once. They defended the lecture system by saying that this very contact with a man like Walker was the best education a student could have.

I still don't believe it. Any assistant could teach a class what happens if you put sulphuric acid on zinc, and why should a good chemist like Walker not spend all his time doing research at the expense of the university or state? I liked chemistry with its practical lab work and passed it easily. But my work must have cost the university something, for I used up all the chloroform cleaning my pipes.

Natural philosophy was double Dutch to me. Professor Mac-Gregor was the worst lecturer I ever encountered, mumbling into his beard as he wrote mysterious formulae on the blackboard, while we passed the time catcalling and tramping tunes with our feet. MacGregor never seemed to mind: I wonder if he even heard us. Our greatest day occurred when the lab assistant, Lindsay, had to turn the handle of an instrument to show the workings of sound waves. Then we all threw pennies at him; but like his master, he stood there quite unperturbed. He had had many years of this, and possibly his only interest was the amount of the collection he would sweep up when class was over.

Lab work in Nat. Phil. was a farce to me. I remember being given some apparatus involving an inclined plane, and repeatedly timing something, so I could write down each result. After getting about fifty of these results, I added them up and took the average. I disliked the dullness of this work and hated my inability to do it quickly. Another man would finish his experiment in about half an hour, and looked to be the class medallist. One day I asked him how he managed to get through his experiments so quickly. 'Take three readings and fake the rest,' he said shortly. After that, my experiments took about twenty minutes each.

I can honestly say that I hardly understood anything about sound, light, and heat – not to mention electricity. When the final exam came round, I stared at a paper that was far beyond my comprehension, and went home for the summer vacation feeling depressed. I passed. Still wondering how and why, I can only conclude that old MacGregor was as absent-minded in correcting papers as he was in the lecture hall, and muddled my paper with someone else's. For all I know, he mixed up mine with that of his medallist, whom he may have failed.

By the end of the first year, I had discovered that science was not in my line, and made up my mind to take a degree in Honours

English. Honours English meant that, with the exception of history, I could spend all of my time taking English classes. I duly entered for history and first-year English.

We had Sir Richard Lodge for English history, and I enjoyed his lectures thoroughly. There was no catcalling in *his* room; one look from him and we all became diligent little boys and girls who were seen and not heard. One youth tried catcalling one day. He sat behind me, and I looked round in annoyance. Suddenly I heard Lodge shout, 'You, sir,' He was looking, I thought, at the man behind me. 'You, you, you, sir,' came the persistent, hard voice of the professor, and he pointed at me. I rose from my seat and silently asked a vital question by indicating myself with my forefinger. 'Yes, you,' thundered Lodge. 'Get out of this classroom, sir.'

Very white, I marched from the room with my head up. After class, I knocked at the door of his private room. 'I thought you would come to apologize,' he said. 'I didn't, sir. I came to tell you I had nothing to do with the noise.'

He eyed me with some suspicion. 'Of course, if you say so . . .' He shrugged his shoulders as if to show he didn't believe me.

Then suddenly I lost all my fear of authority and my temper as well. 'Look here, sir,' I said, 'I had to work for years to save up enough money to come to the university. I am years older than the average student. Do you think, in these circumstances, I came to Edinburgh to behave like a raw schoolboy?'

His eyebrows went up in surprise. Then he smiled, held out his hand, and apologized. My honour was satisfied, but I could have sunk through the floor next day when Lodge began his lecture by offering a public apology, for it wasn't so much an apology as a formal and flowery statement of praise. His word-portrait made me not only a scholar but a super-gentleman – and a prig.

My English professor was George Saintsbury, the renowned English author and critic. I sat under him for three years, but he did not know my name or know me by sight except on one occasion. His lectures were soliloquies: he spoke them like a parrot, and did not seem to care whether we listened or not. That suited us all right, for we did not listen. At least I personally did not, knowing that I could find it all in his voluminous writings a week before the exam. He had a high, squeaky voice, and amused us by his gentle-

manly attitude towards his contemporaries: 'Er – I do not quite
agree with my friend – er – [then quickly] Mr Bridges when he says
– but I must be just and take into consideration what Professor
Raleigh, who by the way in his attitude towards Dryden . . .' We
had great sport trying to stick to the main road through all his
parentheses.

Our course of study was not a creative one. We were supposed
to 'know' literature from Beowulf to Pater. We had to learn Anglo-
Saxon and Middle English. We used set books and studied set
periods – my final exam covered Elizabethan drama. In effect, we
read books about books. For an exam, it was necessary to know
what Coleridge and Hazlitt had said about Shakespeare; in any
question on style, we were supposed to know exactly what Longinus
had said about the subject.

By that time I had discovered Ibsen and was full of enthusiasm
for his plays. When my classwork demanded from me an essay on
Much Ado about Nothing, I quite foolishly wrote a damning criticism of the play, comparing its theatre with the contemporary
theatre of Ibsen. That is, I criticized Shakespeare for not writing a
realistic play – a stupid thing to do, but putting forward the point
of view I held at the time. Saintsbury was very angry with me – the
one time he must have recognized my name.

I held then, and do now, that it is better to write a bad limerick
than be able to recite *Paradise Lost*. That is a fundamental thing in
education. But the university never asked us to compose even a
limerick; it did not ask from us any original opinions about
Shakespeare or about anyone else. In those years, I read Spenser,
Chaucer, Pope, Dryden, most of Shakespeare and much of his
contemporaries; practically all of the Restoration drama, Coleridge,
Tennyson, Dr Johnson, Keats . . . but why go on? I was compelled
to concentrate on whether a blank-verse line had elision or not, or
whether one could trace the rhythm of 'Christabel' in 'The Lotus
Eaters'. It was all piddling stuff, like taking Milan Cathedral to
pieces stone by stone to discover where the beauty lay. I had to
read such a glorious thing as *The Tempest* with annotations, painfully looking up the etymological meaning of some phrase that did
not matter a scrap.

Saintsbury gave me a feeling for prose style, and that's about all.
He knew the beauty of literature, but he could not get it across to

us. I spent three years with him in dreary swamps of prose rhythm and poetic diction, seeing the trees but never the woods beyond. He held that his work had to deal with manner and not matter; otherwise, he said, English literature would bring in every study under the sun. I can see that, but it simply isn't possible to treat Macaulay's 'Essay on Clive' as a piece of literature without giving – or having any opinion on – the historical and political aspects of Clive's life. Saintsbury found it so easy to separate subject from style that he praised Blake as a great technical poet, and Nietzsche as one of the greatest prose writers, while dismissing the subject-matter of both with the words, 'They were, of course, mad.'

Whatever I actually gained from Saintsbury, it was certainly not an appreciation of literature. To this day I cannot read poetry for pleasure, cannot touch the classics. One year I went over to Norway – an MA in Honours English – and my literature for reading on the voyage was a bundle of *Black Mask* magazines – American crook yarns. True they were shoved into my hand by a friend as I left, but if I'd had Keats and Shelley in my bag, I still would have read the *Black Mask*s.

I hasten to add that it would be grossly unfair to blame Edinburgh University for any bad taste acquired; I am merely suggesting that if my years there had been spent in studying matter instead of manner, I might have had a better taste in literature today. I know that anything I could say about Chaucer and Keats would be unimportant and uninformed.

When Professor Chrystal, the celebrated mathematician, died, I went to see Saintsbury about giving me an obituary of the professor for our university magazine, *The Student*.

'I am just going into my Honours class', he said. 'If you are quick at taking notes, I shall allow you to come in, for I mean to say something about my old friend.'

'But, sir, I have been in your Honours class for three years.'

He looked up quickly and asked my name. When I replied, he said, 'Good heavens, how you have grown.'

I had been six feet years before I entered the university, and there weren't a dozen of us in that class. Saintsbury recognized books but not students. Lecturing to a bunch of raw undergraduates must have been hell for him.

On the whole, social life at Edinburgh was pleasant. Being a member of the Union, I always had a meeting place and an armchair of an evening. The difficulty was the shortage of cash. Most of my friends were well off. They wore the same sort of golfing jacket and flannel bags as I did, but they had money to spend; and when drinks went round it was awkward, because I never had more than a few coppers in my pockets.

I could not afford to play any games or even go to see matches. I had to pretend I hated music-halls in order to avoid joining parties going to the King's or the Empire. Nowadays I should tell them the truth, that I was poor. Mainly from my mother, who feared that we might revert to her working-class mother's status, I had the idea that poverty was a crime, a thing to be ashamed of, to hide as skilfully as one could. I must have played my part well, for years afterwards a fellow student, who had been a pal, remarked, 'Yes, it was all very well for you, Neill. You had money and I hadn't.'

The whole question of my attitude towards money is important. Because of the poverty suffered in my young years, I have a queer meanness about money. I grudge paying out small sums, yet can sign a cheque for a large amount without a moment's hesitation. Many other men regard cheques in a similar way: to us, a cheque isn't real money. It is fantasy money, and therefore of no emotional value. When motoring, I pay for petrol without quibbling; but if I have to take a taxi, I sit and watch the meter painfully whenever there is a traffic jam in the street. If I suddenly became a millionaire, I should still travel third class and buy a secondhand car. I dislike borrowing money and dislike more lending it. Only once was a lent fiver paid back to me – by a Scot, of course.

In still another way, money was a problem on occasion. My editorship of *The Student* gave me free dress-circle tickets to all the city theatres on Monday nights, and luckily evening dress was not obligatory. But there was a whole week of opera once – *Die Meistersinger*, *Orpheus*, *Elektra*, some others – and I went every single night to these more formal events. Towards the end of the week, I had to doctor my one dress shirt meticulously with white chalk to make it look decent.

As editor of *The Student*, I also had the privilege of being invited *ex officio* to an inter-university conference in St Andrews. I was allowed a small grant from the Students' Representative Council towards my expenses at the conference. It was not enough, and I drew about a pound more. But Walker, the secretary, stood me on the mat and gave me a thorough dressing-down. 'No other editor ever used more than the allotted amount,' he said, and I stood silent, ashamed of my poverty, hating the man. He was comfortably off, and looked at me as if I were something the cat had dragged into the house. My predecessors in the editorial chair had been gentlemen; that seemed to be what he was trying to tell me. I felt both angry and guilty.

I cannot recall exactly when I began to write, but it must have been some time before becoming editor. I began by submitting drawings and cartoons – awful things that make me blush to remember; my drawing, then as now, was atrocious. At that time, a student advised me to try a comic literary sketch for the *Glasgow Herald*. I sent one in, and a few mornings later found it in the paper. Possibly that was one of the most ecstatic moments of my life, the first time in print. It seemed incredible, wonderful, glorious: I trod on air all that day. Later, I sent in other sketches and received fourteen shillings for each one that was published.

I cannot honestly say that my four years in Edinburgh were very happy. I always return to the city unwillingly and without any interest. It is beautiful – more beautiful perhaps than any other city I have seen – but for me, Edinburgh remains a dead city, parochial and pompous. Its university life had little or no group spirit. We all lived in digs. The only meeting place was the Union, and thousands were not even members of that. A man could take a degree in Edinburgh without speaking to a single student during the time he was there. And some students seemed to do just that, too.

It might be interesting here to contrast my growth with Willie's, since he had been so strong an influence on my early life. Later he veered to the right, while I gradually assumed a more leftist attitude towards politics and other matters. There was one great difference between us as boys. He developed very young, reading the Bible at three, and entered the university when sixteen. My own advancement seemed incredibly slow.

Though I was twenty-eight when editing *The Student*, my editorials might have been written by a boy of fourteen. Their puerility is lamentable and their arrogance - comical is perhaps the best term. As editor, I suffered badly from being the sole authority. There was no need to ask anyone's opinion, and I published my own geese, believing they were swans. Some of my friends called certain articles tripe; alas, that happened after their publication. But editing the magazine was a liberal education in its way. I got to know about spacing, proof-reading, and technical production matters.

My finals were at hand. During my last year, I had given up my time and interest to editing *The Student*, and anticipated a very poor degree – in fact, the poorest possible, a third-class pass. But in the finals I did not do as badly as expected; indeed at the end of the week, I almost dared hope for a first in spite of my frankly bad Anglo-Saxon and Middle English. I got a second and was quite pleased. In due course, I was capped MA; but by then, sad to recall, I did not feel unduly proud or pleased. Everything in life comes too late, we hear.

Whether that is so or not, it was certainly true of my degree. As Robert Louis Stevenson said, 'To travel hopefully is a better thing than to arrive.' The degree, once a glittering peak, had become a minor hill, from the top of which I could look far out and see distant peaks, high and perhaps inaccessible – work, fame, perhaps death. More bluntly stated: I had got my degree and didn't know how to use it. All I knew was that *I didn't want to teach*: to think of going on all my life as English master in some provincial secondary school or academy made me shiver. No, teaching would be the last resort, if every other line failed.

A Profession

Journalism was my future, and I studied the ads in the papers; I applied for a few jobs but got no answers. Then a friend said he could get me some work at T. C. & E. C. Jacks, the Edinburgh publishers. The job was subediting a one-volume encyclopaedia planned to contain something more perhaps than the *Britannica*. Its chief editor was a man named H. C. O'Neill. It turned out to be a lousy job. Half the contributions came from clergymen with unreadable penmanship. When the copy was readable, it ran too long. We often had to throw the stuff into the waste-paper basket and rewrite it ourselves. I recall writing up the Panama Canal in this way, cribbing of course from other encyclopaedias. The work was extremely useful in one way: it gave me a dread of superfluous words.

I had been about a year at this work when O'Neill persuaded the firm to transfer its editorial office to London. Having reached the age of twenty-nine without crossing the border, I found the idea of going to London both wonderful and inevitable; had not Barrie and lesser Scots writers gone south to find wealth and a name? I counted the days before I should set off.

I don't recall how I looked, arriving in King's Cross station on a Sunday morning late in 1912, but I felt much as Keats's baffled Cortez: 'Silent, upon a peak in Darien'. Here was London, the centre of life and everything valuable to life. I made for the Strand and Fleet Street. With a thrill I looked round, trying hard to keep from realizing a slight disappointment. They were meaner streets than I had imagined, less picturesque than the Strand that appeared so colourfully on the jacket of *Strand Magazine*.

During the working day, I divided my time between Long Acre and the British Museum. The encyclopaedia having been finished and published, I had been asked to write the English language and literature portion of a popular-educator reference work that Jacks were then preparing. After completing it, and fearful of losing my job, I did the mathematics section. Then I took on the section on drawing, with my own illustrations, which fortunately never saw the light of a bookseller's shop, for O'Neill wisely decided to cut out that subject. At last, nothing remained for me to write, and I found myself unemployed. I was worried. The one thing I did not want to do was to return to Scotland and – the only possible job there – teaching.

One night, I woke up with a sharp pain in my leg. It was diagnosed as phlebitis – inflammation of a vein. I was alarmed because I knew that such inflammation caused a clot and that if even a tiny fragment of this clot broke away there was a chance of very sudden death. The surgeon at King Edward Hospital ligatured my vein, so that the clot could not move, and I lay in bed for about a fortnight, having the time of my life.

After my recovery I returned to town and answered various ads. One ran: 'Art editor wanted for new magazine in Fleet Street', and gave a box number for reply. Obviously, this was no job for me, but having nothing to lose, I sat down and wrote an application letter, frivolous in tone. My surprise, a few mornings later, when I got a reply asking me to come and see the editor of *Piccadilly Magazine*, 40 Fleet Street, was mixed with trepidation; I knew nothing about art. I went, however, and was interviewed.

Vincent, the editor, took up two letters. 'That one,' he said, 'is from a man who has been on a well-known magazine for ten years as art editor. This one is from the art editor of another well-known magazine, where he has been for twelve years.'

I swallowed hard.

'I am going to offer you the job,' he went on.

I gasped and said, 'In God's name, why?'

'Because,' he said, 'your letter was the only one that amused me. When can you start?'

I accepted his offer of one hundred and fifty pounds a year.

I really liked working on that newly formed magazine, even though, because of my leg, I spent my weekly salary on taxis. My job was to read short stories and hand on my choices to Vincent. If he approved, I had to find the right illustrator for the story: Balliol Salmond, if it was a yarn about a girl in a boat; someone else for a story with shooting; Harry Rountree for animals. When returning a serial to H. G. Wells's agent as unsuitable, I felt myself grow inches higher.

The *Piccadilly Magazine*'s first issue had been scheduled for the end of August 1914. One of the articles, well illustrated with photographs, was entitled 'The Real German Danger – the Crown Prince', but the shot at Sarajevo killed, among other things, the budding *Piccadilly Magazine*. It never appeared.

I was staying with a friend when war was declared, and still remember how the two of us – both socialists – sat up talking about it while the Life Guards nearby cheered all night long. My friend said tensely, 'Oh, the fools, the bloody damn fools. Can't they see it means their death and the death of most things we love?'

I went home to Kingsmuir perturbed in mind. I felt that I really should join up, preferring the artillery because of my bad feet. On the other hand, supporting my cowardice, was the statement of two doctors that I wasn't fit. After a few weeks, I applied for and got the job of temporary headmaster at Gretna Green school. When I arrived there, I found that the permanent head, a hefty he-man, was serving with the King's Own Scottish Borderers, but I did not feel too bad about the situation. My bad leg was swollen and numb, rather than painful, and I think now that the condition must have been, in modern parlance, psychological – my protection against joining the army.

The story of my stay in Gretna Green was told, more or less truly, in my first book, *A Dominie's Log*. But its sequel, *A Dominie Dismissed*, was pure fiction, written during my army service later.

Coming from Fleet Street to a slow village required some adaptation. I had lodgings in a small cottage, and when my landlady brought in the paraffin lamp of an evening and drew the blind of the small window, I felt that I was separated from the whole world. It was characteristic of this gulf separating Gretna from London that she frowned on the use of typewriters on Sundays. I think I began to write books to keep myself from going barmy.

It seems ludicrous that a man who is known as an educational heretic should have taken to this profession merely because journalism and his military courage failed him. Yet I began to think about education for the first time in Gretna. My predecessor had been a disciplinarian, and I arrived to find a silent, obedient school; but I knew that the bigger lads were watching me carefully to see how far they could go. I put on my severest look and glared at them; and on the second day, when the biggest of them tried me out with a semi-insolent answer, I gave him a leathering with the strap. I was still governed by the old dictum of the teaching profession: show you are master at once.

It would be silly to say I could have gone on as a disciplinarian if I had tried, for I couldn't will myself to do that. Gradually, the children discovered that my discipline was a bluff, that I really didn't care if they learned or not. The silent school became a beer garden, full of noise and laughter. But we carried on the usual lessons, and I suppose they learned as much as they would have if they had been afraid of me. Either way, it seemed to me such a futile waste to teach the geography of India to children who were going out to the farms.

The school board did not care very much what I was doing, but some of its members, as individuals, became friends of mine; Stafford, the minister, Dick MacDougall, the board clerk, and their wives, were kind to me. According to general opinion among the villagers, I was quite a nice chap but, of course, half daft. To my horror, I found myself fast becoming countrified – narrow, interested in local gossip, craning my neck to see where the doctor was going. I tried to keep in touch with larger affairs by having the *Nation* and the *New Age* sent weekly by post.

One sunny May morning, a terrible troop-train disaster took place a field's breadth from my lodgings. When my landlady woke me and told me there had been a smash, I jumped on my cycle and went off. The scene resembled a silent film. The only sounds were the hissing of engines and the pops of cartridges as fire crept along the wreckage. Men were lying dead or dying; one soldier with both legs torn off asked me for a cigarette, and he grinned as I lit it for him. 'May as well lose them here as in France,' he said lightly. He died before the cigarette was half smoked.

To me, the whole affair seemed unreal, like a dream. I joined a party that was trying to free a man from under an engine. As we worked, another man said to me, 'They expect the engine to explode any second.' But after an uneasy glance at the hissing steam, I thought no more about it. The quietness of that morning was unbelievable. Hardly a man groaned, and when the dying men called aloud, it was always for their mothers. Women and children were among the injured, but no cries or sobbing seemed to come from them. It was said that the officers shot some of the men who were hopelessly pinned under the blazing wreckage. I never knew if the story was true, but hoped it was.

What impressed me so strongly that morning was my lack of any emotion at all, even pity. To be fair to myself, of course, I was busy all the time doing things for the wounded. I felt uncomfortable about this, however, and late at night, sitting in the minister's house, I said to him, 'I must be the greatest egoist God ever made: nothing to give anyone, selfish to the core. This morning in that field I had not the tiniest suspicion of any feeling. I was just a stone of indifference.'

Stafford stared at me with open eyes. 'I was just about to say the same thing to you. I thought I was a monster because I felt nothing.' We apparently had assumed the attitude that doctors and nurses have. Just as a person's fear changes into positive energy when rowing a boat in a bad swell, so he can absorb terror and pity while assisting others in pain. And one cannot feel deeply for complete strangers.

Contrariwise, I recall how one of my pupils – a boy – was killed that morning, run down by a motor cycle on his way to the disaster. His mother asked me to go and see his body that night, and I felt a real grief. I also felt keenly the plight of the signalman whose mistake had caused the accident; I had his sons in school and liked them, as well as their father. To me, imprisoning him was only one of the many signs of barbarity in our legal code.

It is difficult to return even in fantasy to my Gretna days. I have motored through the village at least once a year but have stopped there only once – and regretted it. Dimly I recall pleasant tea parties with my assistants, May and Christine and Bell, the bustle and chaos of the building of the great munition works, and the transformation of a dull hamlet into a township with cinema and shops.

I went off one Saturday to Dumfries to join the army. I know that I had no real wish to be a soldier, but something must have influenced me; either a bad conscience after a friend had been killed or, just as likely, an order that all men should be examined under the Derby Scheme. I was rejected because of my leg, and given a certificate stating that I was permanently unfit for service. Just as I left the building, however, a sergeant asked me if I had joined the Derby Scheme. I told him that I did not need to, because

I had been rejected. 'But,' he said, 'you get half a crown if you join.' When I asked him how, he took me to an officer, before whom I swore that I would serve 'my King and Country' when called upon to do so. The sergeant got half a crown from me for his pains. Later, when all rejected men were ordered to be re-examined and I was passed as fit, I should have had the disgrace of being drafted, if that sergeant hadn't had a thirst on him and an eye to the main chance.

The Army

In the early spring of 1917, all medically rejected men were ordered to report for re-examination. I was passed A1 by a doctor I had known at the university. This was in Dumfries, and the recruits were sent off the same night to Berwick-upon-Tweed. There we were asked what regiment we wanted to go into. Thinking of my feet, I said the artillery. The sergeant gave me a look.

'Artillery!' – he laughed nastily. 'Hi, youse blokes, here's a guy as wants to join the artillery!' Then to me, he snapped, 'You have two choices, King's Own Scottish Borderers or the Royal Scots Fusiliers.'

I asked where the training camps were situated.

'KOSB, Catterick; RSF, Greenock.'

I chose the RSF simply because Glasgow was nearer to the people I knew. I was given a pass and set off to Ayr, the RSF recruiting base. One other recruit had chosen the RSF, and he advised me to take two days' leave, without asking, before I reported. I was afraid to, but when I got to the barracks in Ayr and found that nobody expected me – the sergeant in fact was annoyed at my turning up on a Saturday night – I much regretted not having taken the man's advice. By this time, my heart was in my boots: I was a walking misery. The incivility and arrogance of the non-commissioned officers with whom I had come in contact, together with the prison appearance of the barracks, gave me a hate of the army that has never left me. I was given a mattress, told to fill it with straw, and then, with other recruits, had to do some fatigue – carrying beds.

My chief associations with the RSF are two; feet and fear. My feet have always been tender and, even today, when I have my shoes specially made, my toes blister if I walk far on a hot day. For years I had worn only shoes, and after an hour's drill in army boots, my ankles were raw flesh. I reported sick again and again, and usually had some dressing put on, but the doctors never seemed to think rest was necessary. I had to go on parade again every time.

I cannot recollect any fear of going to France. I knew that we were supposed to have a few months' training and then go out automatically in drafts, to replace casualties. Strangely enough, that didn't worry me; my fear was attached to the lance-corporal who made my life a hell for weeks. For some reason, he disliked me at sight, and after parades, when there was any fatigue to do, he always chose me, usually addressing me as 'youse big bastard'. He was a cab-driver in civilian life, they said.

One day, while giving out our letters, he stopped and peered at an envelope. 'Jesus Christ, who the hell's this?' he asked. '"A. S. Neill, Esq., MA, author of *A Dominie's Log*." What the hell . . .?' I modestly held up my hand. His mouth opened. 'You an MA?' he gasped. 'My Christ!' The sequel was astonishing. He never gave me fatigue again, never bullied me. On the contrary, he treated me as if I were the colonel himself. Later, I was to find other NCOs who confessed to a great feeling of inferiority when I was in their squads: they were ashamed of their lack of grammar.

We slept twenty men and an NCO to an army hut. Many of the men, who came mostly from Glasgow, were 'Glesga keelies', rough diamonds of the slums. They were fine, friendly lads, always kind to each other, usually cheerful. To them, the army food I found almost uneatable was the best food they had ever had; to them, army discipline seemed not much worse than the discipline of the factory. Their language was almost completely sexual, everything – food, parades, sergeants – described as 'fucking'. They discussed openly the most intimate details of the anatomies of their wives and sweethearts.

Life in the army seemed like one continuous rush: we never had time to do anything properly, even shaving. Worst of all was the duty of mess orderly for the day. One waited in a queue for meals to be carried to the huts. Then one had to wash up after the meal and be spotless for the next parade, with the rifle clean, buttons and boots shining. Behind all this rush was the dread of being late for parade; that was a crime. But one would be 'crimed' for many things – being unshaved, having dirty buttons, unpolished buckles, unwhitened braid. To be crimed was to be given pack drill with full equipment, doubling up and down the square till exhausted.

I managed to avoid being crimed except once. My rifle, a modern one that I cared for as tenderly as a child, had been taken from me and I was given an old-fashioned Lee-Enfield instead. At rifle inspection, the officer crimed me for having a dirty rifle. I went to my sergeant and told him I had spent an hour trying to clean the thing, but the dirt was ingrained. He took me to see the sergeant in charge of musketry, who examined the rifle. 'Nobody could ever clean it,' he pronounced. I don't know what went on behind the scenes, but my name was taken off the crime list.

This incident was exceptional. Generally, one had no redress, and it was this feeling of absolute powerlessness that kept me in the depths. Any corporal could crime you, and you dared not say a word. Theoretically you could, but we all knew that any complaint about a superior officer made you a marked man, and you would get it in the neck ever after. Old soldiers always pleaded guilty without defence, whether justly charged or not.

Hated duties could not be evaded. As a system, the discipline was mistake-proof. You had to be somewhere. If you went sick, your name appeared on the sick list; if you were doing fatigues, your squad sergeant had a note of it. The only man I knew who dodged the system effectively for six weeks was a youth who had been transferred from one squad to another. When he joined his new squad, he found that his name wasn't on the roll; they had forgotten to transfer it. He gave up going on parade. Every morning, he walked out of camp with belt and cane, a large envelope in his hand marked OHMS. When he was finally found out, nothing happened to him, because the NCOs who had left his name off the roll knew that they were 'for it' if they reported him.

My feet were giving me hell. Every night I soaked them in cold water, and every morning I soaped my socks, but the blisters came as before. I was limping during square drill when a major came along. He told me to fall out and asked what was wrong. I told him. He said I should report sick, and I told him it was useless, for they would only send me on parade again. He then ordered me to take off my boots and show him my feet. 'You go back to your hut and rest,' he said. 'By the way, what are you in civil life?'

Two nights later, while I sat tending my feet in the hut as usual, the orderly sergeant came round.

'Neill here? Wanted at the Company bunk.'

I trembled. Wanted at Company headquarters generally meant being put on the mat. I thought of all my crimes, dodging church parade every Sunday, overstaying my leave – there were enough of them – and reported in trepidation. The major who had ordered me to rest sat writing at a table. I saluted and waited at attention. By this time, I was certain that because of my bad feet he would offer me a job clerking in the office. Finally he looked up.

'Know anything about mathematics?' he barked.

'Yes, sir, I wrote a book on mathematics.'

'Oh! You seem to be the very man we want.' He lifted a document. 'I have here a form from the War Office saying they need men of mathematical knowledge as officers in the artillery. I shall put your name forward.'

I was then transferred to the Cadet Corps at Fort Matilda. All sixteen of us had special drill. We were supposed to show the regiment how the best soldiers perform, and our training was modelled on that of the Guards. When slapping our rifle butts in presenting arms, we almost made our hands bleed. We had lectures in huts and out on the hill, and my feet got a chance to recover. My pet aversion was bayonet fighting. We were told to regard the sacks as Huns who had just raped our sisters, and were instructed to stab them with fitting fierceness.

One day, in company orders, there arrived a command that 32703 Private Neill report to Trowbridge Cadet School, Wiltshire. After Fort Matilda, Trowbridge seemed like heaven. Discipline was easy and polished buttons did not seem to matter much. The whole section, including the officer in charge, burst into laughter when I marched with the Guards' swing-of-arm, up to the shoulder; and I was ordered to cut out that swank stuff. Then the section laughed at my cleaning my boots before afternoon parade. Tut, tut, I thought, a pleasant place, but, oh, what soldiers!

For the first time in my army career, the work was interesting to me. We studied map-reading, maths, and laying out lines of fire, and had gun drill with six-inch howitzers. We did much with an instrument called a No. 5 Director, and all of us used the prismatic compass. The other fellows were nearer my level than the men of the RSF, many having been clerks and teachers, and we had some jolly times together.

I had one degrading experience at Trowbridge, involving a major who lectured on bracketing, a most complicated study of range distances in firing practice. He was not a good lecturer, and his voice must have put me on the verge of sleep. Suddenly I started, for he was looking at me and, in an angry voice, was ordering me to the blackboard to explain what bracketing was. I had not the faintest idea; of course I could not say so, but proved my complete ignorance by standing there like an ass with a bit of chalk in my hand. By this time he was livid and red.

'Why brainless idiots like you get to cadet schools is more than I can understand. I don't blame you – you can't help your stupidity; I blame the system that sends you up here. Have you had no education?'

I hung my head.

'Answer me. Where were you educated?'

'Edinburgh University,' I said humbly. A titter round the room was nipped off by the glare of the officer. He never spoke to me again.

Our term ended, we passed our exit exams, and in front of us was Lydd – the real thing, the nightmare lying ahead of a pleasant dream. Trowbridge had been like a university, easy and academic. But Lydd was officered by men just back from the front with no sympathy for the academic in anything. Our three weeks in Lydd were one continuous grind, and we discovered that anything we had learned at Trowbridge was of no value there. Laying out a line of fire no longer suggested a leisurely problem in maths; it was a thing to be done in ten seconds with a slide rule. The men at Lydd knew their jobs and put the wind up us all, for failure meant not only the disgrace of being returned to Trowbridge for a month or two, but also being put into a section of new men. No, that probability we dared not face, so we slaved.

The major at Lydd who taught the bracketing was a fearful man, and we had been warned about him long before we came up. When we were using real shells for the first time, he took us one by one to the observation post. There we all watched the burst of a shell, and had to know at once which directions to telephone to the gunner for his next shot. The major kept firing questions at us, and when we made mistakes – as we did, mainly through fear of him – he called us everything he knew.

We all passed, however, and were duly notified that we had received commissions in the Royal Artillery. After our ten days' leave to collect uniforms and kits, I was posted to an officers' 'pool' in Aldershot, saddened to find that most of my pals had been posted to Farnborough. Our pool consisted of about sixty officers waiting to be sent to France. The life was pleasant enough. I remember clearly the night I arrived, being saluted by the sergeant-major. How hard to believe that I would never again fear an NCO! I had a bitter feeling when I thought of our good food and comforts, and compared them with the food and lack of privacy I had as a non-com. Officers and privates lived poles apart in every way; the old distinction was still there – Eton at one end and slums at the other. The officer planned; the private had no need to think, only to clean with spit and polish.

I had a batman, an independent sort of fellow from Lancashire. He was an active socialist, he said, and to hell with it anyway – what was a bloody officer but the servant of capitalism? So my orderly lay on my bed, smoking my cigarettes, while I polished my leggings and boots for the morrow. He kept assuring me that he bore me no personal grudge because I was an officer. He seemed a nice chap but a born pessimist, who swore that every league football match was faked – sold to the highest bidder – and offered to bring me written evidence if I liked.

Aldershot was a lazy life. We had lectures and occasionally exercises, but we all felt that these were just to keep us from getting too discontented. Every few days, a list of officers for the next draft would go up, but my name never appeared among them. Instead, I was told to attach myself to a training battery where my duties included giving lectures on lines of fire.

One day, I saw a gunner obviously paying no attention as I laboriously, and badly, tried to explain the mathematics of laying out a line of fire. To me, he seemed a stupid sort of fellow.

'Here, you,' I said, 'you don't seem to be taking any interest in what I am teaching. What are you in civil life?'

'I'm a maths master at a secondary school,' he said.

Rising to the occasion, I held out my chalk. 'For the Lord's sake, then, show them how this damn thing is done.'

And he showed them.

I kept hoping to be sent to France on a draft; not because I had miraculously acquired more courage, but simply because the other men were all out, or going out, and I felt left behind, like the lame boy in the Pied Piper story. Then an epidemic of influenza ran through the camp, and I went down with it. Mine was a bad attack, ending in neurasthenia. At Gretna Green, I had once been off work for a month with the same trouble, but this became worse – a complete nervous breakdown, with insomnia, and nightmares when I did fall asleep. In short, I was a dud as a soldier or anything else. The medical orderly worried about me – probably suspected me of being a mental case – and said he would send me up to a nerve specialist in town when I was fit to travel.

The specialist turned out to be Dr William H. Rivers, the famous anthropologist. I did not know anything about him, nor did I know anything about psychology. I recall being mildly surprised when he asked me to tell him a dream, and being more and more surprised at his evident interest while I told it. It was a dream about a snake I had killed that kept coming to life again. I had never heard of Freud then, but apparently Rivers had. Finally he said to me, 'If you go to France you will either win the Victoria Cross or be shot for running away. We won't risk it. I'll recommend that you give up your commission on grounds of ill health.'

So ended my inglorious career as a soldier. I must have cost the nation quite a lot of money, giving back little in duty or work. I realize now that my nervous breakdown was the method used by my unconscious to keep me from danger. On a conscious level, I seemed ready to go to the fighting front without any abnormal fear. In fact, I felt that as an officer it would be easier, because I would be leading men and would have to show them how to face danger.

In the army I had made one good friend. We were always together. A year after the war, we ran into each other in the Strand, delighted to meet again. We made a date to have dinner, and for half an hour we talked about old times: 'Remember Tubby? That morning when he hadn't shaved and the sergeant . . .' We laughed a bit. Then the conversation ceased, and we both realized that we had nothing more to say to each other. Army life had drawn us together because we had to concentrate on military things; in civilian life we hadn't an interest in common. It was a sad dinner party, and although we tried to make an artificial cheerfulness, and promised to meet again, we both knew in our hearts that we never could.

Years after the war, Walter Martin, another friend from the war years, said something to me that was unbelievable.

'Neill, I saved your life.'

'How?'

'I had a pull at the War Office and I arranged that you would not be sent to the front.'

I can scarcely believe this, but if it were so, it would explain why my name never appeared on the draft notices in the officers' pool. Walter died before I could ask him to tell me more, and I still doubt very much if any such influence could have exempted an individual soldier.

A Headmaster

After a long convalescence, I began to think of a job. Back in the Gretna Green period, a lady who was much involved with King Alfred's School in Hampstead had written to me, after having read my *Dominie's Log*, and when I went to see her she told me about Homer Lane, who had founded the unique Little Commonwealth reform camp for juvenile delinquents. She gave me a report of one of his lectures. She also introduced me to John Russell, the headmaster of King Alfred's.

While at the cadet school, I had learned that Lane's Little Commonwealth was in Dorset, not very far from Trowbridge. I wrote to him asking if I could come to see him, and, when he said I could, got weekend leave. Homer Lane was easily the most impressive personality I had met up to then. He told of his cases as I listened, entranced. His young delinquents charmed me, and I got Lane to promise to let me work at Little Commonwealth when I had finished army service.

My first act, when I felt fit enough, was to write to Lane, saying I could come. I got a reply telling me that the Commonwealth had been closed, and that Lane himself was in bad health in London. Disappointed, I thought I should try second best. I wrote to John Russell about a job, got one, and joined the staff of King Alfred's School.

J.R., as we called Russell, was a dear old man; I liked him from the first moment I saw him, and he liked me. Since Russell's beginning as a pioneer thirty years before, King Alfred's School had been regarded as the most advanced school of its kind. While perhaps not the first to practise coeducation, it did more to force the issue upon English opinion than any other school. Long before my time, it had done away with prizes and marks and corporal punishment.

I entered this famous school rather timidly with my very Scottish accent. My reputation as a mad Scots dominie had preceded me, and some of the pupils later told me that they had stared at me the first day, wondering if I were really mad or only a crank.

I liked the atmosphere of the school at once; its free and easy discipline took my heart. But I disliked the staffroom, and often have wondered why it was not a happier place than it was. It did not have the congenial atmosphere of the classrooms; although the staff members were friendly as individuals, they were collectively – what I called them then – bloody.

J.R. got me to ask Homer Lane to come and give the staff a few talks on psychology. Lane sat with a face like vinegar, and after the first talk, said to me, 'My God, Neill, what is wrong with that staff? It gives me the absolute jim-jams. It's full of hate.' In a way, I think that I may have been a fly in the ointment – the young whipper-snapper who had come to tell them how to run their school. Very properly, they put me in my place.

Fundamentally, the problem was J.R. himself. He was God, a lovable old God, but nevertheless God – and a moralist of great force. I first realized this when Patrick, aged eight, kissed Clare, aged seven. J.R. had a 'call-over' about it and spoke for nearly an hour. I came away feeling that kissing must be the main sin against the Holy Ghost.

There was something dead about the pupils; they lacked an interest in life. This seemed most obvious at meetings of former Alfredians, when the 'old boys', girls mostly, sat at the feet of J.R. or George Earle, an English master who served as second-in-command, and listened as if their one-time teachers had all the wisdom in the world.

I learned with mixed feelings that some of the big lads in the school had never heard the word 'shit', and did not know the ordinary swear-words, but that one or two of the girls knew them all. Dimly, I began to sense that I had come to a school whose life attitudes were fundamentally and essentially those which had damned my own life in Scotland – moral standards from without. King Alfred's School was far from being free, and very soon I found myself 'agin the government'.

I had begun to be analysed by Lane and became a frequent visitor to his home. What he said about freedom was the gospel I had been looking for; a scientific foundation for the vague yearnings shown forth in my *Dominie's Log*. Thus it came about that I began to try to 'improve' King Alfred's School in staff meetings. The school wasn't moving with the times, I complained. It should have self-government. Dear old J.R. spread his hands and said, with his usual smile, 'Go on, Neill. Try it. Try it.'

I tried it. The classes changed from one room to another at the ringing of the lessons bell. Thus the Betas would have maths the first period, say, and then come to me when the bell rang. Naturally, all self-government meant to them was a chance to let off steam in my room for an hour. They made a hell of a row, and the teachers in neighbouring rooms got annoyed. At the next staff meeting, they all said it was obvious, of course, that self-government didn't work. It didn't, but it certainly 'played'. The day came when J.R. came to me very perplexed and very sad, and said, 'One of us has to resign, Neill, either you or I.'

I said, 'Me, J.R.; you've been here longer than I have.' Once more I was unemployed.

His name has disappeared from books on education, but in his day he was a pioneer. We differed. He was a moralist but I was very fond of him and, in spite of my rebellion, I think he liked me.

When I had to leave King Alfred's School I was genuinely anxious. I saw no future for myself. True, I might get a job as English teacher in a Scots school, but London had gripped me, and I didn't want to leave it. Mrs Beatrice Ensor stepped in and offered me the job of jointly editing *The New Era* with her. I took up my duties in Tavistock Square, sharing a room with her husband, a non-smoker who hated my smoking all day at work. The Ensors were theosophists.

It was good fun having a paper to edit. Mrs Ensor gave me a free hand to say anything I liked, and I soon saw that the more outrageously I attacked pedants and schools the more delighted she was. Some people found her rather a forbidding person, but I liked her and ragged her most of the time about her theosophical higher-life complex. She was a born organizer, and it was through her that I went to Holland to meet the Austrian children who came to England after the war.

The New Era was no abiding city: I knew that I must move on. In 1921 luck brought me an invitation to take part in a new Educational Fellowship Conference in Calais, and another to go on from there to Salzburg to lecture to an international conference of women. From Salzburg, I went on to Hellerau, a suburb of Dresden, to stay with Dr Otto Neustatter and Frau Doktor Neustatter, who later became my first wife. Together with Karl Baer, an architect, and his American wife Christine we founded the Internationalschule, Hellerau.

Living in Germany gave me much that living at home could not give me. For one thing I lived for nearly three years in an atmosphere of rhythm and dance, of great opera and orchestral music. My stay in Hellerau was the most exciting period of my life. For the first time I mixed with European nationals. I knew not a word of German. When I took out my first English pupil, Derrick, aged eight, I was trying to learn German from the Hugo tutor. In three weeks Derrick was not only talking German; he was speaking Saxon dialect. (I notice that today my German pupils are talking English in a few weeks and if I speak to one in German he or she replies in English.)

Our International School had three divisions – eurythmics, my foreign division, and the German school, which was part day and part boarding. I have told in earlier books of my quarrels with the German teachers over education. They were benevolent moulders of character while I was the opposite. My period in Hellerau gave me a *Weltanschauung*, a world view, and in a way it killed any tendency I had towards nationalism. And it humbled me. Here was I with my Hons. English degree, having to sit silent when the talk was of art and music and philosophy. I felt uneducated and, indeed, would feel the same today, for my ignorance of many subjects is abysmal – meaning that a specialized university education is no education at all.

I was not allowed by the Ministry to teach Germans and my division consisted of English, Norwegians, Belgians and Yugoslavs. I wasn't even allowed to teach English to the German division because I had not taken my degree in a German university. I had to appoint a German woman whose pronunciation was terrible. She kept arguing with me about accent, and when an Irish visitor came with a brogue you could cut with a knife, she cried, '*Wunderbar*; das is the proper Oxford accent.'

In 1923 revolution broke out in Saxony. Shots were fired on the Dresden streets. Our school was emptying. The dance division went to Schloss Laxenburg near Vienna and I took my division to the top of a mountain at the edge of the Tyrol, four hours' train journey from Vienna. It was an old monastery and beside it was a church of pilgrimage.

The church had stone saints all around and when the pilgrims came from all over Catholic Europe our English pupils used to give the saints haloes by shining broken mirrors at them. There was much crossing of themselves by visitors and, when the children's trick was discovered, I wondered why we were not lynched, for the peasants were the most hateful people I ever came across. Few had ever seen a foreigner and the fact that we were heathens was enough to kindle their hatred of us. A German girl of nine sunbathed in a bathing-costume, and we had a policeman up next day saying the village was shocked and angry.

Farmers and their wives threw broken bottles into the pond we bathed in. The climax came when I was summoned to the Education Ministry in Vienna.

'Herr Neill, do you teach religion?'

'No.'

The official took down a hefty volume and read out a law: every Austrian school must teach religion. I explained that I had no Austrian children, but that was no excuse; the law must be obeyed. So in late 1924 I took my little group to England.

Late in the year I rented a house in Lyme Regis, Dorset. It was called Summerhill and stood on the hill going to Charmouth. Lyme was and is a place mostly for retired people, a class-conscious little town. We were outsiders; our dirty little youngsters were looked at down upper-class noses. But one day a Rolls-Royce with a crest on it drove up; the Earl of Sandwich, one of the founders of the Little Commonwealth, had come to visit us for a few days. Then people bowed to us.

We had only five pupils, three paying half fees, two paying nothing. My first wife and I (by this time I had married Frau Doktor Neustatter) would stand looking at an ironmonger's window wondering if we could afford a spade. Because Lyme was a holiday resort we turned the school into a boarding-house in the school holidays and managed to make ends meet.

Bertrand Russell was thinking of setting up his own school with his wife Dora. He came and spent a week with us and we all liked his wit and humour. One starry night he and I went for a walk.

'Russell,' I said, 'the difference between us is this; if we had a boy with us now you would want to tell him about the stars while I would leave him to his own thoughts.' He laughed when I added, 'Maybe I say that because I know damn all about the stars anyway.'

I was not happy in Lyme. The air was so relaxing that walking up the hilly streets was an effort. When we moved to Suffolk the kids' appetite doubled. Our staff was small: George Corkhill taught science, 'Jonesie', who had joined us in Austria, taught maths, and my wife was matron. Then, as now, we got too many problem children, misfits that other schools did not want. It was a stirring time and, because they were so interesting, the problem children gave us more joy than sorrow. One girl, who later became the golf champion of half a dozen countries, had been accustomed to making her parents and teachers angry at her defiance. She decided to take me on. She kicked me for an hour but, in spite of the pain, I refused to react. Finally, she burst into tears, and I expect learned the hard way that her attempts to take the micky out of adults did not always succeed.

At that stage I was a proper fool. I thought that psychology could cure everything barring a broken leg, and I took on children who had been injured at birth, mentally deficient boys and girls. Of course I soon found that I could do nothing to cure them.

When the three-year lease was up we had twenty-seven pupils and could not house them. I bought an old Morris car and set off along the south coast to find a house. I saw some beauties at £50,000 each. Then I went up the east coast and the last house on my list was Newhaven in the small town of Leiston, Suffolk. It was only £3,250, a sum I had not got, but I bought it on a mortgage. I brought the name Summerhill with me and in all these years not one visitor has asked me the reason for the name, although the place is dead flat.

When the Second World War broke out we stayed on in Summerhill during the phoney war period, but after Dunkirk, when we expected invasion, we had to move. We found a big house in Ffestiniog in north Wales; it was dilapidated and local boys had smashed all the lavatories and most of the windows. We were there for five years, the longest years of my life. It rained and rained. I had to give up my car and queue for buses. All around us were

Welsh-speaking people; some of the old people knew no English. I had returned to the atmosphere of my native Scottish village. Chapels and hymns were everywhere, with their accompanying hypocrisy. Shortly after we arrived there one of our bright boys was accidentally drowned, and later my wife had a stroke – her speech went and her mind became confused. She died in a hospital in 1944. No wonder Ffestiniog was a misery to me.

In Wales the house was smaller than in Leiston and we had a hundred on the waiting-list. We couldn't find a bigger house and I had to refuse kids daily. Welsh tradesmen would never come to do a job. The house needed many repairs, the central heating was not working, the hot-water boiler a dud, and no one would come to mend them. We had two months without electric light. Fruit was almost unobtainable, coal and coke only rumours. I had to mend doors, stoke fires, teach maths, cater, and worst of all interview all the damned officials who still thought in peace-time terms. The medical officer of health, an old man, objected because we were overcrowded, and evaded my query as to what he would do about the thousands of kids who had bad air in shelters and tubes.

In Wales I found the staff business hopeless. I had a run of pacifists who were no good at all, all negative, in the clouds, and wanting to tell me how to run the school on Jesus lines. I missed the contacts of old.

At the beginning and end of term the children had a long weary train journey to London from Wales. We were lucky; not once did our pupils get blitzed. But the school was not really Summerhill. Parents sent their children, not to be free, but to be safe, and when peace came those parents withdrew their kids. We were over-crowded. Food was rationed and tobacco was difficult to buy. The pubs closed at 9 p.m. as against 10.30 p.m. in England. Our boys had a perpetual war with the village boys, who were most aggressive in spite of, or perhaps because of, all the chapel-going.

Maybe the most joyous day of my life was the day when I returned to Leiston in 1945 after the disastrous interlude in Wales. The school building was in a bad way. The army had had it for five years and had done more damage in that time than my kids had done in thirteen years, but it did not seem to matter. We were home at dear old Summerhill. We gladly sat and slept on mattresses on the floor until our furniture began to come from Wales about ten days later.

I never regretted coming to Leiston. The air is bracing and the eleven acres are a paradise for kids. I am often asked what the town thinks of us and never know the answer. My staff and I frequent the local pubs – I have never seen a state teacher there, or for that matter a doctor or lawyer, but Summerhill, having no class, belongs to all classes. I don't think the town understands what it is all about, but the people are friendly. One youth of about seventeen hung about our gates for a time, and when I asked him what he wanted he replied, 'A free fuck.' But I don't say he was typical of Leiston inhabitants.

I am 'Neill' without any 'mister' to some of the workmen as I am to staff, domestics, pupils. No one touches his hat to me and some locals may wonder what the crowds of world visitors come to see. I was a member of a local golf club for twenty-five years and I think that only one member knew who I was – the school doctor.

Heroes and Sources

I disclaim any originality in thought. Indeed, if I have any merit it is that I have a flair for spotting the people who matter. I learned a tremendous lot from Homer Lane and, incidentally, point out that I have always acknowledged my debt to him. I discovered Wilhelm Stekel, the psychoanalyst, round about 1923 and our friendship lasted till his death, but his work was curative, and I was gradually drifting away from the therapy side of psychology. I transferred my interest to a later discovery, Wilhelm Reich, who, while doing therapy in a new way, was tackling the much greater question of the analysis of society. I think of all the people who have had an influence on my work, Lane and Reich stand out most prominently.

It is impossible, however, to say what influences condition the life of any man; we gather a million ideas and attitudes, which mostly become unconscious. These may suddenly appear as a new idea or principle after the unconscious has digested them and strung them together. In the early days I read Edmond Holmes's *What Is and What Might Be*, Caldwell Cook's *Playway*, Norman MacMunn's *Path to Freedom in the School*. I fancy that they did not influence me much – they were too much confined to the school, to methods of teaching; for the same reason, Montessori also left me cold.

No, I found my inspirations outside the teaching fraternity, in Freud, Reich, Lane, Wells, Shaw, and, of course, Christ. I admit that last influence with difficulty, owing to my early 'religious' training which made him a god instead of a most human human. All I have gained from the general picture is a vision of the man Jesus, a man giving love, asking none in exchange. He also had charity, condemning no one if we except the money-changers, and there his reaction only showed how human he was. Sin to him appeared to be sickness; he apparently was conscious of man's unconscious two thousand years before Freud was born. He did not have to resist temptation because within himself he did not feel guilty.

As well as finding most educational writers dull I find most educational papers dull. A daydream of mine has been to run an educational journal that would cut out all mention of classes, salaries, pensions, inspectors, and school subjects. A journal that would be full of brightness and humour. There is far too little humour in our schools and certainly in our educational journals. While I say this I know that humour can have its dangers. Some men use humour to cover up more serious matters in life, for it is easy to laugh something off instead of facing it.

For instance, I never could stomach the wit of Gilbert in the Gilbert and Sullivan operas. To me it was shallow and cynical. In the *Self Educator* I wrote: 'Gilbert's wit is based on a superficial view of society . . . Shaw, on the other hand, thinks society rotten at the core.'

I quote this not because Gilbert is of any importance, but because it reminds me that at the age of twenty-nine I was already beginning to form values about what mattered in life. Gilbert ragged society while he approved of it; George Bernard Shaw disapproved of it and I was on the side of Shaw. That may have been the beginning of my challenge to life. It was at that age that Shaw and H. G. Wells were my favourite writers; possibly they had more influence on my career than all the later psychologists had.

And yet, in hindsight, Wells always disappointed. He would labour a theme such as the planlessness of the planners, and I kept looking for the solution that never appeared. When a solution came it was not solution at all, as in *The Shape of Things to Come*, where, after a terrible war, the world was saved by a group of scientists. I wonder what Wells would have made of the scientists today, with their pollution and H-bombs and the ruin of natural life, plants and animals.

Shaw had no solution either. His brilliant analysis of society led to no promise of a new society. It must have been their analysis without synthesis that made me lose interest in Shaw and Wells. They dated themselves; neither accepted the dynamic psychology of Freud.

Wells, the hero of my youth, I met when he was an old man, and my dream was shattered; a little man with a squeaky voice and an arrogant manner.

A hero who did not disappoint was Henry Miller. Someone had sent him one or two of my books and Henry wrote to me and we kept up a desultory correspondence for some years. Then he came to London and we had lunch together. I loved Henry, so warm, so humorous, so obviously genuine. I have often sighed to think that thousands of miles separate us.

I never met J. M. Barrie. He was my youthful hero until I came under the spell of Wells. Our birthplaces were only eight miles apart. He went to Edinburgh University and so did I. He was a famous writer; I also would be a famous writer. It was a clear case of identification. I read and reread his *Sentimental Tommy* and his *Peter Pan*.

My discipleship came to a sudden end when I read that tremendous counterblast to Scottish sentimentality, *The House with the Green Shutters*. Nearly seventy years ago when we young lads and lasses were reading the Scottish novels of the times, George Douglas Brown's book came like a lightning stroke. Its stark realism and its wonderful word painting possibly made Barrie and Ian McLaren and Crockett unreadable for all time. I now saw Barrie as a minor writer with only flashes of insight and humour. *The House* became my Bible; I knew it almost by heart.

I am humbled by Brown's descriptions: 'He was a great fellow, my friend Will; the thumb mark of his Maker was wet in the clay of him.' Gourlay had a chest 'like the heave of a hill'. His anger 'struck life like a black frost'. I still long to be able to write with the word picturing of Douglas Brown but I am sane enough to laugh and accept the truth that it isn't my line.

George Douglas Brown was a great writer and a sincere and potent observer. It is not only in literary style that he can be great. His characters are live, hateful, sting-wasps for the most part, but they are starkly alive. With the exception of the baker they are all either malicious or miserable. The women are sluts or mortally diseased. His village of Barbie is a little hell of hate and spite and malevolent gossip; Brown's radiant word-making does not ever lift the gloom from the situation. Brown wrote one book of genius, a novel that will live as one of Scotland's finest pieces of literature. Probably even if he had not died young he would have remained a one-book man.

I decided to write Brown's life, and via letters to the press I got much material. Alas, it was mostly dull, peddling stuff. I could find no highlights in his life and gave up my project, sending all my material to James Veitch, the Scots novelist, who wrote it instead. But I gained a sweet experience. I visited Brown's friend in Glasgow, then an old woman, very deaf, and fell in love with her. I half think that she was too good for the rather dour Geordie. She was anxious that the life should be written by me and was disappointed that it wasn't.

A few years later I called to see her again and found a boarded-up house for sale. A neighbour told me the dear old lady had died a year before. I have her letters to me, and am sending them to the National Library of Scotland with the proviso that they cannot be shown to the public for twenty years. This in case her relatives might object to their publication. I know they will be placed in the Douglas Brown file with its manuscript of the *House* in penny exercise-books. I used to read them every time I went to Edinburgh.

At another period of my life, in Vienna, I became a patient of Dr Wilhelm Stekel, one of the Freudian school who, like Jung and Adler, broke away from it. I had reviewed a book of his that claimed that analysis was too expensive and too long: Stekel said that an analysis should not take longer than three months, a statement that appealed to my Scottish thrift. Stekel was a brilliant symbolist. He hardly ever asked for an association to a dream. 'Ach, Neill, this dream shows that you are still in lof with your sister.' I cannot recall having had any emotional response to anything Stekel said, it touched my head but never my emotions. I don't think I got a transference to him. Maybe because he was boyish in some ways.

'Neill, your dream shows that you are in lof with my wife.'

'But Stekel, I like your wife but she has no sexual attraction for me.'

He flared up angrily. 'Vot, you do not admire my vife? That is to her an insult. She is admired by many men.'

Another time I asked him if I could use his toilet. When I returned he looked at me in an arch fashion and pointed a finger.

'Ach so! Der Neill wants to be Wilhelm Stekel, the king; he vants to sit on his throne! Naughty Neill.' My explanation that I had diarrhoea he brushed aside with a laugh.

Stekel was one of the great authorities on symbolism; his dream analysis of symbols was fascinating, but I wonder how much it did for his patients.

Stekel used to tell us of a party he went to at an artist's flat. The talk turned to symbolism and Stekel gave his contribution. His host would not have it.

'Nonsense, Stekel, I don't accept a word of it.' He pointed to a picture on the wall. 'Mean to say there is symbolism in that still life I painted?'

Stekel put on his glasses. 'Yes, there is.'

'What sort of symbolism?'

'Ah,' said Stekel, 'I couldn't tell you in public.'

'Nonsense,' cried the artist. 'We're all friends here. Out with it.'

'All right. When you painted that picture you had just seduced a servant girl; she was pregnant and you were looking for an abortionist.'

The artist went white.

'Mein Gott!' he cried.

I asked Stekel how he came to it.

'The picture was of a dining-table. A bottle of port had spilled over – the blood [the abortion]; a sausage on a plate was exactly like a foetus.' But how he got the servant girl I cannot recollect.

Interpreting symbolism is like a crossword, a pleasant game. I feel sure that it never helped a patient, and I guess that many analysts have stopped using it.

Stekel's *A Primer for Mothers* has much non-technical sense in it; in particular, it is full of sane advice about the dangers of prohibiting masturbation at all ages. I disagree with him when he writes, 'Pay no attention to the child at night, regardless of how he screams, unless he is wet and his diapers need to be changed.' I feel that Stekel over-emphasizes the struggle for power that every child indulges in. The danger of any book is that the reader will accept it wholly (or, of course, reject it *in toto*). Any observant mother knows when a night scream is a power one, and she reacts accordingly.

The best book on babies I have come across is an American one, *Baby and Child Care*, by Benjamin Spock, MD. It is nearer to self-regulation than any book I have seen.

Sage Bernal was a scientist with a great imagination. He used to give our pupils talks. He told them that one day the North Sea would be drained and made into arable land; he foresaw the population explosion thirty years ago and pictured the continuation of human life on satellites. During the war Churchill thought highly of him. His first job was to examine unexploded bombs, and the tale went that he arrived at a field with a large crater bounded by barbed wire.

'Sorry, sir,' said the sergeant at the entrance, 'but no one can come in here until a big bug from London sees the bomb.' Sage, never thinking that he was the big bug, went away.

I asked Sage if the story were true.

'Not quite; I crept under the wire when the sergeant was looking the other way.'

He did not seem to know what fear was. When I asked him if he had ever been afraid in his dangerous job, he answered, 'Once, when a bomb began to make a ticking noise, I was so scared that I jumped back a yard.'

He was Sage because he always had an answer, but when I asked him why a razor on a hone sharpened better when the hone was oiled, he shook his head and said he had no idea. I wish I could have seen him dressed in naval uniform commanding a landing ship in the D-Day invasion. He did not know the difference between port and starboard and shocked his crew by crying left and right.

Sage had a stroke and the end of his life was a period of miserable frustration because his brain was clear until he died. I hope that someone will write a life of this fine scientist and most human friend.

So much for heroes. My milieu has been the less exalted classes – the teachers, the students, the parents – the *hoi polloi*, and that has been good; so many never know what ordinary people do and think.

Homer Lane

The most influential factor in my life, the man who has inspired me most, was probably Homer Lane. Lane was an American, but his work is much more widely known in England than in America. After working in a reform school for boys, the Ford Republic, in the USA, he was invited by a few well-known social reformers to open a home for delinquent children in England. It surprises me that the land of his birth does not know of him. To judge from my large mail from America, schools there are as wrong as all the other schools in the world. They hitch their wagon to learning, to college degrees, to success in a world of cheap standards and infantile amusements. Homer Lane showed the other way – if the emotions are free, the intellect looks after itself. Lane was a great pioneer but not a leader. Like others, I took from him what was of value to me and rejected what I did not consider of moment.

I first met him in 1917, when I visited his Little Commonwealth in Dorset, where in 1913 he had been appointed superintendent of a colony of delinquent boys and girls who governed themselves in a small democracy, each person – including Lane himself – having one vote. At that time I knew nothing about child psychology. I had already written three groping books, groping for freedom, motivated by the feeling that education was all wrong, but ignorant of what the basis of that wrongness was. I recall my first visit to the Little Commonwealth, arriving in the middle of a stormy self-government meeting. Then Lane and I sat up talking – no, he talked while I listened. I had never heard of child psychology or for that matter of dynamic psychology of any sort. At that meeting I sat up until three in the morning listening to Lane's descriptions of his methods.

That night he showed me the solution that the only way was to be, as he phrased it, 'on the side of the child'. It meant abolishing all punishment and fear and external discipline; it meant trusting children to grow in their own way without any pressure from

outside, save that of communal self-government. It meant putting
learning in its place – below living. As a schoolmaster I had used
knowledge as the criterion of success. Lane showed me that
emotions were infinitely more powerful and more vital than intellect.

It is true that his Commonwealth was not a school. Most of the
children there had had a poor education and were largely inarticul-
ate, although they weren't so in speaking up at self-government
meetings. And 'school work' did not mean mathematics and history; it meant building houses and milking cows. Thus, although
Lane's work may have little to say to the teacher of school subjects,
he says much to anyone in charge of children – whether in the
home, in school, or in a reformatory. He says much that the
student in training college does not learn: the lesson that one must
go deep, seek motives, approve, live with children without insisting
on dignity or respect – which both generally imply fear.

I was to join him in the Commonwealth after being discharged
from the army, but by that time the Commonwealth was closed by
order of the Home Office. All I really knew about it firsthand,
other than my short visits, was from meeting its citizens at Lane's
house, where for two years I dined every Sunday night. Most of
them had been court cases at one time, but to me they seemed
quiet, social, gentle young men and women who without the Commonwealth, I am sure, would have been in prison. They proved to
me for all time that hate and punishment never cured anyone and
that the only cure was love, which to Lane implied approval, acceptance.

Lane never completely grew up, and that may account for the
simplicity of his message. Any uneducated working man can grasp
at least some of the philosophy that Lane offered. In a way, he
talked in practical parables. Once, when Lane was given a problem
boy from the juvenile courts, he handed him a pound note and told
him how to get down to the Little Commonwealth. Someone said,
'Lane, he'll spend the pound and never get to the Commonwealth.'
Lane smiled. 'He won't,' he said, 'but had I said to him, "I trust
you to take the train," he probably would have spent the money,
for my saying so would have shown him that I didn't trust him at
all.' The lad was waiting for him when he returned.

On another occasion he was building a wall with his boys at the

Commonwealth. The corner he built was excellent (he was good at all manual work), but the boys, discontented with their work, began to fool about and knock down their parts of the wall. Lane immediately knocked down his corner. An uneducated person might not be able to grasp consciously the motive he had, but it is the kind of incident that strikes the unconscious.

After the Commonwealth was closed, Lane set up in London as an analyst. I knew nothing then about analysis and had hardly heard of Freud: I had no thought of being analysed until Lane told me that he thought every teacher should be, and offered to take me on without paying any fees. I had a daily session. It was not a Freudian style of analysis; I did not lie on a couch; we sat and talked.

I wonder if Lane did free me from an inhibiting neurosis. His brilliant analysis of dreams and their symbolism (when I look back now) never touched me below the neck. Later when I went as a patient to Stekel in Vienna I found him also brilliant, but again never touching my guts. But who can assess therapy of any kind? How can I say I'd have run a Summerhill even if Lane had never lived? My own opinion is that I got a hell of a lot from him, but how much was personal (analysis) and how much social (ability to work), I can't say. I am sure that what Lane did for me positively did not come so much from analysis; it came from his treatment of children.

I saw him in his post-Commonwealth days, that is, at the wrong time. He had set up as a therapist in London, and I became one of his first patients to undergo analysis. It was the wrong job for him. Luckily, he also lectured a great deal and gave seminars, and in this he was excellent. Lane had a gift that cannot be described, a charm that disarmed and attracted like a strong magnet. One evil result of this was discipleship that was almost uncritical; what old Homer said in his seminars was gospel, the voice of a new god. We disciples sat at his feet and swallowed everything he said without question. He would bring out statements like: 'Every footballer has a castration complex,' statements that could not be proved, and we lapped them up without challenging them.

We used to challenge him at his seminars about his attitude to sex, why he was so concerned about sex in his Commonwealth. His answer should have been that he could not have his adolescents having a sex life because of social conditions and state control, but he used to give what to us were rationalized replies. His involved argument that it would be bad for adolescents to have a full love life didn't satisfy us. I don't think that Lane ever got over his early New England puritanism.

He made things too simple. When he encouraged Jabez to smash cups and saucers, Jabez threw down the poker and rushed off in tears. Lane claimed that this incident released the boy's inhibitions, that they came tumbling out with a rush. I don't believe it. Looking back now, I think he claimed too much. There is no such thing as a dramatic cure; every cure takes a long time. True, Lane's action was the beginning of a cure, but he should not have claimed that one incident was enough, for we took it for granted that in ten minutes Jabez became a new boy. Yet Lane was not lying to us; he was making a point by giving personal emphasis to an anecdote.

And we were not simpletons: among us were Lord Lytton, J. H. Simpson, John Layard, Dr David, the Bishop of Liverpool. By and large we all looked on Lane as a god, an oracle. Readers of David Wills's biography of Lane will realize that he was no god, nor was he an oracle. What he was was an intuitive genius, a man without much book learning, but a man who, more than any man I have known, had the power of giving out love and understanding to children. His way of treating disturbed children was a model for all workers in the field. I don't think that his theories about psychology had any effect on his delinquent pupils; I am sure that what helped them was the warmth of his personality, his approving smile, and his humour.

Lane told us he had had Freudian analysis in the USA but we didn't believe him, nor do I now. I doubt if he had ever studied Freud deeply. Lane was no scholar. He had, as David Wills says, one of the attributes we attach to genius, the ability to get to fundamentals without, so to say, practising five-finger exercises for hours.

Lane had something else that was unique, the gift of getting behind the facade of conventional behaviour and superficial manners. He often said that crime had a good motive behind it, and I think he meant the attempt of the criminal to find joy in life. But the poor boy reared in a slum without anything joyous in his life seeks the tawdry way of petty pilfering, because all the other gates to freedom and happiness are barred by a poverty of body and mind forced on him by an unequal society. Inspired by Lane in my own treatment of children, I have had many problem pupils in the days before I took only 'normal' children. I can think of only one who did not become a balanced, healthy citizen.

Lane's attitude to me was a complex one. During his Sunday-night dinners Homer was often sour and grumpy and never spoke; at other times full of laying down the law. When he died I brought his daughter Olive Lane here, unofficially adopting her. He liked me but had an attitude I couldn't fathom. Later a woman patient said that he was jealous of me, but I can't believe that, for I was a nobody, a very weak disciple knowing my inferiority to him. I didn't do any good work until he died; then I had to feel 'I am on my own now. I can't run to Lane for advice and guidance. I've got to stand on my own feet.'

In late 1919 Lane attacked me because I had given a lecture and had spoken of his Little Commonwealth work. Someone reported this to Lane and he was wild, said I had misrepresented him and ordered me never to mention him again. I retaliated with anger too and for a few months took my analysis to Maurice Nicoll the Jungian (and got damn all out of it too). Meanwhile I continued to dine at Lane's house every Sunday night. He was quite friendly, asked me how I was getting on with Nicoll, and when I told him said, 'You'd better come back to me.'

What kind of a man was Lane? A man with a wonderful smile, a man with much sympathy and humour. Even his enemies were sometimes taken with his charm. Children loved him. Lane radiated warmth, and must have had a great attraction for women. I think we all had an ambivalent attitude to him, but in my own case I think that the love I had for him overbalanced the hate.

I never thought for a moment that there was any truth in the charges made when the Little Commonwealth was closed by the Home Office. Nor do I want to judge Lane or anyone else. Did he have intercourse with his delinquent girls in the Little Commonwealth? There may have been a few Lolitas among them. Having known Lane for a longish time and having been analysed by him for two years, I cannot think that he would fornicate with a problem girl of eighteen or so, knowing, as he must have done, the dangers. The least caress, the least sympathy can mean to a neurotic girl in her teens a fantasy of seduction.

I found it hard to be critical because I was so overwhelmed with wonder and joy at his treatment of his Little Commonwealth cases. He should never have taken on adults, for, as I have said, he was too ungrown-up, too simple, too trusting. He once accepted gifts of money from a pathological woman. He almost took a sumptuous car from her, but the bank stopped the cheque, since her account was overdrawn. Instances such as these, together with accusations that he was sleeping with his female patients, brought him first to the dock and then to his death.

I had doubts about the later trial and banishment, but John Layard one night quoted the testimony of a few women patients who had told him Lane had slept with them. His stories sounded convincing. Forget as insignificant Lane's weaknesses, his vanities, his littleness. The good that men do lives after them.

I think that David Wills has made a sound analysis of Lane's life lapses, springing originally from his New England puritan mother, his terrible boyish guilt when he failed to look after a wee sister who got drowned, and later his guilt when he took his first wife on a toboggan ride shortly after she had had her baby and she died of pneumonia. Wills argues, and I think rightly, that Lane's subsequent throwing in the sponge and running away from every difficulty stemmed from his early life.

I liked the family a lot. Polly and Allen Lane were sent to King Alfred's School because I was teaching there. The story ran that the girl Lane loved had died, and he then married her sister Mabel. I was sure he never loved Mabel and I had a lot of liking and sympathy for her. I don't think she understood a thing he did or said. Someone told me much later that their son Raymond called me a low-down thief who cadged his Daddy's ideas. True – yet if Lane had lived he would have disapproved of Summerhill. He would, I believe, have thought that it lacked spirituality.

I could never discover what his attitude to religion was. I fancy that his early New England puritanism never died completely. He spoke much about 'spirituality', and my impression was that he meant creativeness, in contrast to possessiveness. Lord Lytton, one of his students, wrote that Lane admired St Paul greatly, but I never heard him mention Paul without intense dislike. He seemed to consider Paul an evil influence that changed the love preached by Jesus into a list of patriarchal, anti-life rules.

I told him of Nietzsche's saying, 'The first and last Christian died on the Cross,' and he nodded agreement. I don't think he had any conscious religion of the church-attendance kind, and I am fairly certain that he did not believe in a heaven and a hell. He often talked about God, meaning, I thought, the 'life force', not the Father who watches what you are doing. Lane did not need a religion; he lived religion, that is, if 'religion' means giving out love and not hate.

The man was an enigma, a great romancer; he told us stories about his boyhood that were all fictional. He was a lover of the good things of life, in short just an ordinary person like you and me, but he had that something that is beyond human frailty, a capacity for getting underneath the skin of humanity – genius, intuition, call it what you will, for it is intangible and cannot be imitated. On the other hand all he taught must not be swallowed uncritically. Luckily, every idol has feet of clay.

Alas, the Establishment has not followed Lane. His influence was limited. Since his death in 1925 the state institutions for problem children have not been changed in favour of freedom and understanding. As I write this today there is no official ban in England on caning handicapped children; it is left to the headmaster's discretion, or more often, his indiscretion. More than four decades after his death, it is apparent that Homer Lane has had little effect on official policy, though I do not intend to slight those teachers in Britain who do take a humane approach.

Lane has had some influence outside state institutions. And, to be fair, some schools in the state system are run with love and not hate. I myself owe much to Lane. He introduced me to child psychology. He was the first man I had heard of who brought depth psychology to the treatment of children, something official treatment rarely does. It was also from Lane that I obtained the idea of self-government at Summerhill. He showed me the necessity of looking deep for the causes of misbehaviour. Yet I doubt whether the thousands of teachers in Great Britain ever knew much about him; when I mention him in lectures, most students and teachers look blank.

To me he was a revelation. Lane showed me the way and I have always acknowledged it. I don't think I am being smug when I say that many have been influenced by Summerhill and have not

acknowledged it in books and articles. It is always the case. I grant
that it does not matter in the long run, but I think that honesty
should admit sources.

Lane was no saviour. Poor man, he couldn't even save himself!
But the fact that he has been neglected by the educational world is
proof that giving children love is also neglected. One evil of humanity is that we persist in telling children how to live. All our
educational systems strive to mould them in the image of their
elders, and the children in turn mould their children, and one result
is a very sick world full of crime and hate and wars. Thus, the
vicious circle persists, and millions of children are unhappy and
tense in mind and body. The weight of this tradition is so heavy
that only one man in a thousand can ever challenge or even want
to challenge the morals and taboos of society.

When such a challenger comes along, society will destroy him, as
it did Homer Lane or Wilhelm Reich. It did not destroy Freud
primarily because it could not find a valid reason. Both Lane and
Reich were accused of crimes and made to appear in court, and
therefore to society they were wicked men. It is the mud that sticks.
Even today Oscar Wilde is rarely the brilliant and kindly wit; too
often he is the homosexual. 'The evil that men do lives after them,
the good is oft interred with their bones.' But Lane and Reich did
no evil. Lane was ruined by his own personality; like Peter Pan, he
never grew up to understand or want to understand such things as
money or legalities or conventions. Reich's life was cut short because he would not compromise with a sick world. Both will be
hailed as great men after we are all dead.

Why does humanity choose a Hitler and not a Homer Lane?
Why does it choose war and not peace, inhumanity towards criminals rather than psychological and social treatment? Perhaps because it is afraid of love, afraid of tenderness.

What a life he had. Time has blunted my memories of him.
As I say, I never believed the story of his seducing delinquent girls
in the Commonwealth. Later when the law accused him of seducing
his adult patients on the analytical couch I had my doubts, but no
feelings of shock. Maybe some female patients got more out of the
seduction than I got out of the dream analysis. Professionally of
course it is wrong, for when a woman becomes the analyst's lover
the analysis stops dead.

The tragedy of Lane's life was that he was associated with social scandal and not with the great work he did with problem children. Scandal cannot kill a man's work for ever, but it can during his lifetime. When I read of Lane's death in the papers I found myself smiling. I thought it hard-heartedness but later I think I got the true explanation: I was free at last. Until then I had relied on him – what would Homer say? Now I had to stand on my own feet.

Wilhelm Reich

If, as I have said, opinions differed about Stekel, they differed much more violently about Wilhelm Reich. I do not pretend to understand his scientific work with 'bions' and 'orgones'. I do understand his thesis that the sickness of humanity is primarily due to sex repression. I freely acknowledge that much of my later writing has been greatly conditioned by my belief in Reich. I ran my school for twenty-six years before I met Reich, and ran it in the same way as I do now. Reich however, made me conscious of things that I had done by intuition.

In the summer of 1947 in Maine I could not grasp his argument that function comes before purpose, until he exclaimed, 'But, Neill, your life work has been founded on the principle that function comes first. You don't have Summerhill *in order that* children should study or learn to work or become "ists" of any kind. You let them function in their own play-work fashion, and you postulate no purpose for them at all.'

For many years my views about sex freedom were only what one might call head ones; intellectually I was completely for freedom, but it was only after a long friendship with Wilhelm Reich that I got a measure of emotional freedom about the question . . . I say a measure because, although I can talk openly and seriously about all sides of sex, if there is one person in the group who is known to me as shockable about sex, then I feel embarrassed, and consciously sugar the raw pill by using medical terminology. If a small child says a word like 'fuck' in front of an unknown visitor or the plumber, I feel embarrassed, rationalizing that it will give outsiders a wrong impression of the school.

My first wife, who did not have a childhood of Calvinism and sex repression, used to laugh and think nothing about the child's expletive, but my present wife, Ena, who had a definite and anti-life training about sex, has the same attitude, so that perhaps there is more in it than early Calvinism. It is in part an identification of self with another, and when recently a visitor began to talk in an anti-Semitic way, I felt very much embarrassed, for one of the party was a Jew.

Getting back to Reich . . . my own opinion is that in psychology Reich is the only original thinker since Freud. For years I had been saying lamely and helplessly that psychology must join up with physiology and biology, and when I met a man who was working that way I was ready to fall for him. I was fascinated with his new theory that neurosis is linked up with bodily tensions.

I have no intention of giving a detailed description of Reich's work; I shall simply tell how he affected and influenced me. I met him first in 1937. I was lecturing in Oslo University and after my lecture the chairman said, 'You had a distinguished man in your audience tonight: Wilhelm Reich.'

'Good God,' I said, 'I was reading his *Mass Psychology of Fascism* on the ship.'

I phoned Reich and he invited me to dinner. We sat talking till late and I was fascinated.

'Reich,' I said, 'you are the man I have been searching for for years, the man to link up the soma and the psyche. Can I come and study under you?'

So for two years I went to Oslo in the three vacations I had each year. He said I could learn only by undergoing his Vegetotherapy, which meant lying naked on a sofa while he attacked my stiff muscles. He refused to touch dreams. It was a hard therapy and often a painful one, but I got more emotional release in a few weeks than I had ever had with Lane, Maurice Nicoll, Stekel. It seemed to me the best kind of therapy and I still think so, even having seen patients after Reichian therapy remain apparently neurotic.

Here I want to say something about Reichian analysis. Some read his books and think it easy. All you have to do is to get the patient to lie naked on a couch, release the stiff tensions in the muscles . . . and wait to see the complexes and infantile memories tumble out. So why can't I set up as an orgone therapist?

This is most dangerous. I can tell from personal experience that the Reichian treatment arouses violent emotions, and unless the therapist has trained in Reichian therapy the patients can be in great danger of suicide or what not. Reich insisted that only trained medical doctors could practise his methods. Here he was right. A lay therapist might find what he thought was a tension of a neck muscle or an abdominal one and try to release the tension, but for all he knew it could be a tubercular lesion or a growth.

Reich had had a roving life. For many years he was one of Freud's inner circle. He fled from Berlin when Hitler came and went to Copenhagen, but was expelled because of his book *The Sexual Struggle of Youth*, in which he argued that sex must follow biology and intercourse should be free to adolescents. Reich then settled in Oslo for several years.

Reich often said, 'Bend the tree when it is a twig and it will be bent when it is fully grown.' He also said, 'What is wrong with psychoanalysis is that it deals with words, while all the damage is done to a child before it can speak.' I doubt if any therapy ever gets down to the roots of neurosis. In the early twenties we were all searching for the famous trauma that caused the sickness. We never found it because there was no trauma, only a plethora of traumatic experiences from the moment of birth. Reich realized that therapy was not the answer, only preventive treatment of disease, and kept up his practice of therapy mainly to raise money for his scientific studies.

When the war came in 1939 I trembled for his fate, for he was a Jew and on the Nazi list for destruction. An American patient, Dr Theodore Wolfe, who later became the translator of his books, managed to get him into the States. His history there until his death in prison is well known. Often he tried to persuade me to bring Summerhill to Rangely, Maine, where he had his clinic, Organon.

'No, Reich, I had my school in a foreign country once and I would never do it again. I don't know the customs, the habits of the USA, and anyway my school would come to be regarded as a Reich school, and that I would never have.' Reich was impossible to work with. He was an all-or-nothing man. One had to go his way, and any dissenter went out on his neck. I knew I could never work with him.

I could not understand Reich's theory of orgone energy. It may exist, but what can one do about it? Reich said it was visible but I had a blind eye to it. He had a small motor which was charged by an orgone accumulator. It ran slowly but when gingered up by volts from a battery it seemed to revolve at a great speed. Reich was in ecstasies: 'The motive force of the future!' he exclaimed. I never heard of its being developed. I did not know enough about his rain-making to form an opinion, but my friend Dr Walter Hoppe in Tel Aviv told me that he has had some wonderful results in cloud bursting. What one might call psychic orgone energy cannot be used in any way I can imagine. But here I admit my ignorance of science of any kind. I was never interested in Reich's later work. To me he was the great man of his earlier books, *Sexual Revolution, Character Analysis, The Function of the Orgasm*, and *The Mass Psychology of Fascism*, which I still think is a masterpiece of crowd analysis.

His widow Ilse's *Wilhelm Reich: A Personal Biography* is a brave and sincere description of a brilliant and complicated man.

Reich, as Ilse points out, was deficient in humour and my friendship with him was marred by the fact that we could not laugh at the same things. He had no liking for ordinary conversation about cars or books, and gossip was anathema to him. His talk was always about his work.

The only time I saw him relax was during his weekly trip to the movies in Rangely, near his clinic. He was completely uncritical of films. Once I said a film was kitsch and he was angry with me: 'I enjoyed every minute of it.'

I still can't see how one can use orgone energy to cure human sickness, world sickness. I can't think that if the whole world had perfect orgasms in the Reichian sense that Arcadia would result. Reich did not have the whole truth. I told him I knew oldish men and women who had never had sex in their lives, but who were happy and charitable and doing good work.

I try in vain to find out if Reich ever solved the mystery of why sex became taboo. Why the Christians made it the big sin. Reich's ideal of free sex for adolescents was not possible at a time when there was no effective contraception. Reich was a puritan in sex. He hated the word 'fuck', which to him was aggressive male sex without tenderness or love. 'Women don't fuck,' he said to me once.

Reich diagnosed brilliantly but he did not know the practical answer, how to get at the perverts who kill the kid in the cradle. That is what I cannot get at, the 'why' of mankind's hate and war and discipline. I can't find an answer to what made man go that way. If Reich gave me one I didn't understand it. Summerhill proves that freedom brings out good and that kids can grow without being made anti-life, but why? Why can't the whole world treat kids that way? I wish I knew.

I am still confused about the role of sex repression. I have had pupils from homes that approved of masturbation, nakedness, and cursing, and still they bullied and destroyed, though to be sure not so much as the kids of stupid parents. All so confusing. Reich, who lived out his sex life fully, was filled with insane jealousy. When Ilse returned home after visiting us, Reich's first words were, 'Did you sleep with Neill?'

I stood in a special relation to Reich. Around him were all his disciples, his doctor trainees, and all was formal. I was the only one who addressed him as Reich. True I had also been his patient, his trainee, but, maybe owing to my age, I was in a category by myself, along with Dr Ola Raknes from Oslo. We had seminars. Reich filled the blackboard with hieroglyphics, equations that meant nothing to me, and I doubt if they meant anything to the others present either.

Reich and I loved each other. When I parted from him in Maine for the last time in 1948 he threw his arms round me. 'Neill, I wish you could stay. You are the only one I can talk to. The others are all patients or disciples.' Then I knew how lonely he was.

Once I said to him, 'Why are you so formal? Why do you address Wolfe as Dr Wolfe? Why aren't you just Reich to them all?'

'Because they would use the familiarity to destroy me as they did in Norway when I was Willy to them all.'

'But Reich, I am Neill to my staff, pupils, domestics, and no one ever takes advantage of the familiarity.'

'Yes, but you aren't dealing with dynamite as I am,' was his cryptic answer.

It is obvious from his wife Ilse's book that Reich in the end lost his reason. That never worried me; many great men went mad – Swift, Nietzsche, Schumann, Ruskin, lots of others. (I know I am not a genius because I haven't.) To me it didn't matter a damn if he had a streak of paranoia . . . who doesn't?

When his son Peter came here as a boy with Ilse and Ola Raknes and sat in my garden, he said, 'Those American planes up there are there to protect me.' I told him they weren't. He went home and must have told Reich what I said because Reich sent a cable to Grethe Hoff saying, 'Don't trust Neill, he is disloyal.' I wrote him a letter and the dear old man replied with much regret and apologies.

In America he was hounded literally to death by smearing scandal-makers. Sick journalists described his orgone accumulator as a means for attaining a sexual orgasm. Why all the bitter enmity shown in the USA? A mere crank does not get abuse and hate. The man who believes the earth is flat is not hounded as Reich was; people laugh at him but they did not laugh at Reich. They smeared him in America; they dismissed him as a paranoic. If a paranoic can give us such brilliant books as *The Mass Psychology of Fascism*, *The Function of the Orgasm*, and *Listen, Little Man!*, then it is high time that psychiatrists were redefining their definitions.

Personally I think that the Reich boycott springs from his uncompromising attitude to life and especially to sex. I am convinced that the question whether orgone energy exists or not has nothing to do with anti-Reichism. I don't know enough science to say whether it exists or not, and I do not care a button about it. But I do care for the Reich I knew and could understand, the man whose analysis of human character was deep and convincing.

We corresponded from the time he went to America until he went to prison. The loneliness of prison must have been hell. I think it was as much the Little Man in him as the great genius that appealed to me, the Reich who stormed at Peter and Ilse, the warm man with whom I emptied many a bottle of rye or Scotch, in short the human guy who enjoyed an exciting film Western as if he were ten years old.

Reich died in prison of a heart attack. I felt his death more acutely than I felt the death of Lane. A bright light had gone out; a great man had died in vile captivity. I think that Reich will not come into his own as a genius until at least the second generation. I was most lucky to know him and learn from him and love him.

Loves and Lovers

When I was a young student teacher in Scotland I fell violently in love with a pupil. Margaret was about sixteen; I, twenty-four. Her voice struck me as the essence of sweetness. To me, she was all that was lovely. Her long lashes almost hid her beautiful eyes, and I found that I could not look at her when she looked at me. She personified the whole school for me. If she happened to be absent, the day was dark, long, and dreary; when she was present, the day was always far too short. Years later, when I told her how much she had meant to me, she seemed much surprised. Wiser now in human motive and behaviour, however, I think she must have known, and no doubt used her dangerous eyes to torment the bashful, half-baked youth who trembled at her glance. Her beauty was not real to me, but something on which to build fantasies. So, of course, I made no advances. Wooing her did not seem to be so important as worshipping her.

The remarkable thing about Margaret was her persistence in my mind. While other girls faded from memory, she continued to haunt my dreams for years. I have found other grown men whose dream-Margarets ever and again came back into their lives as dream-pictures, and I have known women who had their dream-men. This puzzles me still. I have had long periods of psycho-analysis with different specialists, but the Margaret image baffled them all. They guessed she was my mother as I first knew her, young and desirable; then they said she must be a substitute for my sister Clunie. Neither explanation gave me any emotional response. I do have a strong feeling that her indifference was her chief attraction. She obviously did not admire me; yet, on the evening before I left the school, she suddenly threw her arms round my neck and said, 'Mr Neill, you are a dear.' Damn the girl. That should have broken the spell. But it only made her more desirable than ever.

For years I heard nothing more of Margaret. Then, when she

was a widow past seventy, I wrote to her and later went to see her. The beautiful eyes were dim, the long eyelashes had gone. I often wrote and phoned her thereafter; she was lonely, living by herself, lame and in pain. She had had a slight stroke and dreaded another. All her life, the lass had remained lower-middle-class, outside the mainstream of new ideas. I laughed at her shock when I used a four-letter word. As time went on, however, the ageing Margaret began to change. 'You have opened up a new world for me,' she would say. And she was a sweet old woman, though too set in her ways to accept modern ideas. One Sunday night, when I phoned her, there was no reply. Neighbours found her in a coma.

Poor Margaret. We agreed that marriage between us would have been a mistake, and I doubt if she ever could have overcome her conventional life in a Scottish suburb. But what is the use of guessing anyway? She was a youthful dream. A young man's fantasy assumes that if a girl is pretty, she has a pretty nature as well. And Margaret was doubly blessed. She had true manners, being considerate of others and hating to offend.

How ignorant, how stupid youth is. At eighteen I fell for a bonny lassie who did not react to my advances – I learned later that she was a lesbian. Her sister was plain. I cultivated the sister, insanely thinking she would tell her beautiful sister what a fine guy I was. I was blind to the fact that she hated her sister like hell. I used to think that the way to a girl's heart was paved with compliments, and it took me a long time to discover that another man won her heart by telling her what a nasty bitch she was.

It took me many years to discover that when a woman glares at a man, stamps her foot, and cries, 'Get out! I hate you,' in most cases she is showing her love for him. But I must have had an elementary feeling for psychology. I recall a dance in the old days of programmes and white gloves, when the women stood around and the swains booked dances with them, each writing the dance in the programme with its silk string. The university beauty was besieged. I was introduced to her and didn't ask for a dance. Later she touched my arm. 'Our dance,' she said. She had cut another dance. 'But,' I said, 'we didn't . . .'

'I know. Damn you, you are the only one who didn't ask me.' And I learned about women from her.

I sigh regretfully when I see the modern girl with her independ-

ence, her frankness about sex, her carelessness in dress with her
blue jeans and blouse, I sigh and wish that women had been as
sincere and honest in my early days. Real companionship between
the sexes was almost impossible then. The red light was sex –
significant that the red light was the sign of the brothel – but in my
youth young women did not give the green go-ahead signal easily.

I call myself normal sexually, even though I fancy I have subordin-
ated sex to ambition. In my student days the nice girls were taboo.
'Who touches me marries me.' So we students picked up shop girls,
girls from the working classes. I never once went to a prostitute –
maybe because there were so many enthusiastic amateurs around.
It was all wrong, all degrading. Once after intercourse with a shop
girl on Blackford Hill she began to cry. I asked her why.

'It isn't fair,' she sobbed. 'You students take us out and we like
your manners and educated speech, but you never marry us. I'll
have to marry some workman who can only talk about football
and beer.'

That was the end of my picking up shop girls.

Twice I nearly got married. Both girls, like myself, were of the
lower middle class. I hesitated. I was in love but reason crept in.
You want to do something important in life. Will she be able to
keep up with you? Stupidly I tried in both cases to educate them,
gave them books, talked of Shaw and Wells and Hardy. Also there
was the economic factor. I was not earning enough to support a
wife and family. Emotionally I was wrong but I could not act in
any other way, not with my grandiose – though unformulated –
plans for success.

I got little pleasure in hole-and-corner affairs: they were sex
without love, without tenderness. My Calvinistic conscience must
have made them dirtier, and it must have been that conscience that
more than once made me impotent. Indeed I sometimes wonder
how anyone reared as a Catholic or a Calvinist can ever get away
from the sex guilt inculcated in early life.

I have never understood women. What man can understand
them? In some ways they are a different species. I grant that if I
had been reared in a different atmosphere I would have had a
better understanding of the psychology of women.

In my youth women were put on a pedestal and we did not
realize that their feet were of common clay. I must have been about

twelve when I read of a woman being killed in a train accident and I thought it could not be true because women were not human like men and not liable to fatalities. And that in spite of the fact that I had four sisters and saw their virtues and faults. Having sisters did not help me one bit to understand other women. The family sex taboo applied to the lassies over the garden wall; they were all the untouchables, mysterious, unattainable.

A mere man can never understand the enormous importance a woman attaches to dress and appearance. If all men were like me the women would be wasting their time and money, for I never see what a woman wears, and at the moment at my desk could not tell what colours my wife and daughter are wearing. I see only faces, eyes in particular. I never see ankles and when some bitchy girl in my school made a remark about another girl's thick ankles I looked and saw them for the first time – she had been in the school for ten years.

In Hellerau I danced with many a pretty girl but remained fancy-free. Violent passion was not for me and that is why I came to marry a woman older than myself. One of my pupils in King Alfred School in London was Walter Lindesay Neustatter, later a well-known psychiatrist. His father was Dr Otto Neustatter and his mother was an Australian, who had been a music student in Leipzig. I got friendly with her: she had the same views on education as I had, and was well-travelled and cultured. Walter and she went to stay with Otto in Hellerau, and I have told how she became matron of my department there and in Sonntagsberg, and later in Lyme Regis.

After her divorce from Otto I married her because of the school: I had to be respectable. But there was another motive; she was an alien and had to register with the police, and, as a Britisher, she was full of misery and resentment. I made her a British subject. My life was full with my work and we got along splendidly. She loved travel and we went on trips to Germany, Italy, France and took cruises. I was always slightly annoyed at the expenditure; I would much rather have spent the money on a precision lathe or a shaping machine, yet the travel must have enlarged my outlook.

She worked hard and was as important in the school as I was, just as my wife Ena is today. I have been lucky in having two wives who were wonderfully competent and understanding. My intention has been to say nothing about people now living and I will say nothing about my second wife, Ena, barring that it was a love match, and Zoë, our daughter, a love child born in wedlock.

I will have to break my resolve to say nothing about people now living in the case of my daughter Zoë. I have mentioned her in more than one of my books and her name must have been read by millions. Many have written asking me about her and her life. Some have asked if she bears out the old Scots saying that the shoemaker's bairns are the worst shod.

I cannot recall my emotion when Zoë was born, only my natural and general feeling of the unfairness that makes the mother have all the pain. I don't think I have ever had a feeling of possession about my daughter, never had the thought she was made of a clay that had a smoother texture than that of the child next door. Seeing your child grow up might be classified as a long, quiet pleasure.

No one has ever seen a completely self-regulated child. Every child living has been moulded by parents, teachers, and society. When my daughter Zoë was two, a magazine, *Picture Post*, published an article about her with photographs, saying that in their opinion, she of all the children of Britain had the best chance of being free. It was not entirely true, for she lived in a school among many children who were not self-regulated. These other children had been more or less conditioned and Zoë found herself in contact with some children who were anti-life.

She was brought up with no fear of animals. Yet one day, when I stopped the car at a farm and said, 'Come on, let's see the moo cows,' she suddenly looked afraid and said, 'No, no; moo cows eat you.' A child of seven had told her so. True, the fear lasted only for a week or two.

It would seem that a self-regulated child is capable of overcoming the influences of conditioned children in a comparatively short time. Zoë's acquired fears and repressed interests never lasted long.

Zoë, when a little over a year old, went through a period of great interest in my glasses, snatching them off my nose to see what they were like. I made no protest, showed no annoyance by look or tone of voice. She soon lost interest in my glasses and never touched them. No doubt, if I had sternly told her not to – or worse, spanked her little hand – her interest in my glasses would have survived, mingled with fear of me and rebellion against me.

Ena and I let her play with breakable ornaments. The child handled them carefully and seldom broke anything. She found things out for herself. Of course, there is a limit to self-regulation. We cannot allow a baby of six months to discover that a lighted cigarette burns painfully.

Under self-regulation, there is no final authority in the home. Thus I could say to my daughter, 'You can't bring that mud and water into our parlour.' But she can say to me, 'Get out of my room, Daddy. I don't want you here now' – a wish that I, of course, would obey without a word.

It is true that there must be some discipline in the home. Generally, it is the type of discipline that safeguards the individual rights of each member of the family. For example, I did not allow my daughter to play with my typewriter. But in a happy family this kind of discipline usually looks after itself.

Zoë was always allowed to choose what she wanted to eat. Whenever she had a cold, she ate only fruit and drank only fruit juices without any suggestion on our part. I never before had seen a child who had so little interest in eating as Zoë.

In my own family, the biggest difficulty with self-regulation centred on the matter of clothing. Zoë would have liked to run about naked all day long if she had been permitted to do so. Zoë shivered until her nose and cheeks turned blue, and then resisted all our efforts to get her to put on more clothes.

Courageous parents might say, 'Her own organism will guide her. Let her shiver, she'll be all right!' But we were not courageous enough to risk pneumonia, so we bullied her into wearing what we thought she ought to wear.

With children and sex there is no sitting on the fence, no neutrality. The choice is between guilty-secret sex or open, healthy sex. When Zoë was six she came to me and said, 'Willie has the biggest cock among the small kids, but Mrs X [a visitor] says it is rude to say cock.' I at once told her that it was not rude. Inwardly, I cursed that woman for her ignorant and narrow understanding of children. I might tolerate propaganda about politics or manners, but when anyone has attacked a child by making that child guilty about sex, I have fought back vigorously.

Ena and I never had to think twice about Zoë and her sex education. It all seemed so simple, so obvious, and so charming –

even if it had its awkward moments, as when Zoë informed a
spinster visitor that she, Zoë, had come into the world because
Daddy fertilized Mummy, adding with interest, 'And who fertilizes
you?'

Zoë could speak thus at three and a half; but at five our daughter
began to realize that some things must not be said to some people.
When we were interviewing a prospective parent – a conventional
businessman – she was trying unsuccessfully to fit some toy together
and at each failure she exclaimed, 'Oh, fuck it!' Later, we told her
that some people did not like that word, and that she should not
use it when visitors were present. 'Okay,' she said.

A week later, she was doing something difficult to accomplish.
She looked up and asked a teacher, 'Are you a visitor?'

The lady replied, 'Of course not!'

Zoë gave a sigh of relief and cried, 'Oh, fuck it!'

Every analyst must feel, even if dimly, that the hours spent in
analysing a patient would never have been necessary if the patient
had been self-regulated as a baby. I say dimly, because we cannot
be really sure of anything.

My daughter, reared in freedom, may have to go to an analyst
one day and say, 'Doctor, I need treatment. I am suffering from a
father complex. I am fed up with being introduced as the daughter
of A. S. Neill. People expect far too much of me; they seem to
think I should be perfect. The old man is dead now, but I can't
forgive him for parading me in his books. And now, do I lie down
on this sofa? . . .' One never knows.

Her school-days were difficult. She fell between home and school.
When she lived in our cottage she was an outsider to the children
who boarded in the main school, and when we made her a boarder
she felt that she hadn't a home. And she suffered much from the
jealousy of others. Ena and I had long been convinced that teachers
should never have their own children in a boarding-school in which
the parents work, so when she was eleven we sent her to a foreign
boarding-school. After her first term she said, 'Daddy, you are a
swindle; you give freedom to other kids but not to your own
daughter. I hate school; it is fake freedom and has no real self-
government.' I visited the school and brought her home.

Zoë is not an academic; from earliest infancy she has had one
great interest – horses. In her early twenties she qualified as a

riding mistress and set up a large stable in the school grounds. Zoë's methods are gentle and kind. Her prize-winning stallion, Karthage, did not need to be broken; when she first jumped on his back he took it as another natural show of kindness.

I suppose at the back of my mind was the wish that Zoë would choose my own line of work and interest and run Summerhill after me. Many parents have indulged in such wishful thinking, especially fathers with big businesses. Luckily we are all wrong; luckily we have no control over our children. Luckily I came to feel that if horses were Zoë's life then her happiness was all that mattered. And after all, to be an expert on horses is as important as to be an expert in education, maybe more important, for you can ruin generations of kids by a false education of fear and authority, whereas only cruel trainers can ruin horses.

In September 1971 she married a young farmer and they now own a farm near the school. At the wedding I had to propose the health of Tony and Zoë Readhead and although I can lecture for hours without any nervousness I was a little anxious about making a short speech where emotion was involved. Luckily I had a vague memory of a passage in one of my books, *The Free Child*. I read it aloud . . .

Yesterday was my birthday. My Zoë, who will be six next month, said, 'Daddy, you are old, aren't you? You'll die before me, won't you? I'll cry when you die.'

'Hey, wait,' I said, 'I will maybe wait to see you married.'

'In that case,' she said, 'I won't need to cry, will I?'

I did not go on to read further: 'It strikes me that if a small child can take it for granted that she won't need her father when she grows up, she has automatically solved the dear old Oedipus complex.'

Other Schools

I am no prophet, but I fear that progressive schools are doomed. Under Communism they could not exist, and under the mild socialism of Britain their life is likely to be short; not that the state will deliberately kill the progressive school directly and openly, but its heavy taxation will soon prevent any parents but the very rich from sending their children to boarding-schools. And the boarding-schools of the rich are not likely to be pioneering schools.

Summerhill has been a scientific experiment in one respect, in that we strove to impose nothing, we simply stood by and observed what children were and did when left to themselves. Here we differed from many a progressive school, the kind of school that is founded to carry out some ideal of an adult or a body of adults.

Here I feel uneasy, I feel slightly disloyal to my fellow progressive teachers. After all, if there is honour among thieves, there is honour among scoundrels. We meet at conferences and we differ in a friendly way. Each of us thinks we are the best. I know some of them well, like them, feel their sincerity and appreciate their worth. Most of them are doing a very good job, and even the worst of them are miles ahead of conventional schools, which too often serve up fear and punishment and character moulding with their discipline.

I know that we can still differ and continue to be friends. I do think that we have more freedom than they have; Summerhill is probably the only progressive school in England that has no compulsory lessons. When one headmaster says that his pupils love Beethoven and won't have rock and roll, I am convinced that he has used his influence, because my pupils by a large majority favour rock and roll. I think he is wrong, but I also think he is a good fellow and an honest one. I hasten to say that the rock and roll epidemic has nothing to do with me, for I hate the noisy, quacking stuff. He and his fellows influence children because they think they know what children ought to have; some of them think they know what children ought to be.

In our International School in Hellerau we had three divisions: eurythmics, my Auslander division, and, much the biggest, the German school for boarders and local children. Our life together was one long wrangle but without bitterness. I claimed to follow child psychology, not knowing what a child was or what it should be. Would it work in the garden? Like maths? Like jazz better than Bach? What would it do when left to play all day with no compulsion to attend lessons? How would it react to self-government? It was all empirical. The Germans took the other line. They knew what a child should be, what he should become. They believed that he must be guided to reach manhood balanced and happy. So they moulded, inspired; they led from jazz to Beethoven. They were examples to their pupils. They didn't smoke or drink. Many belonged to the Wandervogel movement and tried to bring back old-time dances and habits.

Unfortunately we shared a hostel – I had the upper storey; the German boarders had the lower one. Of an evening my lot would be foxtrotting to a gramophone, while downstairs a teacher was reading from Nietzsche or Goethe. One by one his children crept up the back stairs and, well, the atmosphere between us was not good. There was no way of solving our basic difference – to mould or not to mould. Mind you, I hasten to add that one moulds without being aware of it. In our General Meeting I complain when tools are being damaged and the children must get the notion that Neill thinks tools are valuable. But tools go on being damaged.

When I taught in King Alfred's School under John Russell around 1919, I can't recall any damage being done. I am sure I never heard a four-letter word. I can't recall any instance of theft. Dear old J.R., a most lovable man, was a father-figure, really a god to some of his old pupils who used to sit at his feet literally and romantically. His influence for 'good' was so potent that 'evil' things like damaging, swearing, etc., never showed their heads.

So it was in Hellerau. Their self-government meetings dealt mainly with questions about work. Our meetings dealt mainly with social behaviour. The German children were better behaved than our lot because their conditioning was thorough, but it was significant that, if and when a pupil from the German school was transferred to our division, his or her behaviour became worse, meaning that freedom was a means of living out all their repressions.

I think, to come home again, the same situation might well arise if we had pupils coming to us from the progressive schools in England. Not every child requires this, but most newcomers have to react to freedom by being antisocial or at least asocial, and I guess that our repair bill in Summerhill is higher than that of some coed school with three times our numbers. Even coming from a school with mild authority a child very often lets off steam.

Summerhill isn't a school; it is a way of life. It could be that one difference between us and other coed schools is that we have more interest in the child's unconscious, in his emotional conflicts. I am not saying that other schools neglect such factors, and maybe I am prejudiced because I came to education via Homer Lane and the dynamic psychologists, rather than through the apostles of learning. I do think we are the only school that makes play of the highest importance. To me that is fundamental.

Why say to a school: 'You are all free. The staff does not make the laws. You are self-governing. You are left to develop your own philosophy of life ... but you must attend lessons'? Oh, I know none of us can be consistent all the time. In Summerhill we don't allow children of six to sit up till ten at night; we don't ask a child with a high temperature to pack away a few mince pies. But on the other hand we never give the slightest hint about going to lessons or washing hands before a meal ... I never do, have never done.

In Summerhill we have shed outside authorities. In a way Summerhill is trying to undo previous moulding all the time, but I fear that many progressive schools are unconsciously and kindly perpetuating the moulding pattern by their standards of good form and gentlemanly behaviour. I fancy there is more swearing in Summerhill than in all the other coed schools lumped together Why? Because swear words belong to deep interests. The pupils in the other schools have the same interests but they have inhibitions about showing those interests in their speech. Why again? Because 'nice' people don't use them ... I occasionally get a new little boy or girl who says the words are 'rude'. If I am wrong, then why does every new child from an authority school begin to swear? Why do so many want to cease taking baths? Why do they bring a masturbation guilt with them? Why, in short, do they come behaving like little hypocrites, scared of teacher's opinion, and moral about other children: 'In my last school we didn't have kids stealing: I think they are awful ...'?

Another way in which Summerhill differs from many progressive schools lies in the fact that they have much larger numbers. We can have our seventy or more pupils in one room at a General Meeting, so that government is direct; a show of hands decides a motion. When a school has three hundred this mode cannot be used. Self-government then means delegated authority, a council of twelve or so. I hear of such councils where the headmaster is always present and can use his veto; I have never used a veto, never had a veto, have never seen any occasion on which I wanted to have one. And I think that my small numbers have this advantage, that there is more contact between young and older pupils, a contact that tends to foster understanding and patience and charity.

Possibly Summerhill has less anxiety about sex than most other schools. A moral atmosphere can, of course, inhibit sex, but some headmasters and headmistresses worry a lot about what they consider dangers. In most schools there is a definite plan to separate boys from girls, especially in their sleeping quarters. Love affairs are not encouraged; they are not encouraged in Summerhill, but they are left alone because an adolescent love affair is so tender and lovely and natural.

Incidentally I cannot stand that word 'progressive'; I prefer the word 'pioneer' with its association with lusty fellows with axes cutting their way through the jungle, so that later the wagons will roll up with their profiteers and exploiters, meaning that, whatever you do, someone is to follow and turn the wilderness you found into a town of electric signs and saloon bars.

As to boarding-schools, I know that the mass of citizens would not miss them if they all perished. They have been class affairs for the rich and comparatively well-off parents. It has always been a sad fact that pioneering in education has been mostly confined to the middle classes who can afford boarding-school fees. In the end the day-school may be the only one to survive, and I think that a great pity. I believe in boarding-schools but only those that have freedom. Since children are not young adults it seems to be desirable that they should live their lives in their own community, measuring themselves against their own peers, especially in these modern days of small families.

The boarding-school is more necessary today than it was in the past when big families made a home a community with much give and take. Today, with small families, there is a danger that the children, not having their peers to live with, will be too much in an adult environment most of the time. It is not fair to keep an only child in a situation wherein he can measure himself only against his parents. He is apt to get too old for his years.

I see the parents' point of view of course. To be deprived of your little child for eight months of the year is a strain. Only yesterday one of my old girls, happily married, said to me, 'I was sent to Summerhill when I was far too young. I was only four, and I have often thought that I should have been with my parents then and a few years later.'

We occasionally take British children at five when the home situation demands it – both parents may be working – but we refuse young children from America on the grounds that a child at least up to seven should not be a few thousand miles from its parents.

No, I do not believe the future lies with the boarding-school. Naturally I think that if all boarding-schools were as happy places as Summerhill many children would benefit from them, but I understand the feelings of parents who want to see their family growing up around them. One snag our old pupils find sometimes is the impossibility of finding a local day-school that will not indoctrinate and mould their children, but that difficulty may slowly solve itself; already many kindergarten schools are excellent and on the side of the child.

Still, one cannot compare a day-school with a boarding one. Suppose a day-school decides to have self-government. What can meetings discuss? What laws can be passed? In a day-school there is nothing to govern about. The timetable is there, the subjects, the exams. The important part of the day pupil's life is lived outside of the school walls. In a boarding-school, on the other hand, thirty-six weeks of the year are spent entirely in school.

In Summerhill one hardly ever hears lessons mentioned at our General Meeting; most subjects dealt with are outside the classroom. In a General Meeting the topics dealt with are nearly all topics that would not even appear in a day-school – children breaking their bedtime rules, noises at meal times, the social programme – how to proportion the time given to seniors and juniors, should the Saturday night dance end at ten or eleven? All are concerned with social activities, with relationships between pupil and pupil, staff and pupil, staff and staff.

Such situations hardly arise in a day-school. The home automatically settles the bedtime question, thus depriving children of the opportunity of thinking about it and acting on it. The boarding-school on the other hand can give the child the opportunity to live in a big family, a family without a father and mother, can give the chance to decide what is usually decided for him. To me this community living is infinitely more important in a child's development than all the textbooks in the world.

To go back to progressive schools, I am not going to be so daft as to argue that an old Summerhillian is a better individual than an ex-pupil of St X or St Y school. One cannot think in terms of individuals. Nor am I thinking in terms of numbers; I am thinking of ultimates. The average progressive school has what could be called ordered freedom; freedom within definite limits. A continuance of this type of school will result in ordered lives, in half-free citizens, in a compromise. While a continuance of education with real freedom must result finally in free men and women – not in a generation, not in two generations, but in the end people will be free.

Free to be what? Themselves. Themselves without hate and fear and authoritarianism. And I am not saying this with my head in the clouds; I am saying it after experience of the incredible results that freedom has on unhappy and warped children.

Many have said to me that Summerhill has done much to make other schools more human and less authoritative. I have said that I have had little success in spite of the fact that things are changing. We have our new primary schools with their happy faces and chatter, their individual interests. Fine but not quite satisfying to me, for the play instinct is not fully recognized. The child must be doing something, learning by doing, but still learning, while play has and should not have any conscious element of learning. We do have the outcrop of new free schools in the USA; and we have the de-schooling movement. Americans like John Holt, Paul Goodman, Ivan Illich, George Dennison and others have influenced American schools bravely.

There are instances where state schools have been allowed to carry out experiments ... E. F. O'Neill in Lancashire. A. A. Bloom in Stepney, but these two excellent men can only experiment marginally within the state system. O'Neill could saw up his ugly desks and make serviceable benches and tables; he could teach in a new and practical way. What he could not do (I assume) was to make all lessons voluntary. Twenty years ago I visited Bloom's school and was delighted with the obvious love and approval of the children. I saw no sign of fear in that school, and I could not see how Bloom could go further than he has gone under state control. True, the state will allow a teacher to pioneer in – say – methods of teaching history, but not in methods of living. Attempts made in state schools have usually run into difficulties.

Some time ago the headmaster of a secondary school told his pupils they could make their own timetables, and the press gave the idea publicity. His education authority met and decided that such an innovation should not be approved. If so mild an experiment in freedom is officially condemned, what hope is there for pioneering in state schools? I cannot see any future for pioneering if it is to be bound and shackled and conditional.

Any young teacher in a big school would find that it is impossible to vary from the school tradition and custom, but that is not to say that a teacher cannot use as much freedom as he dare. He can be on the side of the child; he can dispense with punishment; he can be human and jolly. Yet he will find himself in all sorts of difficulties. One of our old boys became a teacher in a school in which were many tough boys. He said to me, 'I began with Summerhill ideas but had to drop them. If I were nice to a kid he thought I was a softy, and my classroom became a bedlam.'

One drawback about giving freedom in a big state school is that most of the parents do not believe in freedom; too many of them look at a school as a place in which their erring offspring can be disciplined. I experienced this in a Scottish village school over fifty years ago. I had a succession of angry parents: 'I send my laddie to the schule to lairn lessons, no' to play a' day.' Freedom is easy in Summerhill because all the parents are with us.

In a state school the main work is learning school subjects. Attendance at classes is compulsory; duffers at maths have to sit there and do their best. There has to be discipline and absence of noise, but free children make a lot of noise. Everything is against the teacher – the buildings, the lack of space for real play, the marshalling, indeed the whole system of education. There can be no freedom so long as the educational Establishment rules that there must not be.

If Summerhill has had any influence I fancy that it was in most cases modified. Some schools accept freedom but they call it ordered freedom, to me a contradiction in terms, and, in any case what freedom can a poor teacher introduce into a barrack-like school with forty in a class? Yet much can be done even under adverse circumstances. Rising Hill School was an example. Michael Duane took over a comprehensive school in a very tough London area. Something like two hundred boys and girls were on probation. Duane refused to use the cane when urged by LCC inspectors to do so. In two years the number on probation was reduced to six. This means that one can use love and not hate in a state school, and is one answer to those who say that freedom is possible only in a boarding-school for middle-class children.

One objection I have to comprehensive schools in England is that they are too big. In a small town everyone has a personality; everyone is known by his neighbours, but in a big city one is in a huge impersonal crowd. So with the big school; the children become just numbers, and there cannot be much contact with the staff, for in a school of 1,200 pupils how can the headmaster know the names of all his pupils? But every child likes to be a personality, to be someone known and liked, and this he cannot be in a large school.

I should like to see a Department of Education plan to erase every big school in – say – London, build one-storey schools out in the country with acres of field and woods, and cart the children out of the city by bus every day.

I wish I could get people to understand that Joey Brown, aged ten, is not just a little boy to be disciplined and moulded by teachers and parents. Joe is a personality; he seeks approval and love and fun and games. In a small school he feels he is appreciated as a person, but in a big crowd he must feel as a private does in a brigade . . . just a unit, a number. So I suggest that one way to cure juvenile delinquents, or rather to prevent children from becoming delinquents, is to break up the large schools into small units. I have already mentioned Michael Duane's success with problem children in a big comprehensive school, but I think that he would have had even more success if he had had them in a small one. His school, Rising Hill, by the way, was eventually killed off by the anti-lifers.

It is rather sad that so much of the good work for freedom is done outside the state system. I think of men who deal with problem children . . . George Lyward, Otto Shaw, David Wills and others that I know less about. These men are far ahead of those officials, legal and otherwise, who believe that the cure for delinquents is a hard, disciplined life in some detention home with military discipline. The men I have mentioned were not inspired by Summerhill, barring Otto Shaw who, years ago, after many visits to my school, decided to start one of his own. Nor were any of the well-known coed schools like Bedales, Dartington Hall or St Christopher's.

Summerhill has always had a struggle to keep going. These are days of uncertainty, of fear; parents no longer have the patience and faith to send their children to a school in which they can play as an alternative to learning. They tremble to think that their son may not be capable of earning a living. Pioneering in education can flourish only in a period of security. I could possibly keep up my numbers if I announced that lessons would be made compulsory as in other schools, but if I did so the base of the system would be shattered. Educational history would say, 'Summerhill had freedom to study or not to study for fifty years, and it failed; Neill by introducing compulsion proved that children will not study unless under authority.'

It would of course be a false deduction, but it would be made and registered. It would be no defence to reply that taxation and insecurity made parents chary of risking their children's future, for the answer would be: 'A good thing can't be killed by economic factors.' Another fallacy. Tom Smith in my father's village school sixty years ago was brilliant, but his father was a ploughman and Tom went on the land, and when I met him years later he was dull and narrow.

Other progressive schools are having a similar struggle to survive. I think then that the prospective demise of the pioneer school makes the subject of freedom a very vital one. Already the freedom of the pioneer school has, to some extent, permeated other schools, state and private. Many and many a teacher has said to me, 'We can't do what Summerhill does, but the mere fact that it lives and works is an inspiration to us who are under a rigid system.'

When the pioneer schools die, where will the stimulus come from? I say: from parents who believe in self-regulation for their children. I can visualize a time when so many parents will be using self-regulation that they will not tolerate a school system that will undo their work with their children at home.

Here I am inclined to laugh at myself. I am tired of the nostrum that promises to save humanity . . . food reformers, political agitators, drugs combines, schools of psychology, religious panaceas. I laugh because I am adding another panacea to the regiment of soap-box orators and their wares, adding self-regulation. Yet I claim that of all these nostrums self-regulation is about the only one that has not been tried. All the others deal with adulthood. To begin with infants may seem ludicrous to many, and yet it is not too fanciful to say that Christianity began to fail because its advocates dropped the suffer-little-children component and adopted the adult, hateful gospel according to St Paul. Communism also dropped its little-children component in favour of a patriarchal authority. Hence from my little soap-box in the park I implore the passing and unheeding pedestrians to seek in our treatment of children the solution of human frustration and misery.

Recent Changes

Now that I am in my eighty-eighth year, I feel that I shall not write another book about education, for I have little new to say. But what I have to say has something in my favour; I have not spent the last fifty years writing down *theories* about children. Most of what I have written has been based on observing children, living with them. True, I have derived inspiration from Freud, Homer Lane, Wilhelm Reich, and others; but gradually, I have tended to drop theories when the test of reality proved them invalid.

It is a queer job, that of an author. As with broadcasting, an author sends out some sort of message to people he does not see, people he cannot count. My public has been a special one. What might be called the official public knows me not. The BBC would certainly never think of inviting me to give a broadcast talk on education. When I lecture to Oxford and Cambridge students, no professor, no don comes to hear me. At one time, I resented the fact that *The Times* would never publish any letter I sent in; but today, I feel their refusal is a compliment. Altogether, I think I am rather proud of these facts, feeling that to be acknowledged by the officials would suggest that I was out of date.

If I were Lord Summerhill I should blush when any shopkeeper called me 'My Lord', realizing what a stuffed shirt I should be. Now that I have recently received three honorary degrees I have to wonder if I am becoming out of date. I did have a bit of conscience about accepting these honorary degrees, seeing that I don't know what education is: I only know what it isn't.

I discovered long ago where a teacher really stands socially. When I was headmaster of a village school and some function took place the laird came first, then the minister, then the doctor. I was down the table with the head gardener. A teacher is almost a gentleman. I suppose my honorary degrees have made me one at last.

I do not claim that I have quite outgrown the wish for

recognition; yet age brings changes – especially changes in values. Recently I lectured to seven hundred teachers, packing a hall built for six hundred, and I had no feeling of elation or conceit. I thought I was really indifferent until I asked myself the question, 'How would you have felt if the audience had consisted of ten?' The answer was 'Damned annoyed,' so that if positive pride is lacking, negative chagrin is not.

Ambition dies with age. Recognition is a different matter. I do not like to see a book with the title of, say, 'The History of Progressive Schools' when such a book ignores my work. I have never yet met anyone who was honestly indifferent to recognition.

Of course it is easy to lay the flattering unction to our souls that we are far too ahead of the times to be recognized, that in a hundred years we shall come into our own. That is a pleasant daydream, one that I cannot be content with now that I am old. No, I am not really troubled by being unmentioned in other books. What does disturb me is plagiarism. I have had a man visit us for a few weeks, studying our self-government. Later he had a full-page article on the wonderful self-government he had established in his own school, without once mentioning that he had got the idea from Summerhill. I got my self-government from Homer Lane and his Little Commonwealth, and I have never hesitated to acknowledge my debt in books and lectures. A good plagiarist should be like a good liar . . . he should be clever enough not to be found out.

No man does anything off his own bat; every man is a conglomeration of outside influences with, of course, something personal added. Many have influenced me . . . H. G. Wells, Bernard Shaw, Freud, Homer Lane, Wilhelm Reich, but not, as I have said, the educationists. I have often been called a disciple of Rousseau, but I did not read *Émile* until fifty years after opening Summerhill. Then I felt very humble to discover that what a man wrote in theory two hundred years ago I had been practising in ignorance of his ideas. Also I was somewhat disappointed. Émile was free but only in the set environment prescribed by his tutor. Summerhill is a set environment but it is the community that decides, not the individual tutor.

I sometimes think that critics are too glib about attributing influence; only a man himself can know who influenced him. The great educators had no influence on me whatever. I have tried reading John Dewey with little success, and am ignorant of Pestalozzi and Froebel. So many who write about education are dull or long-winded or both. I find Dewey such a writer, plus 90 per cent of those who write for *The Times Educational Supplement.*

I read Montessori, but she had only a negative influence on me, because I disapproved of her separation of work and play, her condemnation of fantasy in a child's life. I saw children in a Montessori school fitting triangles into triangles when they should have been plastering the wall with their paintings. Many years ago I saw Montessori's chief lieutenant, Signorina Maccheroni, snatch the Long Stair (a learning apparatus) from a child who was playing trains with it. The child was furious. So was I. From that moment I disliked the rigidity, discipline, and morality of the system.

There is a comical aspect of age. For years I have been trying to reach the young – young students, young teachers, young parents – seeing age as a brake on progress. Now that I am old – one of the Old Men I have preached against so long – I feel differently. Recently, when I talked to three hundred students in Cambridge, I felt myself the youngest person in the hall. I *did*. I said to them, 'Why do you need an old man like me to come and tell *you* about freedom?' Nowadays, I do not think in terms of youth and age. I feel that years have little to do with one's thinking. I know lads of twenty who are ninety, and men of sixty who are twenty. I am thinking in terms of freshness, enthusiasm, of lack of conservatism, of deadness, of pessimism.

I do not know if I have mellowed or not. I suffer fools less gladly than I used to do, am more irritated by boring conversations, and less interested in people's personal histories. But then, I've had far too many imposed on me these last fifty years. I also find less interest in things, and seldom want to buy anything. I haven't looked in a clothes-shop window for years. And even my beloved tool shops in Euston Road do not attract me nowadays.

If I have now reached the stage when children's noise tires me more than it used to, I cannot say that age has brought impatience. I can still see a child do all the wrong things, live out all the old complexes, knowing that in good time the child will be a good citizen. Age lessens fear. But age also lessens courage. Years ago, I could easily tell a boy who threatened to jump from a high window if he did not get his own way to go on and jump. I am not so sure I could do so today.

I have seen many changes in my long life, not only in material things like motors, films, radio, TV, but what one might call cultural things, changes in human outlook. In my youth, we had to wear costumes when bathing, and sex and swearing were taboo. When Shaw's play *Pygmalion* was produced with Eliza Dolittle's 'not bloody likely', every paper printed the word as b—y. Today even the highbrow papers will print words like 'shit', 'fart', 'fuck'. But why good old Anglo-Saxon words were considered obscene I never knew.

I have lived to see a great release of sex in women. In my early days a woman was not supposed to have any pleasure in sex, a belief sponsored by many women who had no orgastic life owing to the ignorance or selfishness of their men. Today women openly acknowledge their demand for as much freedom in sex as men. Virginity has even lost its air of sanctity.

In my lifetime the world has become more sinister, more dangerous, and here I am not thinking of wars, I am thinking of the diminishing power of the people and the growing power of the big businesses, the combines, the dehumanization of industry. At the beginning of the century small businesses were common. The boss was Bill Smith who knew his hands and their families. Today workmen have no Bill Smith to approach with any difficulties they may have: they have the great bureaucratic, humanless company.

I have lived to see – I won't say the death of God since there are many millions of Moslems and Catholics around – lived to see the decline of Protestant religion. In England the churches are not full; youth is largely indifferent to organized religion. It does not believe in sin and heaven and hell. Its gods are more or less harmless – pop stars, disc jockeys, football heroes – but the 'new religion' has one characteristic in common with the old: the hate and violence between the supporters of football teams compares with the hate and violence in religious Ulster with its Roman Catholic and Protestant teams wanting to murder each other.

It is a known fact that with age comes conservatism. Without patting myself on the back I think I have escaped becoming conservative. That does not mean that I have accepted the mores and tastes of the young. My pupils play records that almost pain me, pop music, cheap songs. They read books that to me are childish. They look at TV shows that to me are pre-adolescent. Dating from the days of slow tango and foxtrot, I cannot stand their monstrous dancing. Even their jazz is not my jazz of the Bix Beiderbecke period.

Youth does not want our culture. How many young teenagers know even the names of Ibsen, Proust, Strindberg, Dante? I am not saying that this is a bad thing. Our culture was static, absorbing books and plays and ideas, but today youth's culture tends towards doing, movement, relaxation, so that one has to ask: Which is better, to sit and read D. H. Lawrence or to go out and dance all night?

Gulfs are inevitable. If conservatism means retaining what is past I am a conservative about, say, silent films, but to me it does not mean that; it means refusing to look at new facts and factors, following father's footsteps, supporting reactionary habits and measures. Britain is full of conservatives, whether they label themselves Tories or Liberals or Labour. To me a conservative is one who accepted the dictates of father and hence all authority, and as I say, even the young radicals often later regress to follow the old Oedipus tradition. One compromises, becomes conservative when one has not enough belief in what one is doing or thinking, when one lacks sincerity, integrity.

I find I can still make contact with the young in many ways, in serious discussions, for example, about life and love and social questions. There can of course be no bridge if the old persist in trying to give the young their previous-generation values. The parents *know* what is right, but the children *feel* what is right for them. There is a natural bridge in a family in which there is a mutual sympathy between old and young, a family in which parents and children do not need to lie to each other, a family with trust and understanding. I love Wagner. My wife Ena dislikes Wagner. I play my beloved *Meistersinger* when she is in another room. My stepson Peter Wood loves Bach. I don't. I walk out of the room. Family life must be give and take.

If a gulf is there it is not made by music or other tastes: it arises from the inability of the old to understand the young. And it arises largely through fear, fear that the young will stray, fear that they are not studying enough, fear that they will not succeed in life. We can disapprove of some of the things the young do, but we must not disapprove of the young themselves.

I think that in Summerhill we do not have the usual generation gap. Though gap there would have to be if drugs came into the school. To take drugs is to escape from a miserable life, and it is the easy way. I am afraid that, instead of seeking freedom by living naturally, youth will use the quick method of the trip, and we cannot be moral about it.

The changes in education have been too slow for me. Freedom in schools has grown, but not so fast as belief in book learning and examinations; the old patriarchal demand of obedience and discipline is as strong as ever in all state systems.

Have I changed my system in any way? I cannot think of any specific change on my part, but there have been changes on the part of children. Before the war we had certain out-of-bounds rules made by the staff. Pupils were forbidden to use the front stairs and the staff lavatory; the round lawn at the front door was out of bounds. The staffroom was made free from invasion. Gradually these prohibitions have disappeared. Gradually the staffroom furniture goes the dilapidated way of the pupils' sitting-room furniture.

Children have changed in some indefinable ways. Thirty years ago I could begin the cure of a young thief by giving him sixpence every time he stole, but I doubt if that method would work today. The new children appear to have a sophistication that I cannot analyse. Maybe due to the increased sickness of the world, to having too much money without doing a thing to earn it. Subtly and unconsciously they may be reacting to the hate that is in racism, anti-Semitism, possibly to the uncertainty of the future in an unemployed world; maybe deeper, the feeling that life itself is uncertain with atom bombs and pollution. I do not know, but I feel that I cannot understand the new generation as I did the older one.

Maybe they have heard too many glib psychological terms . . . as too many American children have done. Perhaps new material values have changed them, giving them a false orientation. Life was simpler in the past. When I started to drive forty-five years ago I might meet two cars in a mile. Today I seem to meet two in ten yards.

My pupils today seem to me to be less communal, less able to grasp and practise self-government than formerly. Some get too much money from their parents, so that saving for a rainy day is something unknown to them. Children demand more now; the old rag doll has been replaced by the talking doll, but I rejoice to notice that most girls still prefer the lower-class model. The question of this new shallow sophistication is so complicated. I have a vague feeling that it has a lot to do with money. Today I don't see the young, even those in their twenties, saving money. It burns a hole in their pockets. This may be due partly to the insecurity of modern life with its wars and crimes and hatreds, and its possible ultimate nuclear destruction. Fundamentally the change in youth must be due to its loss of faith in age, in authority, in power, and for that I can cry hurrah to the new generation.

The young have come to see through the pretences and morals of their elders. They realize that they have been lied to and cheated. Youth today challenges more loudly than the past generation did. It was not youth that made the H bomb: it was age. But youth knows that it is powerless. Their lives are in the hands of the old men – the politicians, the military, the nationalists, the rich and powerful. Events and fear have made youth adult before its time, and that may be one explanation of the new sophistication.

A few generations ago youth accepted its lower status, accepted the directions of the fathers and their symbols. Today youth rebels but in a futile way. Its weird haircuts, its leather jackets, its blue jeans, its motor bikes are all symbols of rebellion but symbols that remain symbols. Nearly every child hates school subjects but every child knows that it can do nothing to change the system. In essentials youth is still docile, obedient, inferior; it challenges the things that do not matter – clothes, manners, and hairstyles.

All the talk about teenage wickedness is rubbish. Teenagers are no more wicked than you or I. They seek the joy of life in an era that does not know joy; all it knows are TV and sports and the sensational press. Its ideals are wealth and big cars and expensive restaurants; its glamour is attached to film and TV stars and ephemeral pop music. Youth sees mostly an acquisitive society that is trite and cheap and tawdry, and the schools, by separating themselves from after-school life, do nothing for the young.

What makes me almost despair is that children never get a chance to live; their love for life is killed by an adult world that 'trains' – that is castrates – youth. True, freedom is growing but oh, so slowly. The bitter truth is that man's thinking and invention have gone far ahead of his inhibited emotions, and that is the real danger of the bomb, for wars are not caused by thinking; they are caused by emotion. A crowd goes mad if its national flag is insulted.

I am pessimistic about the slow growth of freedom. Have we time to bring up children who will be free emotionally? Free from hate and aggression, free to live and let others live? So that the question resolves itself into this one: can humanity evolve in such a way that all people will feel free inside, free from the fatal wish to mould other people?

Who can answer?

I have had to change my ideas on many things in recent years. I used to think that boys and girls stuck to traditional ways, the boys liking woodwork, the girls sewing and knitting. Today the workshop has as many girls as boys in it, but I still never see girls taking their bikes to pieces as boys do.

I have had to change my ideas on handiwork. My kids made things to which they could attach a fantasy – boats, guns, swords – and they smiled at my hobby, hammered brass and copper. I thought that such work could not attract them because it takes a lot of imagination to attach a fantasy to a brass bowl. But when Peter Wood opened his pottery shop, the rage for making vases and teapots was great. I had to conclude that I was wrong, for I cannot imagine what fantasy can be linked up with a teapot.

I too often erred by keeping bullies who frightened younger children. Mostly because I did not know where to send them, fearing that a fear school would ruin them for life. Today I would throw out a confirmed bully of fourteen if small pupils were anxious. Too many problems are dumped on us and the parents do not tell us. Fifty years of pulling parental chestnuts out of the fire have been enough for me.

One thing I cannot make up my mind about. Is Summerhill better for the bright child than for the one with a low IQ? (By the way we do not use IQs in Summerhill, possibly because when a teacher gave the whole school a test, two boys and a girl beat me.) One thing is sure, our academic successes all come from fairly free homes with intelligent parents.

I have reluctantly come to the conclusion that a few children, very few, cannot take freedom and would be better at a school with benign discipline, children who seem to need a shove. Yet often we have pupils who hardly ever attend a lesson in ten years and are now successful people, so maybe I am wrong about that kick in the pants. I must be, for although naturally I am not in touch with all my old pupils, I know of only one who cannot hold down a job.

Fundamentally I have changed nothing. If I could begin another fifty years of Summerhill I would retain self-government, freedom to go or stay away from lessons, no indoctrination in morality or religion, no fear in the school.

But how can anyone be free when we were all moulded in our cradles? Freedom is a relative term. The freedom we think about in Summerhill is individual freedom, inner freedom. Few of us can have that inner freedom. In our school freedom means doing what you like so long as you do not interfere with the freedom of others. That is the outer meaning, but deeper down we strive to see that children are free internally, free from fear, from hypocrisy, from hate, from intolerance.

The whole set-up of society is against such freedom; every man seeks freedom, but is afraid of it at the same time . . , Erich Fromm's *Fear of Freedom* makes this clear. National freedom so often results in blood baths; individual freedom can end in tragedy – Wilhelm Reich, for instance, in our time and many martyrs in past days. Reich, by the way, in his book *The Murder of Christ*, argues that Christ himself was crucified because he was pro-life and pro-freedom.

Ibsen says, 'The strongest man is he who stands most alone.' The man who seeks freedom for the world does stand alone . . . if he is a danger to the entrenched society. No authority has attacked Summerhill, but if many free schools sprang up and the established order were threatened, it could happen that Summerhill would be closed. The first motive of a crowd is to preserve itself, yet the rebels manage to permeate the armour even if slightly, and in the long run the crowd changes, but ever so slowly. Ibsen says somewhere that a truth remains a truth for twenty years; then the majority gets hold of it and it becomes a lie.

I do not think that the world will use the Summerhill method of education for a very long time – if it ever uses it. The world may find a better way. Only an empty windbag would assume that his work is the last word on the subject. The world *must* find a better way. For politics will not save humanity. It never has done so.

How can we have happy homes with love in them when the home is a tiny corner of a homeland that shows hate socially in a hundred ways? You can see why I cannot look upon education as a matter of exams and classes and learning. The school evades the basic issue – all the science and maths and history in the world will not help to make the home more loving, the child free from inhibitions, the parents free from neurosis.

The future of Summerhill itself may be of little import. But the future of the Summerhill idea is of the greatest importance to humanity. New generations must be given the chance to grow in freedom. The bestowal of freedom is the bestowal of love. And only love can save the world.

World Wide

Is Summerhill known throughout the world? Hardly. And only to a comparative handful of educators. For many years Summerhill was best known in Scandinavia. For thirty years, we had pupils from Norway, Sweden, Denmark – sometimes twenty at a time. The educational standard of these countries is an academic one and they worship examinations. I said to an audience in Stockholm, 'You Swedes come out in crowds to hear me talk about freedom. At the same time your schools are factories for turning out children who can pass examinations. Why don't you do something about it?'

One teacher got up. 'You see, Neill, the men who control education do not come to your lectures.'

One handicap for them is that private schools have been much more under state control than they are with us, and I know that the noble pioneer, Gustav Johnsson, has had much opposition in carrying out his work with delinquents. Since Reich lived for some time in Scandinavia there are quite a few teachers and parents who have been influenced by his doctrine of self-regulation.

During those early years we also had pupils from Australia, New Zealand, South Africa, and Canada. My books have been translated into many languages, including Japanese, Hebrew, Hindustani, and Gujarati. A principal of a school in the Sudan tells me that Summerhill is of great interest to some teachers there.

There are translations into two Indian languages, with what results I do not know, but make the guess that they do not have much influence, for India is almost certain to think that illiteracy is the main problem to be tackled. When in 1936 I talked with semi-literate South African natives, their one idea was to get a white man's education in school subjects.

I question if Summerhill is well known in Scotland. I was once introduced to the owner of a big bookshop there. He gripped my hand firmly and said, 'Man, it is an honour to meet the author of

The Booming of Bunkie' (the title of a farcical and poor novel I wrote in 1918). Scots who trek south are never very much honoured in their native land, and any Scot who returns to his home town expecting to be received as an honoured visitor is ignorant of his own national characteristics.

The way to go back to Scotland is to dress humbly, talk dialect, and on no account mention that England exists, for to many Scots it does not, just as Scotland is only a name to some English people. John Aitkenhead followed Summerhill when he set up his Kilquhanity School in Scotland, but then wisely went his own way, although the two schools retained their fundamental belief in self-government.

One pleasant feature about Summerhill has been its influence in Japan. Over forty years ago we had a visit from Seishi Shimod a, an outstanding educationist. He has translated all my books since the days of *The Problem Child* and, according to my royalty account, a large quantity has been sold. I hear about teachers in Tokyo meeting to discuss our methods. I gather that the Japanese system of education is a strong and authoritative one, with discipline strict and unbending. It is rather embarrassing to have a line of books in Japanese on my shelves; one of them, entitled *A. S. Neill and his Work*, intrigues me, and my little joke when I ask my music teacher to play it for me hides a curiosity that cannot be satisfied. Mr Shimoda again spent a month with us in 1958.

In recent years Summerhill has had Americans (over half the pupils in 1971), Swedes, Norwegians, Danes, Germans, Dutch, and French. They all learn English and adapt themselves to our way of life. None of us tries to learn their languages, nor do we adapt ourselves to their manner of living ... their food for example. When we had an International School in Hellerau, and later in Austria, we all had to learn German and had to adapt ourselves to German diet and customs ... I had to teach at seven in the morning in the summer term. I hated the early rising.

In Hellerau we were in the main internationally minded. We had every nationality in Europe except Spanish. There was no anti-Semitism at the school. In Dresden in 1921 the big shops had notices, 'No Jews Will Be Served', but their prejudice began decades before then. I look back on those days with much sadness, for many of our pupils were Jewish and they must all have ended in the gas chambers.

I cannot judge what effect the school at Hellerau had on the pupils; I can only know what the experience did for me. It made me an internationalist; it did not destroy my attachment to Scotland or England – indeed what I got was intangible, perhaps a feeling of brotherhood that the stay-at-home cannot achieve. Even when later, in the Templehof in Berlin, I listened to Hitler's roaring hate I still could not hate the Germans, and when I read of German casualties in the Second World War, I wondered sadly if Fritz and Hermann were among them.

I recall my first trip abroad, to Holland. I thought to myself: 'In this landscape, with its coloured barges and cheap cigars and plethora of butter and cheese, every native must be happy.' I felt the same, to a lesser extent, in the USA: why, even the Babbits I picked up, or rather who picked me up in pullmans, had a touch of that glamour that tints the unknown. Damon Runyan and his romantic train of crooks and pimps on the one side; Damon Runyan dying wretchedly of cancer of the throat on the other. Every promised country has a touch of the promised land, of Arcadia.

I have no illusion about internationalism. I cannot think that world peace will be saved by a hundred international schools. The powers that make war have no connection with the workers for world peace. Peace can come only when we abolish nationalism and exploitation of oil and gold. Did the men who died in the Boer War die for the honour of Britain or for the profits of the diamond and gold shareholders? Perhaps the most puzzling feature in man is his capacity for sacrificing himself for objects he is unconscious of.

Sixty million Germans followed a madman. Thousands in the USA have cried, 'Better dead than red,' a most silly war cry, for Communism changes every day; the young in Russia, I hear, won't read Karl Marx. If one must fight Communism it should be by proving that capitalism is the better horse, that it gives more happiness to more people. I cannot understand the alarm and fury the word Communism arouses in America. The main difference between the two systems seems to be that one allows profit and the other doesn't. Both systems mould their children in home and school; both emphasize nationalism; both think that peace depends on the H bomb; both inhibit the individual. A Russian cannot buy a western daily paper, barring the London Communist Party paper, the *Morning Star*, and an American cannot call himself a Communist.

Originally my politics were mixed up with emotion. When Winston Churchill came to contest Dundee as a Liberal I was still a young student-teacher. I rejoiced at a Tory handbill: 'What is the use of a WC without a seat?' and threw things at young Winston when he spoke at an open-air meeting, mainly because a girl called Ella Robertson dared me to. Later, in 1913, when I first went to live in London I joined the Labour Party and spoke ignorant rubbish in Hyde Park.

After the Russian Revolution, when reports told of new freedom in schools (children could apparently choose to learn or play and they had self-government in their schools), I fondly imagined that Utopia had suddenly arrived for good, but, as a canny Scot, I did not join the Party. For years I had a blind spot; I simply would not accept the stories of Stalin's mass murder by starvation of a million or more peasants who would not fit into his state farming scheme. But I did wonder why Bolsheviks of the old brigade were confessing to crimes they had not committed before they were shot in the back of the neck. The truth is that I *wanted* to believe in the new order; I wanted to think that the new education in Russia was wonderful, hence my blind eye. My disillusionment took many years.

In 1937 I applied for a visa to visit Russia. It was refused, no reason being given. By that time I had given up my hope that Communism was a cure for world sickness. I ceased to be interested in politics of any kind, but voted Labour in the belief that it was more pro-life than was Conservative, and I still hold that belief in spite of my disappointment with Labour rule. Labour, at least, is against class distinctions. I should really vote Tory because the Tories will never give up their public schools. And as long as Eton and Harrow exist my own school is safe.

Your voice and mine never reach the war makers and the statesmen. They have the power and we have only our dreams of freedom for mankind.

I was not really conscious of politics until in 1950 I applied to the American Embassy for a visa. I had already lectured in the USA in 1947 and 1948 and the 1950 tour had been arranged by Reich. I was kept waiting for an hour and suspected that something was wrong. Then I was called before an official.

'Are you a Communist?'

'No, I am not.'

'Have you ever written anything in favour of Communism?'

Then I knew he had phoned the Home Office and asked for my dossier.

'I have written about eighteen books but I never read them and have no idea what is in them; I have a vague idea that I praised Russian education as it was after the Revolution. Then it was for freedom but today it is like your and our education, against freedom.'

My application was refused and my lecture tour cancelled. These were the McCarthy days of course.

I recall saying to the consul, 'I am a communist in the way Jesus Christ was one, communist with a small c.' He gave me a look of shock and I guessed he was a Catholic. I found out later that he was. The sequel came when in December 1969 Orson Bean invited me to go over to take part in the Johnny Carson TV show. Again I went to the embassy.

'It won't take more than twenty minutes, Mr Neill; please fill in this form.'

Question: Have you ever been refused a visa by the American government. I sighed and wrote yes, in 1950, which meant that the twenty minutes was more like two hours. I was asked to fill in the complete form, and then more waits, more interviews. Finally I was given a visa for four years. The annoying thing was that the consul said; 'We have no record of your being refused a visa.' Then I felt like kicking myself for my useless honesty.

But this is gossip, not politics. I know that some have to deal with government, finance, foreign policy. I know that democracy is phoney; our last election in Britain gave the Tories a majority but the Labour and Liberal parties combined got more votes than those cast for the Tories. But since the alternative to democracy is dictatorship we cannot give it up. It is all so sinister. When I see on TV the primary elections in the USA, with their infantile parades and bands and flags, I feel dejected and hopeless. I see behind them the self-seeking lobbyists, the rat-race of capitalism. When a President makes some gesture – Nixon going to China, for example – who knows what the motive is? Some Americans say he is thinking of the next presidential election.

I often think that the USA is on the verge of fascism. Since the fascist mentality controls the mass media – press, TV, radio – and feeds the masses on kitsch, I tremble for the future. I fear that fascist Reagan reaches a much wider public than I do, and I don't get much comfort in thinking that Summerhill will live long after he is forgotten.

At the moment the Tory government is hiving off industries that the previous Labour government nationalized. The old saying was that trade follows the flag. It is the other way round; often trade seems to control politics.

The title of the German edition of *Summerhill* is *Theory and Practice in Anti-authoritarian Education*, the publisher's title, not mine. Various young Germans try to use the book in their fight for Communism or Social Democracy or what not. I tell them that the book has nothing to do with politics. Politics means democracy. Democracy, the votes of the masses castrated in their cradles. Without the castration we might get politics that were sincere and pro-life. All my life I could never catch crowd emotion. I could never wave a flag, never shout a slogan, never become active in any party, political or otherwise. A rank individualist dealing with crowds of kids.

No, I cannot see the honesty in most politics or politicians. My politics, happily, are mostly confined to our school democracy, which is as near real democracy as it can be. We meet in a big room and make our laws by general show of hands. I know that this system could not be applied to the mass of voters across the country, yet to me a democracy in which one man is supposed to represent the opinions of thirty thousand is a fake democracy. I am aware that many politicians do much good work. What puts me off politics is the indifference of the ruling people, whatever their party.

For instance, in Britain our prison system is a disgrace. Men are treated with little humaneness, they are deprived of sex, of culture, of everything that makes life life. The barbarous system is accepted not only by politicians but by the clergy, the doctors, the lawyers, indeed by people in general. A well-fed judge will sentence men to thirty years for robbing a train and no politician protests in Parliament. Another judge will sentence a murderer to life imprisonment, which in practice means nine or ten years.

I suddenly realize that I am quite proud of having been refused a visa by the USSR and by the USA. Maybe this is my claim to immortality.

I think that in some ways Britain is freer than the United States. I have had Summerhill in England for forty-six years and I have had no trouble from the state or the church. But I am afraid that had I tried to have a free school in the States I might have had trouble with the Catholics or the Baptists or the Daughters of the American Revolution. And the school could not have avoided the racists, for a free school must take all colours and races. None of my Americans seem to have come from anti-race homes, so perhaps I cannot judge the average American child by my experience of them.

The name of Harold Hart, my American publisher, should live if only because he saved Summerhill. In 1960, when he published *Summerhill*, we were down to twenty-five pupils and wondered if we could carry on. The publication of the book brought the invasion of American pupils and eleven years later the German translation brought the Teutonic invasion. In the preface of *Summerhill, For and Against* Hart tells of his struggle to get the book on the market; he spent quite a few thousands on publicizing it because he believed in it and was ready to take the risk.

I notice that my American pupils have an anxiety about their future for, with the exception of the very young ones, they have all experienced the pressurizing of American schools; they all know that their future depends on college training and degrees. Britain has not imitated their insane drive to examinations, but, alas, the drive is coming quickly. My stepson Peter Wood trained with Bernard Leach, one of the best potters in the world. He applied for a job teaching evening classes in a city. The job went to a teacher who knew little about ceramics but who had a Handiwork Teacher's Certificate.

Many of our American pupils read *Summerhill* and demanded to come. Most American pupils adapt well. In half a term 'I'm going to the beth room' becomes 'Fuck off, I'm going to the bogs.' We began to find difficulties, especially with the older ones. Their attitude was: 'This is a free school: I'll do what I like.' It took them some time to grasp the fact that freedom does not mean doing exactly as you like. They found that in a self-governing school they had to obey thc laws made by the whole community. And it was hard for some of them to conform.

Now we make the upper age limit for entry twelve. Most pupils over fourteen have come too late to freedom; they have had too long a period of repression and they too often express their new-found freedom in antisocial behaviour, boredom, idleness with a bad conscience.

American adolescents seem to have a stronger reaction to their homes than our children have. Family ties, or should I say pressures, are stronger in the USA, and that is one reason why my home pupils seem to go home for vacations more eagerly than their American fellows do. Some say that they are not happy at home, that their parents do not understand them; in some cases this is due to the horrid American system that makes a college career seem essential to so many young people. The parents get alarmed about the children's future and in a few cases this alarm has prevented their children from getting the full benefit from Summerhill. The child is in a conflict.

The school says, 'You are free to go to lessons or stay away. The wish to learn must come from inside yourself,' but when a parent writes hoping that the child is attending lessons, the result is unhappiness, with a complete absence of desire to attend any classes. Recently I asked one father either to stop telling his son to attend lessons or to take him away. He took him away.

American pupils don't know their own slang. I asked a lad of thirteen how many names he knew for a revolver. He said gun, automatic, pistol. Never heard of gat, iron, rod, Betsy, John Roscoe, or the Old Equalizer. He'd never heard of Damon Runyan or O'Henry. Still, our home lot never read Jerome K. Jerome or W. W. Jacobs. Makes me feel my age.

When one of my American pupils has to go home and enter an American school I get a long form to fill up with dozens of questions: motivation, industry, self-confidence, etc. I draw my pen through the lot and on the back of the form I give my opinion of the child in a few lines.

American parents, as well as having more anxiety about the economic future of their children, also seem more frightened about sex than English parents. I get more fussiness from American parents than from British ones, but that may be due partly to the anxiety of parents three thousand miles from their children.

For some reason it hurts me when some new school in the USA calls itself a Summerhill. Often I heard Reich say, 'I want no disciples,' and I feel as he did. More than once I have sent letters to new educational journals in America imploring teachers to stand on their own feet and not copy Summerhill. Of late, I am glad to say, I seldom see the word Summerhill on their pages. I heard of a school in the USA that claimed to run on Summerhill lines. It had half an hour's compulsory religious lesson every morning. At one school there were stories of promiscuous fucking amongst the adolescents with the ten-year-olds trying to imitate them. I have heard other stories of young pupils using dope.

I have been called a pioneer, and if a pioneer is one who does not accept crowd values, I suppose I am one. New ideas come from individuals; Marx was greater than the Fabian Society; Simpson was greater than the diehard doctors who rejected his chloroform. Both of these, of course, were in a category far above mine. The prophet's voice always cries in the wilderness. And that makes me pessimistic about humanity. For man is a herd animal and herds seek leaders. They are also like wolves, pack animals.

The powers above cleverly exploit our herd instinct. It is a platitude today to say that they castrate children by making them fearful of authority and making them guilty about religion and sex, so that when adult they are neutral sheep with no guts to challenge anything. Hitler castrated a nation but our overlords are much more subtle; their equivalent of *'Heil Hitler'* is 'Law and Order', which means the defence of property and the stifling of life.

Our schools' chief function is to kill the life of children. Otherwise the Establishment would be powerless. Would millions of free men allow themselves to be sacrificed to causes they had no interest in and did not understand? Is the future of humanity one of slaves ruled by an élite of powerful masters?

But now let me be more optimistic. In fifty years of free children I have detected not only an absence of the competitive spirit, but also a total indifference to leaders. One can reason with free children but one cannot lead them. True, my pupils lived in their own herd, but not with leadership.

A headmaster can be, indeed is, a father-figure but no child can make its school self-government a father-figure. I say that the future success of the world will come from the rejection of the father, the crowd leader. Most people accept father and mother, meaning that the great majority joins the Establishment, the anti-progress and usually anti-life majority. Our school systems, whether capitalist or Communist, foster this early moulding of the masses because wolf leaders are tough and powerful and ruthless, and their main aim is to kill and eat. In the human herd we have it in replica. The wars for gold or whatnot, the takeover bids which often make thousands unemployed, the bludgeoning of the young by sadistic cops. If the people were free such barbarities could not live.

What I do know is that as long as his long helpless childhood is conditioned by adults who accept the crowd attitude to life, man will not be free. It is good to see so many young people challenge authority in the West, but so depressing to see a TV film on China when a million children wave their little red books, their individuality crushed out in their cradles. Communism is the super-manipulator of mass psychology; the crowd does not think: it feels.

I know that the herd instinct can never be abolished. My concern is to see it so modified that it will cease to be a danger. Man seeks freedom and at the same time is afraid of it. Many Southern slaves were scared when they were given freedom. Old prison inmates, after a long stretch inside, find life outside terrifying. Yet I like to think that in a thousand years the masses will have modified their crowd instinct so that competition will have been overcome by co-operation, hate by love, pornography by natural love. There will be no more lone wolves, only leaderless pack wolves seeking a common good.

Last Words

I wrote my autobiography in Norway in 1939. My then publishers did not think it would sell so I dumped the manuscript in a drawer and forgot about it until my good friend and translator Shimoda asked if he could translate it into Japanese. He did. I see the volume on my shelves, but, for all I can tell, it could be *Lady Chatterley's Lover*.

Every autobiography is, if not a lie, an evasion of the truth. Indeed I wonder what value an autobiography has. To know that J. M. Barrie and Ruskin and Carlyle were impotent, to know that Freud, when catching a train, had to be in the station an hour beforehand, to know that Reich was over-jealous or that Oscar Wilde was homosexual: I cannot see how such knowledge affects our judgement of their work. Luckily we know almost nothing of Shakespeare.

Not my life but only what I have done seems to me cogent, and what have I done anyway? The great ones, the Freuds, the Einsteins, made new discoveries: I discovered nothing. The new dynamic psychology showed that the emotions are the driving force in life, not the intellect, so I founded a school in which the emotions would come first. For years I have wondered why a million teachers did not grasp the simple truth and leave kids to grow up in their own way and at their own speed. Maybe they could not because they had to bring their own personalities into their work.

If I have any special talent it is that of staying in the background. Often I sit through a Summerhill General Meeting without saying a word. Without boasting, I think that here I go one better than Homer Lane, whose strong personality coloured the Little Commonwealth. I was never a strong man and I don't like strong men who sway crowds or families or classrooms.

I ask myself what sort of man am I? Folks call me amiable and it may be so, for I am pretty equable and placid, never flying off the handle as Reich used to do.

I have no idea how I look. I can't recall looking into a mirror since I took to an electric razor some years ago. It takes a long time to realize that no one cares a damn how one looks. The lovelorn swain of twenty really thinks that the desired one will be impressed by his having socks and tie that match in colour.

I have had fame, or maybe I should call it publicity, with thousands of visitors to Summerhill in recent years and a large fan mail. Unfortunately most things in life come too late. Barrie put it: 'They give you nuts to chew when your teeth have gone.'

When one is old praise is sweet to be sure but blame has no special emotional impact. A recent rather nasty article in a Sunday paper about the Summerhill fiftieth anniversary party in London did not make me angry or even concerned. Perhaps because I have not been accustomed to enmity. I know of no one who is my enemy, though there must be a few thousand parents in the USA, Germany, Brazil, etc., who hate my guts. I hear of some from their children . . . 'When I quote your *Summerhill* to my parents they go haywire. Daddy has forbidden me to read it.'

I am often spoken of as the man who loves children. Love is hardly the word to use when a problem boy is breaking my school windows. One cannot love masses, only individuals, and not all individuals are lovable. No, I reject the word love; I prefer Homer Lane's 'being on the side of the child', which means approval, sympathy, kindness, plus a complete absence of adult authority. It is of more value to understand children than to love them.

I read recently that a coward is always an introvert. The hero is brave because he is one of a crowd. An interesting theory. It may be that while the brave extrovert is courageous physically, the introvert is brave morally. Ibsen, like myself, was a physical coward but one does not long for a big he-man in *An Enemy of the People* when the morally brave doctor challenges the iniquity of the town Establishment. But then who is wholly introverted or extroverted? We are all a combination of both. I fancy that most people lean towards the extrovert side.

The extrovert is he who accepted father and followed his ways, while the introvert rebelled against father. I rejected my father because in my childhood he rejected me, made me frightened, inferior, obedient. But why my brothers did not react as I did I cannot guess, for one of them was more scared of Father than I was, and he did not challenge anything later. My sisters never challenged him; they accepted the mores and talk of the home and only Clunie was a rebel.

But yet, doubts again. Clunie and I had the same anti-life Calvinistic environment. I became an atheist later in life than she did and I doubt very much that on my death-bed I'll mutter the prayers of long ago as she did. It is so difficult to know whether a belief has both intellect and emotion behind it. Is the rabid radical marching with his red flag because he loves the poor, or because he hates the rich? Alas, to look for motives is as useless as to look for a life plan.

I have a strong belief in justice, and children when free have this belief. I have never shown favouritism in my school – not that I didn't like some kids better than others, but I hope I never betrayed any preference. Once I heard some kids discussing the staff and their favourites. One girl said, 'Who are Neill's favourites?' Two names were given – the two pupils I liked least. I should have been an actor.

Fame is a mirage. A few millions, mostly in the USA and Germany, have read one or two of my books. Many schools in the USA have been inspired by Summerhill, yet I know that after a few obituary notices I shall be forgotten. The truth is that I don't think I am very important, taking the long view. Bertrand Russell is already forgotten, just as I shall be. But his books and mine will go on for a few years.

And yet there is sadness in the knowledge that Keats did not live to realize his fame, which he said was writ in water. Keats lamented that his name was writ in water, but had it been writ in great golden letters, would it have eased the agony of leaving life so young? George Douglas Brown died just after his great novel *The House with the Green Shutters* was published and never knew that he had written a masterpiece. The thought that one day I may be put in a book of famous educationists does not give me the smallest thrill. As Sam Goldwyn cried, when asked to think of posterity: 'What the hell has posterity done for me?'

A man's dream life should show him how small he is. In the daydream we are in control and we dream of success, courage, conquest; but the night dream is beyond control. I doubt if Freud was right in claiming that every dream expresses a wish, however complicated the symbolism. Having had hundreds of my dreams analysed in therapy, having analysed hundreds of children's dreams, I cannot believe that all are wish-fulfilments. In any case, I give the opinion that I don't think the analysis of any of my dreams helped me one bit.

I mention dreams because they get behind the image a man has made for himself, behind what Reich called his armour. Big men can be little men in their dreams. I knew a high churchman who often dreamt that he stood in his pulpit naked. I have dreamt that I was shitting in a pot in a crowded ballroom – an odd kind of wishful thinking.

My own dreams I cannot analyse. They have no connection with people I know. I never dream of my family, my school, my early life. I did when younger. For years after the death of my dear sister Clunie and after Homer Lane's death I dreamt of them again and again. They were unpleasant dreams; the sun did not shine in them. Vaguely I knew they were dead and the contact with them was not a happy one. Twice since Reich died I have talked with him in dreams, again with no happiness. In these cases the wish-fulfilment was not disguised by symbolism.

Dreams of course depend on the glands. Octogenarians do not have sex dreams or prowess dreams – they don't run races, don't drive fast cars. My anxiety dreams have gone with the years. I used to dream of standing before a large audience unable to say a word. For many years I dreamt about travelling to my childhood home in Scotland. My parents were expecting me on a certain day by a certain train. I never got there. Everything seemed to stand in my way . . . the taxi was late or the train was late or I couldn't go because of a forgotten lecture date. It was all misery and frustration.

I must have had a very bad conscience about my parents, although consciously I did not neglect them. I wrote to them regularly every week, with difficulty to be sure, for their interests and mine were different. They were weather letters. In my time the gulf between parents and children was a very wide one; contact about real and deep matters was impossible.

Here I am gropingly trying to say that I am a split personality. I am the pioneer educationist and I am a child still bound emotionally to my parents, to my environment. I made images and never could destroy them. In my dreams, Newport, Fife, for instance, where I taught for the first time in a school with easy discipline and where I fell in love with Margaret, became a heaven to which I kept returning. Possibly my situation is that of millions, a conscious busy life in the daytime and a regression at night to a past life romanticized in fantasy. Many men and women have long-lost loves that have lived on unconsciously, and it is likely that many a marriage has been wrecked by this romantic fixation on the past.

So when one writes about one's life what side of one's personality is being described? Usually the conscious one, too often the name-dropping snob one frequently sees in the lives of actors and showmen – 'Dined with the Duchess of Theberton last night.' And we cannot sniff and be superior about this kind of snobbery. I have written about 'my old friend Bertrand Russell' but apart from his spending a week in Summerhill nearly fifty years ago I saw him only once again, although we corresponded.

No, self-analysis is impossible. You cannot psychoanalyse yourself because you cannot face the factors that would offend your own opinion of your ego.

Reich spoke of armouring, acquiring an outer shell to show to the world, hiding the depths of the personality. We all armour ourselves. Introspection is limited, and that is the real reason why a man cannot psychoanalyse himself; he dare not face his inner conflicts, his repressions. It would not be easy for, say, a prominent evangelist to face his naked soul, to find that he was selfish, mean, sadistic, and an unconscious womanizer. A balanced man is one who is prepared to discover the little man in himself, and from that angle none of us is balanced. The principle works both ways of course; Gestapo torturers of Jews petted their children and their dogs.

Armouring does not matter if one is conscious of using it; as Reich often said, 'You have to be a conscious hypocrite on occasion.' It is the armouring that is unconscious that does the damage.

Conceit is an armour against admitting to oneself that one is a dud. It fades with the years but never quite expires. Reich's desire to have an elaborate tomb in Organon was a kind of posthumous conceit; in life he scorned display and honours and pageantry of all kinds. I myself have no feelings about tombstones or monuments after my death. All I want is a quiet cremation with no fuss, no flowers, no black clothes, no epitaph. I should like my body to be taken away by the undertaker and have no funeral at all, but I fear that there would be criticism of my family. 'The hard-boiled lot, not even giving the old man the respect of a decent burial.'

I am ignorant about psychology. Where does the truth lie? In Freud, Jung, Reich, Marcuse, Fromm, Rogers? Is sex repression the main cause of world wickedness? If Adler's power motive is right why do the masses have no power and no desire to obtain it? If original sin exists why aren't we all crooks and murderers?

For fifty years I have run my school on the assumption that environment is the main factor in conditioning human behaviour, but I get two brothers, one of whom is social, the other antisocial. True, the environment is not exactly the same for both; it does not counteract the jealousy in a family. I have to conclude that environment is not enough, and sadly accept the fact that no one can do a thing about heredity.

My ignorance about books is abysmal, especially foreign books. I know more about tools, although I was never a good craftsman. In spite of getting a high mark in my final exam in history at the university I know hardly anything about it. My honours degree in English literature has no significance; my views on Keats or Milton are not worth a scrap. Statistics make me flee. When I lectured in the USA there was always some earnest questioner – 'Mr Neill, what percentage of children under ten are interested in mathematics?'

One of the regrets of my life is that I never learned French. In books most French passages are not translated; German ones are but I don't need them for I can read German. In my youth I learned small Latin and less Greek, and they are long forgotten. I learned German simply because my stay in Germany compelled me to. I cannot speak it well, for I have never mastered the articles – *der*, *die* and *das*. I taught maths for many years but today have no idea what modern maths means. The truth is that I am not educated.

It may be because of my ignorances that I like to ask folks about their jobs. I can listen attentively to a beekeeper, a farmer, an explorer but not to a teacher. I would like to ask an explorer a question I have had more than once from kids – how does anyone in the Arctic Circle do his business? Does he take his pants down in the deep freeze? I would like to ask a historian another kids' question – what did people use in the lavatory before the invention of paper? History to kids means answering the most interesting questions.

Does ignorance matter? They say that maths teaches one to reason, but I have yet to see a school staffroom in which teachers rush to the maths man for advice. Most of us know nothing of zoology, botany, astronomy, mathematics, physics, philosophy. It is a fallacy that knowledge means power. I have known men who seemed to know everything, and understood nothing. Oscar Wilde wrote, 'A cynic is one who knows the price of everything and the value of nothing.' Often very knowledgeable men are anti-Semitic, using their knowledge to rationalize their hatred. It is no wonder that the masses distrust the intellectuals.

I am not saying that knowledge is valueless. My old pupil Professor Gordon Leff writes thick books on medieval history and spends many hours researching in places like the Vatican Library. It is his job to know and, knowing, to understand.

Nay, the important thing is not ultimately to know, it is to feel, and all the university degrees in the world do not help one to feel. The ideal is to know and feel at the same time. In my own case it is not my knowledge of psychology that helps a kid; it is my ability to be a kid again myself and see his point of view. 'Genius is the power of being a boy again at will,' said Barrie. Not genius, which can mean anything, just ability, talent if you like.

I do not regret my plethora of ignorances. I know enough to let me carry on my job. To understand Einstein would not help me a bit when Johnny is stealing from our larder. I won't say ignorance is bliss but it is not a calamity, else we would all be morons.

Philosophy means the study of what is important in life, and, as we all have different interests, our philosophies are legion. That makes for universal misunderstanding. I think my own philosophy, by and large, is to let people live in their own way, and really this sums up Summerhill. I have written again and again that no man is good enough, wise enough to tell another how to live, but I am conscious of the fact that by running a school with freedom for kids and then writing about it I am assuming that I am trying to tell readers how to live, meaning that I am conscious of being a humbug.

In these pages I have had something to say about the fears that ruled my early life. At eighty-nine I naturally know that death cannot be far away and I hate the idea of going out like a candle to the nothingness beyond. But whether that is a fear of death I am not sure; more likely it is a fear of not living, of leaving people and things that I hold dear. And there is curiosity. I want to live to see what is to happen to children, to humanity, to the world with its hate and crime and thwarted love. It is a sobering thought that when I die the postman and the milkman will come as usual, my demise meaning nothing to them, nothing really unless to the ones around me.

I have been lucky in having a long life with the minimum of fear stimulus from the outside. The Ministry of Education, possibly disliking my views, has been tolerant. No churchman has attacked me for keeping children from religion, or at least not giving them any. Our small town in Suffolk is peaceful and our children are safe from hoodlums and rapists. My pupils are much more fearless than I was at their age.

If one lives to be very old nature seems to make the passing easy. I find that I have gradually lost interest in things and to a lesser degree in people. I see the gardener use the scythe I used to keep so clean and sharp and it means nothing. When I get up in the morning I feel I am a hundred and have no interest in anything or anyone, but when I go to bed I am fifty. The morning mail brings nothing to excite me; the morning papers have little interest. In old age there is nothing to look forward to. I can think of no promising event that would give me a thrill, not a cheque for a million from a rich American, not an offer of a title (which I could not accept) or a new honorary degree from a university.

If the weakness of old age did not come I wonder how long a man could live happily, how long he could retain his interest, say, in the beauty of flowers and landscapes. I have had my school in two places of great beauty – the Austrian Tyrol and the Welsh mountains. After a few weeks I ceased to see the beauty, just as the director of a musical comedy ceases to see the beauty of his chorus girls. Hence if I say to myself, 'Soon you will not see the Summerhill trees and flowers, the happy faces of the kids; soon you will leave your friends for ever, how very sad,' I am not being quite sincere.

In Scotland we laughed more than somewhat about death. A

farmer's wife died. As they carried the coffin down the awkward stair it hit a corner. The lid flew open and the woman woke up from her trance. Twenty years later she died a second time and the farmer stood anxiously by as they carried the coffin down the stairs. 'Canny wi' that corner, lads.'

I have my office in the Cottage now and don't have to climb stairs any longer. Summerhill pupils, tired of being a zoo to over a hundred visitors a week, made a law: No More Visitors. I am too old and too tired of visitors' questions so it suits me as well. I want to help Ena to carry on but I am so easily tired. Gradually I have come to accept the idea of death. I still hate the idea that I'll never know what happened to Summerhill or Zoë or the world.

Someone recently asked me what incidents in my life stand out as blissful moments. In childhood there must have been many, for youth is the time for ecstasy . . . and terrible depression, say after a day at the circus. I cannot recall the early delights, the occasions when time stood still when a beloved lass smiled on me. My greatest pleasure of all was comparatively recent: my return to Summerhill after the war. The mess the army had made of the premises was forgotten in the joy of quiet happiness in being at last back in the place I loved. I had never had any emotional attachment to a place before. It may be that Summerhill is my own; I bought it, improved it; it became an extension of my own personality. It was my *House with the Green Shutters*. When I think of death now I think of it not as leaving life so much as leaving Summerhill, which after all has been my life.